DOCTORS

An Industry Accounting and Auditing Guide

DOCTORS

An Industry Accounting and Auditing Guide

Second edition

John Dean

John Dean Associates

Accountancy Books
Gloucester House
399 Silbury Boulevard
Central Milton Keynes
MK9 2HL
Tel: 01908 248000

ISBN 1 85355 668 8

British Library Cataloguing-in-Publication Data.

A catalogue record for this book is available from the British Library.

Throughout this book the male pronoun has been used to cover references to both the male and female.

Typeset by Type Study, Scarborough
Printed in Great Britain by Bell & Bain

Contents

		page
List of abbreviations		xii
Preface to the second edition		xiii

1 The profession of General Practice — 1
- 1.1 Introduction — 1
- 1.2 Organisation of the NHS — 3
- 1.3 Independent contractor status — 4
- 1.4 Management and efficiency — 5
  - 1.4.1 Internal management and controls — 7
- 1.5 Statutory framework — 8

2 Principles of GP finance — 9
- 2.1 The Statement of Fees and Allowances (SFA) — 9
- 2.2 GPs' pay and the Review Body — 10
  - 2.2.1 How GPs' pay is calculated — 11
  - 2.2.2 Indirectly reimbursed expenses — 12
  - 2.2.3 The sampling process and the Inland Revenue enquiry — 13
- 2.3 Fees and allowances — 15
  - 2.3.1 Basic practice allowance (BPA) — 15
  - 2.3.2 Seniority awards — 16
  - 2.3.3 Post graduate education allowance (PGEA) — 16
  - 2.3.4 Capitation fees — 17
  - 2.3.5 Registration fees — 17
  - 2.3.6 Child health surveillance — 17
  - 2.3.7 Deprivation payments — 17
  - 2.3.8 Payments on account — 18
- 2.4 Reimbursement of direct refunds — 18
  - 2.4.1 Rents — 19
  - 2.4.2 Rates — 19
  - 2.4.3 Ancillary staff refunds — 20
  - 2.4.4 GPs in health centres — 21
  - 2.4.5 GP trainees — 21
  - 2.4.6 Car parking — 22
  - 2.4.7 Drug refunds — 22
  - 2.4.8 Computer grants — 22

Contents

	2.4.9	Payments on account	22
2.5	Target payments		23
2.6	Item of service fees		24
	2.6.1	Night visit fees	24
	2.6.2	Maternity medical services (MMS)	25
	2.6.3	Anaesthetic/dental haemorrhage	26
	2.6.4	Contraceptive services	26
	2.6.5	Temporary residents	26
	2.6.6	Vaccinations and immunisations	26
2.7	Sessional payments		27
	2.7.1	Health promotion	27
	2.7.2	Minor surgery	28
	2.7.3	Training of medical students	28
2.8	The dispensing practice		28
	2.8.1	Profitability	29
	2.8.2	Payments by HA	30
	2.8.3	Superannuation	30
	2.8.4	Stock on hand	30
	2.8.5	Private prescriptions	31
	2.8.6	Prescribing doctors	31
2.9	The training practice		32
	2.9.1	Income tax	33
	2.9.2	National Insurance	33
	2.9.3	Superannuation	33
	2.9.4	The trainee supervision grant	34
	2.9.5	Other payments and refunds	34
2.10	Non-NHS earnings		35
2.11	The use of statistics		36
	2.11.1	Expenditure levels	36
	2.11.2	Proportions of NHS income	36
	2.11.3	Item of service fees	36
	2.11.4	Gross and net incomes	37
	2.11.5	Other statistics	38
	2.11.6	Average list sizes	38
	2.11.7	Case study	40
	2.11.8	Keeping up to date	41
2.12	Abatement rule		41
2.13	Goodwill		42
2.14	Part-time working		43
	2.14.1	Part-time practice	43
	2.14.2	Job sharing	44
2.15	Computer grants and reimbursements		45
2.16	Payments during sickness and confinement		45
2.17	The doctors' retainer scheme		47
2.18	GP co-operatives		47

3   The ownership of surgeries   **49**
   3.1   Principles and practice   49
   3.2   The notional rent allowance   50
   3.3   Outline of the cost rent scheme   52
   3.4   Establishment of cost limits   53
       3.4.1   Calcuating the total cost   53
       3.4.2   Area bands and factors   54
   3.5   Fixed and variable rates   55
   3.6   Financing the project   56
       3.6.1   What will it cost?   58
   3.7   The sale and leaseback scheme   59
   3.8   Negative equity   60
       3.8.1   Existing surgeries   61
       3.8.2   Ownership by trust   63
   3.9   Basis of valuation   63
       3.9.1   The incoming partner   65
   3.10   Improvement grants   65

4   Acting for doctors   **67**
   4.1   Acquiring a speciality   68
   4.2   Internal organisation   69
   4.3   Working papers   69
   4.4   Planning the work   70
   4.5   Progressing the work   71
   4.6   Reviewing files   74
   4.7   Permanent files   74
   4.8   The charging of fees   75
       4.8.1   Fee budgeting   75
   4.9   Action on new clients   77
   4.10   Letters of representation   79
   4.11   Nominated partners   80
   4.12   The partnership and personal accountant   81
   4.13   Avoiding problems   81

5   The GP partnership   **84**
   5.1   How the partnership is organised   84
       5.1.1   Pooling of income   85
   5.2   Partnership changes   86
   5.3   Organising the profit-sharing ratios   87
   5.4   'Fixed-share' partners   89
   5.5   Prior shares of profit   91
   5.6   Partnership deeds   92
   5.7   The surgery-owning partnership   94
       5.7.1   Retiring partners   97
       5.7.2   Property capital accounts   97

5.8	Organising the capital structure	98
	5.8.1 Fixed capital accounts	100
5.9	The outgoing partner	103
5.10	The incoming partner	103
5.11	Current accounts	105
5.12	Drawings and tax reserves	105
	5.12.1 Income tax reserve accounts	109
	5.12.2 Tax reserves: future policy	110

6 General practitioner accounts: principles and practice 111
6.1	Introduction	111
6.2	Choice of year ends	112
6.3	Several major principles	113
	6.3.1 Grossing up	113
	6.3.2 Partnership changes	113
	6.3.3 Prior shares	115
	6.3.4 Profit allocation	116
	6.3.5 Surgery ownership	117
	6.3.6 Capital grants	117
	6.3.7 Fundholding	117
	6.3.8 Dispensing practices	117
	6.3.9 Stock on hand	118
	6.3.10 Superannuation	118
	6.3.11 Personal expenses claims	118
	6.3.12 Debtors	118
	6.3.13 Pre-payments	119
	6.3.14 Creditors	119
6.4	Potential problems	119
	6.4.1 Locum and maternity leave	120
	6.4.2 Current accounts	121
	6.4.3 Drawings	121
	6.4.4 Negative equity	121
	6.4.5 Tax provisions	122
	6.4.6 Business rates	123
	6.4.7 Trainees' salaries	123
6.5	Management information	123
6.6	Accountant's certificate	124

7 Taxation 125
7.1	Introduction	125
7.2	Partnership taxation and the preceding year basis	126
7.3	Assessments on partnership changes	127
	7.3.1 Allocation of 'prior share' items	127
	7.3.2 Personal practice expenses claims	128
7.4	Taxation on surgery ownership	134

7.4.1	Partnership allocations	134
7.4.2	Relief for interest paid	134
7.4.3	Capital allowances: new surgery developments	135
7.5	Unlocking the partnership capital	135
7.5.1	Division of partnership mortgage	136
7.5.2	Tax-efficient borrowing	137
7.6	Claims for practice expenses	140
7.6.1	The Inland Revenue attitude	141
7.6.2	Preparing the claim	141
7.6.3	Partnership or personal expenses?	142
7.6.4	Practice use of the home	142
7.6.5	Study allowance	144
7.6.6	Capital gains tax	145
7.6.7	Locum fees, etc.	145
7.6.8	Accountancy fees	145
7.6.9	Security expenses	145
7.6.10	Private telephone bills	146
7.6.11	Computers and videos	146
7.6.12	Permanent health/locum insurance	146
7.6.13	Courses and conferences	147
7.6.14	Conclusion	147
7.7	Motoring expenses	147
7.7.1	'Private use' factor	148
7.7.2	Capital allowances	149
7.8	Spouses and families	149
7.8.1	Wives' salaries	150
7.8.2	Method of payment	151
7.8.3	GPs in partnership	151
7.8.4	The female GP	151
7.8.5	Pension schemes	152
7.8.6	Medical insurance premiums	152
7.9	Schedule E remuneration in partnerships	153
7.10	National Insurance	156
7.11	VAT and the GP	158
7.11.1	VAT exemptions	158
7.11.2	New surgeries and self-supply	159
7.11.3	Partial exemption and the *de-minimis* rule	159
7.11.4	Dispensing practices	159
7.12	Avoiding Inland Revenue enquiries	160
7.12.1	Expenses claims	160
7.12.2	Non-disclosure of income	160
7.12.3	The client	161
7.13	The trainee car allowance	162
7.14	Gifts and donations	164
7.15	Bank interest and charges	165

	7.15.1	Overdrawn current accounts	165
7.16		Capital expenditure	166
7.17		Domestic mortgage interest relief	166

8 GP fundholding — **168**

8.1		Origin	168
8.2		Eligibility rules	168
8.3		Setting the budget and scope of the fund	169
8.4		Community fundholding	170
8.5		The role of the accountant	170
8.6		Fundholding accounts	171
8.7		The practice fund management allowance (PFMA)	174
8.8		Connections with practice accounts	177
8.9		Computer reimbursement scheme	178
8.10		Fund savings	178
	8.10.1	Ownership of assets	179
	8.10.2	Surgery buildings	179
	8.10.3	Doctors leaving the practice	179
8.11		Taxation implications	180

9 Superannuation, pensions and retirement — **182**

9.1		The NHS scheme	183
9.2		The two schemes	183
9.3		Membership of the scheme	183
9.4		Opting out of the scheme	184
9.5		Contributions levels	184
	9.5.1	GP partnerships	186
9.6		Tax relief on contributions	186
9.7		The dynamising factor	188
9.8		Benefits of the scheme	189
9.9		Purchase of additional benefits	190
	9.9.1	Added years	190
	9.9.2	The unreduced lump sum	191
	9.9.3	Additional voluntary contributions (AVCs)	193
9.10		Death and sickness benefits	193
9.11		Leaving the scheme: refunds and transfers	193
9.12		Hospital service	194
9.13		Voluntary early retirement	194
9.14		Partial retirement	195
	9.14.1	Abatement	196
9.15		The private options	196
	9.15.1	The 'grossing-up' formula (also known as 'topping-up')	197
	9.15.2	Renunciation of concessionary tax relief	198

	9.15.3	Free-standing additional voluntary contributions (FSAVCs)	200
	9.15.4	Pensions for spouses	200
9.16		Investing the lump sum	200
9.17		Timing of retirement	201
9.18		Superannuation on outside appointments	201

Appendix 1	Specimen partnership accounts	204
Appendix 2	Fees and allowances for GPs: 1995/96 and 1996/97	220
Appendix 3	Inland Revenue: enquiry into GPs' expenses	222
Appendix 4	Sample partnership agreement	227
Appendix 5	Internal control questionnaire for medical practices	243
Appendix 6	Specimen master index: working papers file	246
Appendix 7	Accounts preparation checklist	247
Appendix 8	Reconciliation of list sizes	252
Appendix 9	Specimen letter of engagement	253
Appendix 10	Specimen letter of representation	257
Appendix 11	Specimen 'year-end' preparatory letter	260
Appendix 12	Specimen appointment of nominated partner letter	263
Appendix 13	Current (from April 1995) cost rent limits (building costs)	264
Appendix 14	1995/96 cost rent limit variations: building cost location factors	265
Appendix 15	Claim for personal practice expenses	270
Appendix 16	Personal practice expenses: confirmation letter	272
Appendix 17	Inland Revenue Extra-Statutory Concession: doctors' and dentists' superannuation contributions (ESC A9)	274
Appendix 18	NHS pension scheme: early retirement factors by age attained	276
Appendix 19	Inland Revenue press release 30 April 1996	278
Appendix 20	Recommended reading	280

| *Index* | 282 |

List of abbreviations

Within this book, for the sake of brevity, a number of acronyms have been used. These are set out below:

AA	Automobile Association
AISMA	Association of Independent Specialist Medical Accountants
BMA	British Medical Association
BPA	Basic Practice Allowance
CGT	Capital Gains Tax
DHA	District Health Authority
DoH	Department of Health
DSS	Department of Social Security
FHSA	Family Health Service Authority (to 31 March 1996)
FSAVC	Free-Standing Additional Voluntary Contribution
GDP	General Dental Practitioners
GMP	General Medical Practice (Practitioners)
GMSC	General Medical Services Committee of the BMA
GP	General Medical Practitioner (in the NHS)
GPFH	GP Fundholding
HA	Health Authority (from 1 April 1996)
IOS	Item of Service fees
LMC	Local Medical Committee
MPC	Medical Practices Committee
NHSPS	NHS Pension Scheme
NIC	National Insurance Contributions
PAYE	Pay-as-you-Earn Tax
PGEA	Post Graduate Education Allowance
PPC	Personal Pension Contributions
PPEC	Personal Practice Expenses Claim
RHA	Regional Health Authority
SFA	Statement of Fees and Allowances ('Red Book')
TB	Trial Balance
VAT	Value Added Tax

Preface to the second edition

As a result of the success of the first edition of *Doctors Accounts*, published in late 1993, it is a pleasure to be invited to prepare a second edition of what, together with its accompanying sections in *Business Briefings* and *Tax Briefings*, has become the definitive text on the subject.

It is perhaps surprising that no publication of this type, addressed to professional advisers rather than to doctors, has previously been published and the success of this has effectively proved the need for such a service.

It has famously been said that 'a week is a long time in politics' and, whilst perhaps with not exactly that level of immediacy, the same is unquestionably true of GP finance, where changes continue to be made on a regular basis and both the GP and his adviser, not surprisingly, find great difficulty in keeping up to date with these.

This is no less of a problem for those who prepare books of this nature, where regular updates must be issued so that readers are able to keep their knowledge up to date and help readers to ensure that advice of this level is made available to their clients on a regular basis.

Since the first edition of this book, in particular, there have been radical changes in the way in which the GP Fundholding Scheme is administered and financed. These are set out in a wholly rewritten Chapter 8. Radical and far-reaching changes in GPs' pension arrangements are set out in a new Chapter 9. Trends in the manner in which out of hours responsibilities are catered for and financed are also covered extensively, as are changes in surgery finance, VAT and certain aspects of taxation.

The last few years have also seen for the first time the establishment of a professional association catering for accountants who specialise in work for GPs. The formation in 1995 of the Association of Independent Specialist Medical Accountants (AISMA) has already attracted a wide range of membership and they offer training, information updates and regular support to firms falling into this category. Readers wishing to contact AISMA can do so via the Secretary, Liz Densley FCA of Honey Barrett, on 014124 730345.

John Dean
June 1996

Chapter 1 – The profession of General Practice

1.1 Introduction

The three years or so since the original preparation of this book have served further to polarise the speciality by a number of firms in dealing with general medical practitioners. The establishment of AISMA (see preface), together with evidence of a larger number of reputable local firms operating in this field, has meant that many GPs now recognise the existence of such a speciality within the accountancy profession, and are more inclined to trust the conduct of their financial affairs to a firm which is able to demonstrate such a speciality.

As we have seen, one of these acknowledged specialities is that of providing advice for medical and dental practitioners, of various types. Within this broad heading, it is possible to identify a number of separate disciplines, each of which has its own experts and adherents. These are, broadly speaking:

(a) general medical practitioners;
(b) hospital consultants, both part-time and full-time;
(c) doctors in private practice;
(d) general dental practitioners;
(e) other practitioners within this general field, such as osteopaths, physiotherapists and chiropodists;
(f) retired doctors.

Whilst doctors in private practice have their own specific problems which need expert advice, those are significantly different from their colleagues in NHS practices and it is to those individuals, general medical practitioners within the National Health Service, that this book is devoted. It is their finances which are increasingly complex, drawn up to a separate set of rules from those in force elsewhere, which give rise to the numerous problems which the practitioner can encounter and with which, as we shall see, he must be familiar before he can hope to advise his client in a competent and effective manner. (This book is not relevant to the needs of general dental practitioners, although the NHS pension scheme (Chapter 9) is to a large degree identical in its application to both NHS doctors and dentists.)

All examples of doctors' accounts, tax computations and other items shown in this book do not refer to any known practice and the figures used are for illustration purposes only.

While every care is taken to ensure that figures and examples included in this book are up to date at the time of preparation, readers should understand that these can change at short notice and are advised to make sure current information is made available to them on a regular basis (see Appendix 20).

Over the last 10 years or so, the need for accountants to specialise in the world of GP finance has become both evident and desirable. With some 33,000 GPs in the country, more or less evenly spread over a cross-section of accounting firms, it is evident that many accountants have GPs among their clients, who are perfectly capable of asking all manner of leading questions, and requiring advice at the drop of a hat. An accountant who is unable to deal with these is likely to lose quickly both the confidence of his client, and, as a natural progression, the client himself.

Since 1985, there has been published in several editions the booklet *Doctors Accounts* in the Accountancy Books *Business Briefings* series. Now available in a looseleaf format and updated at least three times annually, this enables up-to-date information to be presented in an easy-to-read manner so that the busy practitioner, who may well not feel able to devote time to regular reading, can easily assimilate current changes as they occur and provide advice to his clients on such a basis.

Since 1993, this principle has been expanded into the *Tax Briefings* looseleaf series, also published by Accountancy Books. A section entitled *Doctors* is again updated on a regular basis and enables practitioners to keep up to date with taxation developments as and when these occur.

The reforms and changes which occur in medical finance on a regular basis have made even more necessary the availability of publications of this nature which ensure that a high standard of knowledgeable professional advice is available to those GPs requiring such a service.

The pending reforms in the taxation system, which for GPs consist of the change to current year basis and the introduction of self-assessment, are covered in this book only insofar as they affect GPs to the exclusion of other members of the taxpaying community. In general, advice on these topics is available in other learned publications and it is not proposed to cover these here in full detail.

Most GPs practise as members of partnerships and this, to a large degree, both in the accountancy and taxation aspect, is covered comprehensively in this book. Indeed, experience tends to show that the majority of problems arising in medical practice derive from the formation of partnerships, introduction of new partners, organisation of capital and the like. Again, this is fully covered.

For the sake of brevity alone, throughout this book doctors and their professional advisers will be referred to in the male gender, although an increasing number of both are in fact female. Similarly, practice managers will be assumed to be female, although an increasing number of highly qualified men are now making their way in this side of the profession. The word practitioner, where used, will refer generally to an accountant or other professional adviser rather than to a medical practitioner.

Although the publication of books of this nature can, it is hoped, go a long way in assisting practitioners to be aware of the rules and ever-changing finances in medical practices, these changes can and do come along at fairly frequent intervals and the reader is strongly advised to do whatever possible to keep up to date. A number of books and journals circulate within the speciality, some of them devoted to medical finance and a list of these is shown in Appendix 20.

1.2   Organisation of the NHS

Before going on to look at the manner in which GPs' finances are organised and the manner in which income is earned and received, it is necessary to look at how the NHS is organised, specifically so far as it concerns GPs.

The NHS, in more or less its present form, has been in existence since 1948. Since then there have been numerous changes in the way in which GP finances are organised. The most radical of these in recent years have been the introduction of GP fundholding as a result of the National Health Service and Community Care Act 1990 and the introduction of the new GP Contract from 1 April 1990. These reforms have already had considerable effect on the organisation and management of the NHS.

The ultimate authority for organisation of the Health Service within the United Kingdom is the Secretary of State at the Department of Health. Below that level, a number of separate tiers of Health Authority operate. Regional Health Authorities (RHA) are responsible directly to the Secretary of State and their duties encompass far more than those concerning GPs. They are, for instance, the controlling authorities for the newly constituted self-governing trusts, hospital services in their area and GP fundholding.

The immediate tier below the RHA level are Health Authorities (formerly Family Health Service Authorities) which are the bodies responsible for the discharge of contractual obligations in respect of payments to general medical, dental, ophthalmic and other practitioners; for the payments to pharmacists and others for certain services and drugs dispensed; for the collection of prescription income; for the collection for DHAs of the cost of hospital prescriptions dispensed in the community and for the approval, monitoring and control of expenditure on certain items of general medical services. From 1 April 1991, FHSAs (as they were then) were given additional duties involving the setting and monitoring of indicative drug prescribing benefits, the monitoring on behalf of the RHA of the budgets of GP fundholders (see Chapter 8), providing advice and support for those practices and making various payments to service providers on their behalf.

Since 1 April 1996, the former FHSAs have been known as Health Authorities and will be referred to as such in this book.

From 1 April 1990, cash limits were imposed on many headings of general medical services expenditure and these limits are set and monitored by the HA. The HA, in fact, will be the public body with which the GP is most in contact; the chief officers will act in the role of guide, philosopher and friend, as well as, to some degree, controller and to a much larger degree, paymaster. All this, of course, is bound up with the GP's unique status as independent contractor to the Health Service.

In Wales, the role of the RHA is performed by the Welsh Office and in Scotland by the Scottish Office, where the role of the HAs are the responsibility of the various Health Boards. In Northern Ireland, a similar role is carried out by the Central Services Agency.

1.3 Independent contractor status

The somewhat unique status of a GP as an independent contractor to the National Health Service goes back to the formation of the NHS in 1948 and, in a rather different guise, for many years before that. In conjunction with other health service professionals, this is a unique status and is only bestowed on the general medical practitioner, together with his colleagues in general dental and general ophthalmic services.

This independent contractor status is not to be lightly cast aside; over the years there have been movements of very limited influence attempting to have GPs transferred to a salaried status, not unlike their colleagues in the hospital service. These have received little support and at the time of writing there is no realistic possibility of a change in this status, apart from a minority of GPs in certain inner-city areas.

This independent contractor status is, in a way, a 'halfway' house, between a genuine self-employed businessman and a salaried employee of the State. On the one hand, as with other self-employed individuals, the GP pays tax under Schedule D; he pays Class 2 and Class 4 National Insurance, he is responsible for his own business, including the hiring and firing of staff, running his own finances and the like. On the other hand he is not, as any other professional person would be, entirely independent in the manner in which his income is calculated. As we shall see, this is based upon a formula produced by the Review Body each year and the GP has little alternative but to accept it. While he can obtain income from other, non-NHS sources, the likelihood is that the preponderance of his income will come from the National Health Service and this level of control limits his independence in a manner which would not be appropriate to other self-employed individuals, who are perfectly free to set their own level of fees and prices, subject only to market forces.

It is in the provision for retirement that the GP appears to obtain the best of both worlds. As the only people in the country who are simultaneously self-employed and members of an occupational pension scheme, the financially aware and well-advised GP finds it possible to maximise his retirement income in a manner not open to most other individuals. This is considered at some length in Chapter 9.

As independent contractors, GPs are responsible not only for the clinical care they provide to patients but also for the organisation and finances of their practices. This allows them to exercise discretion and a large element of freedom in how their practices are run. This autonomy brings with it the administrative and financial responsibility for running the practice as a business, as well as that of providing a high level of medical care to patients.

In some practices, rather sadly, given their lack of training and – in all too many cases – lack of interest in financial and administrative matters, one frequently finds practices which may well run as models of efficiency so far as medical care is concerned, but are significantly lacking in financial efficiency. This is essentially, and, in the broader term, the role of the advising professional.

1.4 Management and efficiency

Having set the scene and looked at the status of the GP in the community, it follows that the GP who runs an efficient practice, both clinically and financially, is likely to be the one with the higher level of earnings and who, with the security of an adequate living, is able to run the medical side of his practice without the constant worry and stress about such relatively routine matters as how his drawings are calculated, how his bills are to be paid, agreement of income tax assessments and demands, and the like. Running a large medical practice these days is an exacting and demanding task, requiring a high level of management expertise and business acumen. Gone are the days of the 'cottage industry'-type medical practice, probably operating from a room in the house of the GP. Whilst such practices do exist, they are becoming fewer and fewer and the norm is now a group practice of upwards of six partners, practising from a new surgery developed under the cost rent scheme, with a high level of staffing and an acceptable level of earnings by the partners.

The current levels of GPs' incomes, particularly taking into account the new sources of income introduced by the 1990 GP Contract, means that practices with turnover in excess of £500,000 are now becoming relatively commonplace, while the practice with a turnover in excess of £1 million, excluding the fundholding budget, is by no means unknown.

These practices are medium-sized businesses in anyone's language; translated into a more commercial environment they would be attractive prospects for any accountant. In the case of medical practice, the other side of the coin is that the adviser will be expected to understand all the complexities and vagaries of how GPs' finances work.

The question of efficiency is at the heart of the successful medical practice. It is well evidenced that an efficient practice will be a remunerative one, and vice versa. The question of financial efficiency in medical practices is not easily defined and, indeed, the difference between a remunerative and an unremunerative practice is not as clear-cut as one might think. The achievement of this level of efficiency has, however, been set out under six headings:

(a) The maximisation of income levels, generally through high earnings from item of service fees, meeting targets and health promotion work.
(b) The timely and accurate claiming of refunds.
(c) Correct staffing levels.
(d) An up-to-date and accurate internal accounting system.
(e) Computerisation.
(f) A commitment to management efficiency by all the partners in the practice.

It is frequently postulated that an additional factor in ensuring high income levels is above average list sizes, particularly since the introduction of the 1990 Contract with its emphasis towards earnings from capitation and performance-based sources. This is by no means always the case;

higher list sizes invariably result in the partners being unable to cover their workload sufficiently without recourse to outside assistance, including expensive locums and deputising services.

Where these high lists apply and doctors are able to derive high earnings from them, as at times occurs, this is invariably due to long working hours and a high level of commitment. Whilst this is in many ways to be commended, nevertheless one finds it is likely to be done at a high cost to the doctor's quality of life, leaving little time for a normal family life and leisure activities. It is no coincidence that the incidence of marital breakdown among GPs is above the national average. This is a choice which only the GP can make, so long as he is made aware of the options open to him.

1.4.1 Internal management and controls

One of the most radical changes over the last few years in the manner in which individual practices are managed has come about by the increasing status of the practice manager. To a large degree the time has gone when the manager of possibly a sizeable business enterprise would be a secretary or receptionist promoted above her ability level but who nevertheless was expected to deal with the whole of the administration of the practice. Not surprisingly, accidents and tragedies were by no means unknown. We now find, particularly with the advent of fundholding (see Chapter 8), that the professional status of practice managers has increased significantly and many practices are now employing able and qualified individuals, possibly with a business/health administration background, who are able to run the practice as a forward-looking business enterprise, with all that this implies.

The ideal management structure of a medical practice, in a nutshell and again using a commercial analogy, is that the practice manager equates with a company secretary/finance director role, running the whole of the management and the finances of the practice, leaving the doctors to deal with the clinical care side of the practice, for which they have been trained. Needless to say, this happy situation does not always apply and inevitably the practice manager will become frustrated at being unable to fulfil her true potential.

Practices are strongly advised to bring into force a Management Chart, possibly within the framework of a business planning operation. Examples of these are illustrated in Chapter 8.

One of the prime arts of management is the successful delegation of responsibility and the practice manager must be prepared to delegate a large part of her workload to more junior staff, whom it will be generally more cost-effective to employ for that purpose.

While it will generally not be part of his basic duties, the accountant advising the medical practice should, with sufficient experience, be able to highlight problems which arise in the management of a practice and make suitable recommendations. A basic example of this would be the introduction of an efficient book-keeping system, possibly on a computerised basis.

1.5   Statutory framework

Only recently, as we shall see, have GPs become exposed to formal audit procedures. Those doctors who are members of fundholding practices will find that their accounts are subject to audit at triennial intervals, if not more frequently (see **8.6**).

Apart from this, however, GPs, whether in sole practice or partnership, are unincorporated businesses and there is no statutory requirement for their accounts to be audited. In the majority of cases, apart from the provision of management information for the partners and maintaining parity between them, the main purpose of the accounts will be for agreement of the tax liability with the Inland Revenue and, where appropriate, in support of loan applications. Some practices (see **2.2**) will have these accounts examined by the Review Body in determining statistics to be used in formulating annual pay awards.

Some years ago there was a suggestion that accounts should be presented on a regular basis to HAs. This was subjected to sufficient opposition that it appears to have been quietly shelved. GPs guard their independence very jealously!

Apart from this, the accountant may well be asked to certify that tax relief is not to be claimed on certain headings of expenditure in support of applications for improvement grants (see **3.10**) and he may well be asked to provide evidence of income levels in support of mortgage applications.

It is unlikely that a practice would wish to have certain audit functions performed and where this applies these should be clearly set out in a letter of engagement (see **4.10** and Appendix 9). This in practice is highly unlikely to be the case, for reasons of cost alone.

Chapter 2 – Principles of GP finance

Having looked at the general framework both of the NHS and individual practices, we must now look at the manner in which a GP earns his income and the complex system of fees and allowances through which this is delivered.

2.1 The Statement of Fees and Allowances (SFA)

The Statement of Fees and Allowances for General Medical Practitioners in England and Wales is the definitive reference book on the manner in which GPs' fees, allowances, refunds, etc. are calculated. Separate but almost identical publications are issued by the Scottish Office and the Northern Ireland Office.

The book is, however, for reasons of brevity apart from anything else, known as the 'Red Book', by reference to the colour of its binder and as such (or SFA) it will be referred to throughout these pages.

It goes without saying that the practitioner who wishes to advise GPs will find life extremely difficult without a copy of the Red Book for easy reference. GPs are perfectly capable of telephoning and expecting advice on interpretation of the book at fairly short notice and there can be an instant loss of confidence if this is not immediately available.

The Red Book has now been made available to interested parties and can be purchased from:

Department of Health
PO Box 410
Wetherby,
Yorks LS23 7EL (Tel: 01937 840250).

The cost of the basic Red Book is £4.00, together with £2.50 for the binder. Amendments cost £2.00 each on issue. There are to the date of writing (March 1996) 17 such amendments. In particular, there are invariably lengthy delays between Red Book changes being first announced, and the actual issue of the appropriate amendment. Requests should be made to be placed on the mailing list so that notification will be given as and when amendments are issued.

2.2   GPs' pay and the Review Body

We have seen how GPs, while not a salaried service, are nevertheless not entirely in control of their own income levels. This income, in a unique situation, is determined by the Doctors and Dentists Review Body, which normally reports each year, making recommendations as to the level of GPs' pay increases for the ensuing year.

For the last few years, Review Body pay awards have been granted more or less in line with fiscal policy of the Government of the day and, not surprisingly, doctors and their representatives have been alienated by the low figures of these awards. This has culminated in a rather higher rise in fees and allowances of about 4 per cent for the 1996/97 year, although even this was phased in to have full effect from 1 December 1996.

There are those that insist that the generosity of pay awards in the public sector tend to take place in the year immediately preceding a General Election. Readers of *Doctors*, however, are likely to pay little heed to such cynicism.

The Review Body was formulated in 1960 following the recommendations of a Royal Commission, charged with making recommendations to the Prime Minister of the day as regards levels of remuneration for doctors and dentists working within the NHS. Their work extends not only to general dental and medical practitioners but also to doctors and dentists who are employed in the Health Service. The Royal Commission recommended finally the establishment of an independent Review Body and laid down certain ground rules by which this should operate.

The Review Body receives evidence from all interested parties, but in practice concentrates upon that received from a number of established sources. Figure 2.1 shows the principal items of evidence considered by the Review Body.

The major interested parties normally submit their written evidence to the Review Body simultaneously, when documents are also exchanged. By this means, each party has prepared its evidence without knowledge of that to be produced by others. Eventually, oral discussions take place in which the Review Body meets the various sides in order to seek clarification as required, and to discuss other points at issue. When its enquiries are complete, the Review Body reports in confidence to the Prime Minister, after which further time normally elapses before the report is published and a decision announced.

Figure 2.1 *Principal sources of evidence to the Review Body*

(a) Written evidence from the profession, prepared by a committee of the BMA.
(b) Written evidence from Health Departments.
(c) Joint written evidence agreed between the profession and the Health Departments, usually dealing with matters which have been agreed by negotiation.
(d) Jointly agreed statistical information, for example evidence on GPs' earnings and expenses.
(e) Independent evidence prepared by the Review Body's Secretariat, the Office of Manpower Economics, for example various surveys conducted at the request of the Review Body.

2.2.1   How GPs' pay is calculated

The system on which GPs' remuneration is based is that known as 'cost plus'; by which an intended average net remuneration is calculated each year, which is then upgraded with the intention of adding such a figure as will cover the anticipated level of expenses for the year under review. It is the manner in which these expenses are calculated and figures formulated by the Review Body 'sampling process' which is the subject of much controversy and, quite rightly, GPs' representatives try to insist that this figure is maximised by the drawing up of accounts under correct guidelines (this is discussed further in Chapter 6).

Given the system in force, the Review Body recommends what appears to be an appropriate level of net income for GPs and by addition of the putative expenses refund, there is calculated by this means the intended gross remuneration, which in turn is directly reflected in the scales of pay for the various items of fees and allowances which a GP will receive.

The word 'average', although used a great deal in this context, should not be taken as anything other than an intended level of income; by no means does it represent an actual achieved level of income for GPs. In practice, many GPs achieve income levels at greatly higher or lower than the intended average, which as we have seen, is largely the result of the financial efficiency with which the practice is organised and managed. It should also not be forgotten that this 'intended average net remuneration' represents NHS income only and does not include non-NHS income, which GPs are free to earn as and to whatever extent they wish. Figure 2.2 gives details of the calculation of intended net remuneration for the 1995/96 and 1996/97 years. The manner in which this manifests itself into separate fees and allowances is shown in Appendix 2.

Figure 2.2 *Review Body award 1996/97*

	1995/ 96 £	From 1 April 1996 £	From 1 Dec 1996 £	Overall increase %
Gross remuneration	64,648	66,568	66,998	+3.6%
Received by reimbursed expenses	21,700	23,000	23,000	+6.0%
	42,948	43,568	43,998	
Adjustment for earlier years	217	772	772	–
Net intended remuneration	43,165	44,340	44,770	+3.7%

2.2.2 Indirectly reimbursed expenses

Perhaps the most difficult and contentious item in this rather complex remuneration package is that by which the GPs' expenses are indirectly refunded to them. The principle here is that all expenses incurred by GPs in providing services for their patients are repaid to the profession in full: some are repaid directly to the individual GP who incurs them (or his practice), while the remainder is reimbursed indirectly on an average basis through adjustment of fees and allowances (see Figure 2.2). One effect of this is that the exact amount an individual GP receives in respect of indirectly reimbursed expenses will not, other than by coincidence, equal his own expenditure.

In practice, there is a strong incentive for a GP to economise in respect of the expense of running his practice. It is at times said that because these expenses are repaid, directly or indirectly, the less an individual GP spends, the greater will be his own profit. This, however, does not represent the full picture; many of these refunds apply to surgery premises and staff and a GP who permanently seeks to exercise economy by limiting expenditure under these headings could well find his practice falling behind standards set by neighbouring and competitive practices, with a consequent loss of both patients and income.

Perhaps a more positive view is that if all GPs were prepared to invest in their own practices, the profession as a whole would benefit through the indirect reimbursement system and general practice would not continue to be underfunded and undercapitalised, as is now the case with many small practices.

There is a great deal of evidence to suggest, in fact, that GPs are woefully underpaid through this indirect expenses element of their pay, given the system as it stands. In fact, the percentage which the indirectly reimbursed expenses (which are intended also to include expenses which are directly reimbursed to the practice) bear to gross intended income for the 1996/97 year is 34.3 per cent. This is intended not only to cover expenses paid by partnerships but also those personal practice expenses (see **7.6**) which are claimed by GPs personally, including their own cars, houses, spouses' salaries and the like. More realistic figures are difficult to obtain, but exercises which have been done on this basis over the years suggest that in fact the true percentage is very much higher – somewhere between 40 per cent and 60 per cent. This would tend to be the greater in the case of dispensing, training, fundholding practices, etc., which tend to have a higher incidence of directly reimbursed expenses. It is clear that the major reason for this apparent under-refund is due principally to two factors:

(a)   the 'netting out' of GPs' directly reimbursed expenses (see **6.3.1**); and
(b)   the under-recording of expenses.

To a large degree the solution to both these problems lies in the hands of the professional adviser; to draw up the accounts in the prescribed manner and to encourage GPs to record systematically all their expenditure so that this ultimately finds its way through their accounts. The various direct refunds which practices can claim are set out in more detail in **2.4**.

2.2.3   The sampling process and the Inland Revenue enquiry

Tax practitioners in particular will be relieved to hear that the term 'Inland Revenue enquiry', used in this context, is rather different to the interpretation they are more used to placing upon it.

We have seen that an essential component of a GP's remuneration award is the indirect reimbursement of expenses. How this figure is arrived at and eventually finds its way into each year's remuneration award is of importance in appreciating how the system works and, of more direct relevance, why the GP's accounts should be prepared in the manner prescribed.

It is obvious that obtaining details of GPs' expenditure on a national basis can only be done by extracting information of this type either from their own records or accounts in some manner. The only practical source of such information is from accounts submitted to the Inland Revenue for agreement of GPs' taxation liabilities and this is effectively the starting point for the figures which will ultimately find their way into the annual pay award.

Problems arise because this data is not held centrally, but retained by individual tax offices. The question of time delays poses a problem and for that reason the expenses information is considered to be three years prior to the year in which the award refers and four years prior to that for which the recommendation is being made. An estimate, therefore, has to be made and actual movements in expenses between the base date and the year in question are adjusted in a subsequent review award.

A sample of GPs is drawn from centrally held records on a random basis. The names of the GPs within the sample are then submitted to tax offices concerned, which complete a statistical return using the latest agreed accounts of the GP concerned. This applies to both the partnership accounts and personal expenses claims. A copy of the latest such form (GP 96) is set out in Appendix 3. This form is then returned to the statistical division of the Inland Revenue, which produces computerised averages for total income and expenses for the year under review. During this process, one adjustment which is made is the removal of expenses which are known to have been directly reimbursed in the year concerned. This can only be done on a national basis, rather than on the basis of individual practices, so that in making this deduction there is a built-in assumption that all practices have in fact properly 'grossed up' their directly reimbursed expenses, by including these as items of expense in their accounts. It follows naturally that if practices have not done so and their accounts are used in the sampling process, then the profession as a whole will suffer.

It follows also that expenses estimates prepared on this basis are estimates only and that when accurate figures are available an adjustment will have to be made. For that reason, retrospective adjustments, sometimes covering several years, are built into the annual Review Body award.

It is important to note that the only accounts included within this sampling process are those ending within the March quarter of each year. For that reason GP negotiators recommend that accounts be drawn up to such a year end, normally March.

This frequently falls contrary to advice given by accountants to their client practices and there is a clear conflict in principle between the two sections of interest, which shows little sign of resolution.

The sampling process seems destined to face further difficulties during the coming years. The transitional year of assessment on the change to current year basis of assessment means that, effectively, for one year accounts will not be submitted to local tax offices. For one year, therefore, there will be little information from which such statistics can be obtained.

Furthermore, when self-assessment is fully in operation, it will no longer be necessary to submit full partnership accounts to tax offices and it must remain to be seen whether the information to be provided for partnerships will give the high level of information required.

2.3　Fees and allowances

Payments made to GPs for work done can generally be divided into two main headings: fees and allowances. Allowances, broadly speaking, are normally items of a lump sum nature, which are paid to GPs who fulfil certain criteria. Fees, on the other hand are those payments which are made either on a 'per capita' basis, such as capitation fees, or for providing distinct services which attract a fee, such as item of service fees, sessional payments and the like.

The detailed GPs' fees and allowances are set out in the Red Book (SFA), for which updates are issued from time to time (see **2.1**). References below are to paragraphs in the SFA.

It is necessary that the practitioner dealing with GPs' finances has a clear understanding of how these items of income are received and how a GP qualifies to receive them. As we shall see, it is necessary, if the eventual accounts are to provide a high level of management information, that the income derived by a GP from each of these sources is clearly set out and compared with statistical information available in order to see exactly how the practice has performed in these areas.

Let us first, therefore, look at the various allowances which a GP might reasonably expect to receive.

2.3.1　Basic practice allowance (BPA) (SFA 12)

GPs qualify for the BPA provided they have lists of at least 400 patients. This is the minimum; to qualify for the full practice allowance a GP must have 1,200 patients. Where a GP has a smaller list, the BPA is proportionately adjusted to reflect his lower list size. Further adjustments to the BPA are available in respect of part-time GPs; this is considered in more detail in **2.14**.

In a partnership, qualification for the BPA will be based upon the average list size of doctors in partnership. Thus, in a practice with four full-time GPs and a list of 5,600 patients, this will give an average of 1,400 per

15

doctor and they will all qualify for the BPA, notwithstanding the fact that one partner's personal list may be below the individual threshold.

2.3.2 Seniority awards (SFA 16)

A supplement to the BPA will be paid to GPs in recognition of length of service. These payments are made to every GP who is eligible for the BPA:

(a)   a first level payment to a GP who has been registered for 11 years or more and has been providing GMS for at least 7 years;

(b)   a second level payment to a GP who has been registered for 18 years or more and has been providing GMS for at least 14 years; and

(c)   a third level payment to a GP who has been registered for 25 years or more and has been providing GMS for at least 21 years.

Where for some reason a GP receives a BPA at less than full rate, the seniority award will be scaled down accordingly.

For the accountant drawing up accounts for his client practice, it is important to ensure that the accounts show clearly the partners' intention as to the allocation of these seniority payments. In many – but by no means all – cases, these are retained by the partners in whose names they are paid, rather than being pooled with the partnership profits for division in agreed ratios. In such cases, the seniority payments should be allocated as prior shares of profit (see **5.5**).

2.3.3 Post graduate education allowance (PGEA) (SFA 37)

This is paid to any GP (or associate practitioner), who maintains a balanced programme of continuing education.

To claim the PGEA, GPs are required to submit to the HA (or Health Board) evidence that they have attended an average five days' training a year over the past five years. Courses are divided into three areas:

- health promotion and prevention;
- disease management;
- service management, which includes practice management.

Similar comments apply with regard to showing this allowance in partnership accounts. It is frequent for this allowance to be retained by individual partners, although it is initially paid to the partnership by the

HA. In such cases the accounts must be designed accordingly (see Appendix 1 and **5.5**).

Let us now, therefore, look at the various fees which GPs are able to claim. Target payments (**2.5**), item of service fees (**2.6**) and sessional payments (**2.7**) are dealt with separately.

2.3.4   Capitation fees (SFA 21)

The majority of income in most practices will derive from capitation fees paid to GPs on the basis of the number of patients on their lists. These fees are paid under three rates:

- to 64 years;
- 65 to 74 years;
- 75 years and over.

This refers to the patient's age during the quarter for which the fee is paid.

2.3.5   Registration fees (SFA 23)

A separate fee is paid to practices resulting from all new registrations (except for patients under five years). To qualify for this fee, a GP must carry out certain specified procedures in respect of patients joining their lists for the first time. These must normally be carried out within three months of the patient joining the list.

2.3.6   Child health surveillance (SFA 22)

Any GP who proposes to be paid for providing child health surveillance services must apply to the HA to be included in the Child Health Surveillance list. To do so, he must demonstrate that he is suitably trained and experienced, in accordance with certain criteria laid down.

A capitation supplement is paid for each child patient under the age of five years, to whom a GP provides developmental surveillance. The child must be registered with the GP for this purpose.

2.3.7   Deprivation payments (SFA 20)

One effect of the 1990 GP Contract, with its emphasis largely on capitation-based sources of income, was to the detriment of inner-city practices, which may well be unable to attract or cater for larger list sizes, due largely to patient demand and for demographic reasons. As a result of this, there was formulated, by means of a 'Jarman Index', a list of deprived areas, which in effect are allocated by reference to wards in urban areas.

Those GPs who provide services to these deprived areas are paid a capitation supplement to the BPA in respect of all patients resident there.

These payments have provided a necessary fillip to a number of such inner-city practices and have effectively ensured that their income has kept pace with their colleagues practising in more prosperous areas.

2.3.8   Payments on account (SFA 76)

The above are the main sources of fees and allowances (apart from those discussed separately below) payable to GPs. These are calculated quarterly by the HA and paid to GPs on that basis. However, practices should ensure that they obtain a payment on account at the end of each month, which will normally represent one-third of the total standard payments at the end of each intervening month, with a balancing payment at the end of each quarter. Care should be taken to ensure that all practices obtain these payments on account, not only for fees and allowances but also for certain refunds such as ancillary staff payments, trainees' salaries, rent allowances, drug dispensing, etc.

Readers who wish to refer to the full conditions of payments of these fees and allowances are referred to the appropriate paragraphs of the Red Book.

2.4   Reimbursement of direct refunds

An integral feature of any GP's remuneration package is the element of expenses which are refunded to him, which must be identified properly and shown correctly in his practice accounts if those are to show a proper reflection of the working for the year, while at the same time maximising expenses for the purpose of the Review Body sampling process. We have also seen (**2.2**) how much of GPs' presumed average expenses are refunded through their remuneration award in the form of indirect refunds. A whole range of expenses paid directly by GPs for their practices are, however, reimbursed directly to them, wholly or in part, by the HA and it is important that these are understood, both to ensure that full refunds are received, with consequent effects on ultimate profit-ability.

General practice is the only profession inside or outside the National Health Service which has this extremely beneficial system of direct refunds. GPs are 'cushioned', effectively, against the effects of rises in expenditure during times of high inflation but also during periods of low remuneration rises, during which high cost items such as rates, drugs and trainees' salaries, which would otherwise have to be borne fully, are repaid to them so that there is no residual net cost to the practice.

It is, however, surprising how many practices fail to take maximum benefit from this system, usually by inadequate claiming procedures, which have lost practices many thousands of pounds for precisely that reason. The accountant drawing up accounts for a general practice should make it his business to ensure that all qualifying expenditure is matched by appropriate refunds, or satisfy himself that any apparent deficiency can be explained. Where relevant, a debtor should be provided (see **6.2**).

Every effort should be made to ensure that all practices have in place an efficient system for claiming these refunds. Where possible, responsibility for this should be delegated to the practice manager or one of her staff, who will be responsible for ensuring that correct claims are submitted and accurate refunds obtained from the HA.

2.4.1   Rents (SFA 51)

Where a practice rents a surgery from a third party, i.e., a landlord, the rent paid will normally be reimbursed in full. However, in some cases GPs will not use the whole of the leased building for NHS purposes and in those cases a restriction will be applied so as to reflect the proportion of the rent which is reimbursable. Where this applies, the District Valuer will visit the premises and assess the proportion qualifying for refund.

In some cases also, the District Valuer may consider the rent paid to be above the market rental value and in those cases a lower notional refund figure may be substituted. GPs do not therefore have a 'carte blanche' facility to pay out whatever they will in rent; the amount paid will always be relevant both to the level of accommodation provided and known rental values.

In many cases, however, GPs will own their own surgeries. In those cases, they will receive either a notional or cost rent allowance, which is dealt with at some length in Chapter 3.

2.4.2   Rates (SFA 51.13(b))

GPs can also claim a full refund of all rates paid on behalf of their surgery, whether the building is owned or leased. This will include such items as:

(a)   uniform business rates;
(b)   water rates;

(c)   water (metered) charges (SFA 51.13(c));
(d)   drainage rates;
(e)   sewerage rates;
(f)   trade refuse collection charges.

Some of these items will only be paid by practices in certain areas. In some urban areas, a charge may be made by the local authority for disposal of trade refuse. Where this occurs a refund should be claimed from the HA (SFA 51.13(d)). Rates will not be reimbursed where the rental paid includes a charge for rates.

Some practices will choose to make payments of business rates by monthly standing orders, normally by 10 such payments between the months of May to February inclusive. Care must be taken to see that these instalments are recovered on a regular basis, normally quarterly.

In some areas, HAs have agreed to make payments of this nature, normally for business and water rates, direct to the local authority or water company concerned, without any cash passing through the practice. This is attractive to practices which do not have to concern themselves with making payments of this nature and dealing with the claiming and receipt of the refund. However, it does impose on the practice an obligation to ensure that these figures are included on both sides of the accounts, for reasons outlined above. The mere fact that they are not passed physically through the accounts does not mean that they can be ignored.

2.4.3   Ancillary staff refunds

It was common until recently for practices to have refunded to them 70 per cent of the gross salary of all ancillary staff, together with 100 per cent of the employer's share of the National Insurance contribution. To a large degree, and following the imposition of cash limiting procedures, this remains subject to negotiation with the HA concerning levels of salary scales, etc. For this purpose, ancillary staff must be engaged to carry out certain qualifying duties:

- nursing and treatment;
- secretarial and clerical work, including records and filing;
- receiving patients;
- making appointments;
- dispensing.

Receiving and passing messages will also rank as a qualifying duty so long as the major part of the employee's time is taken up on duties as specified above.

It should be noted that this does not include the salaries of cleaners, who are regarded as non-qualified for this purpose. Salaries of practice managers, although not specifically quoted, are generally held to fall within the qualifying duties.

Where cash limits are imposed, an HA will usually quote a standard figure for the ensuing year and this will be paid in monthly instalments, regardless of the staff engaged by that particular practice. Different considerations do, however, apply in various parts of the country and all practices should be aware of the policy of their particular HA.

2.4.4   GPs in health centres (SFA 53)

Those doctors practising from publicly-owned health centres, normally owned and administered by a District Health Authority, will find that no direct charge is made on them for rent and rates, in the sense that they must draw a cheque on the practice bank account and recover this by submission of an eventual claim, possibly some weeks later.

Nevertheless, a charge is made and this is dealt with internally without passing through the practice bank account. In those cases it must be emphasised as strongly as possible that the figure for rent and rates should be obtained and included as an item of both expense and refund on both sides of the annual practice accounts. This serves the purpose of maximising expenses in case these accounts are required for production to the Review Body (see **2.2**). Accountants preparing accounts for general practices may encounter difficulty in obtaining from Health Authorities such details for inclusion in their accounts. Such figures, if all else fails, should be shown as estimates, although this should only be done as a last resort.

Similarly, some practices in health centres do not employ their own staff, these being administered and paid by the Health Authority. In these cases a doctor will normally be charged a net 30 per cent of those staff salaries, with a full remission of National Insurance contributions. Again, it is necessary for similar reasons that this expenditure is grossed up with, in the case of salaries, 100 per cent being shown on the expenditure side and 70 per cent as a refund, leaving the net cost of 30 per cent. Similarly, National Insurance contributions should be shown fully on both sides of the accounts. This information should be automatically supplied to the practice at regular intervals. Variations may apply where 'cash limiting' has been imposed on a practice.

2.4.5   GP trainees (SFA 38)

Frequently, doctors undertake the work of training young doctors who will eventually become principals in general practice. A fee will be paid to the trainer in the form of the trainee supervision grant.

For practice purposes, the GP trainee, during his year with the practice, will be paid a salary based upon a scale negotiated from time to time and advised to the practice by the HA. This salary will be paid to the trainee as if he were a normal employee of the practice, with the full range of PAYE and Class 1 National Insurance deductions being imposed.

A refund will, however, be made to the practice of the amount of the gross salary, plus the car allowance and the employer's share of Class 1 NIC. Again, the salary cost and refunds should be shown on both sides of the accounts (see also **6.2**).

The question of training practices is dealt with in some detail in **2.9**.

2.4.6   Car parking

In some urban areas, where it is necessary for the doctors to use a municipal car park, a refund of car parking charges can be claimed from the HA. This will normally be in the form of a refund of fees charged for contract parking tickets.

2.4.7   Drug refunds (SFA 44)

Many practices make claims for repayments of drugs dispensed or provided for patients. Again, claims can be made for these and GPs should ensure that this is done on a regular basis. Normally refunds will be made in arrear, probably by as much as three months. The question of dispensing practices is a separate issue and is dealt with in **2.8**.

2.4.8   Computer grants (SFA 58)

In recent years a scheme has been introduced whereby GPs can obtain refunds of part of the cost of installing computers in their practices, as well as for leasing and maintenance costs. See also **2.15**.

A well drawn-up set of practice accounts should demonstrate the fact that all these refunds are receivable and the payment on one side matches the refund on the other (see Chapter 6).

2.4.9   Payments on account

GPs can obtain by right monthly payments on account of all these items except rates (unless paid by monthly standing order) or rental payments, which are normally repaid on presentation of the necessary receipt. However, in respect of ancillary staff and trainee refunds, payments on account should be received monthly with a balancing-up at the end of the quarter. If properly done this can have a significant effect on the practice's cash flow position.

Once agreed with the HA, such a facility will not normally be withdrawn.

2.5 Target payments (SFA 25, 26, 28)

A major new source of income introduced in the 1990 Contract was in respect of payments to be made to GPs in return for achieving certain targets. These targets are in the area of preventive medicine and are intended to encourage GPs to embark upon certain procedures with this in mind.

Generally, these target payments offer two levels of achievement and payment is based upon a higher or lower level, depending on the percentage of cover achieved.

These target payments fall into three groups:

(a) *Child immunisation (SFA 25)* Two target levels are available, 70 per cent and 90 per cent, representing average coverage levels within certain groups. The targets will be achieved if, on the first day of any quarter, on average across the three groups, 70 per cent and 90 per cent of children aged two on a GP's list have had complete courses of immunisation.

(b) *Pre-school boosters (children under 5) (SFA 26)* Two target levels are available, 70 per cent and 90 per cent, which will be achieved if on the first day of a quarter at least 70 per cent and 90 per cent respectively of children aged five on a GP's list have been given certain reinforced immunisations.

(c) *Cervical cytology (SFA 28)* Offering cervical smear tests to women in the age group 25–64 in England and Wales (or 20–60 in Scotland). Target payments are made where 50 per cent or 80 per cent of women in those groups have had an adequate smear test during the previous five-and-a-half years.
There are two target levels, 50 per cent and 80 per cent which are achieved if on the first day of the quarter 50 per cent and 80 per cent respectively on a GP's list within those age groups have had a cervical smear test during the previous five-and-a-half years.

To a large degree the achievement of these targets represents a reflection on the efficiency of the practice in identifying groups qualifying for these payments on their list, operating successful notification and recall systems and above all, making sure that the procedures are applied. Detailed scales of payment are set out in Appendix 2.

2.6 Item of service fees

To a large degree, the financial success of a practice depends upon the efficient claiming of item of service fees. These are in total intended to account for some 16 per cent of GPs' income from NHS sources. The 1994/95 actual returned averages for England and Wales showed that the average return per patient was some £4.72.

Some practices achieve higher returns, usually through practising in a special area; for instance, one would expect practices in a holiday resort to have a much higher than average incidence of temporary resident's fees, whereas those in a relatively rural backwater are likely to show below-average returns from maternity and family planning fees. Nevertheless, taken as a whole, the average is a useful means of judging the financial efficiency of a practice and an aid to generating higher levels of income than may have been possible previously. Further details of statistics of this nature are set out in **2.11**. Item of service fees are divided into five headings:

- night visits;
- maternity medical services;
- contraceptive services;
- temporary residents;
- vaccinations and immunisations (so far not covered by target payments – see **2.5**).

Let us consider these in some detail.

2.6.1 Night visit fees (SFA 24)

A GP will be paid a fee for each visit requested and made between the hours of 10pm and 8am to a patient who is:

(a) on his list of patients; or
(b) a temporary resident; or
(c) a woman for whom he has undertaken to provide maternity medical services and the visit is related to these.

A higher fee is payable if either:

(a) the GP with whom the patient is registered makes the visit personally; or
(b) the visit is made by a partner or another GP from his group practice; or
(c) the visit is made by an assistant employed by the partnership or a member of the group; or

24

(d)   the visit is made by a locum or deputy employed by the partnership or group; or

(e)   the visit is made by a trainee GP employed by the partnership or group; or

(f)   the GP is single-handed or in a group practice or partnership and he is part of a local non-commercial rota which includes GPs, outside of the group or partnership, who may also be single-handed or working in a group, whose total number does not exceed 10 and have agreed to provide out of hours cover for each other. The HA needs to be informed of the details of these arrangements.

In all other cases a lower fee will be payable to the GP with whom the patient requiring the visit is registered.

Out of hours payments

The manner in which night visits are remunerated has been a bone of contention between GP representatives and the Government for many years. In 1995 this dispute was sufficient to hold up the publication of the Review Body report for several months.

Later in 1995, it was announced that a Development Fund had been proposed, which is to be used in making payments to GPs by way of direct remuneration of certain expenses which GPs incur to maintain or improve out of hours service. This reimbursement will apply to any of the following:

(a)   The cost of communications equipment in providing general medical services outside normal hours.

(b)   Part of the cost of membership of a GP rota organised for the purpose of providing general medical services outside normal hours to NHS patients.

(c)   Part of the subscription cost of using a deputising service to provide general medical services outside normal hours to NHS patients.

(d)   Locum costs of isolated rural GPs.

This change was effective from 1 April 1995.

Practitioners should ensure that any reimbursements received under this scheme are shown gross in the practice accounts and payments shown as such in the usual way.

2.6.2   Maternity medical services (MMS) (SFA 31)

A full MMS fee will be paid to a GP who provides comprehensive service during the pregnancy of a patient, including the confinement and post-natal period. In addition, a full post-natal examination at or about 6 weeks after confinement and in any event no later than 12 weeks must be carried out. The full fee is payable provided that the GP accepts his patient's application to receive these services, provided that the application is accepted no less than 6 weeks before the date of confinement.

The MMS fee is paid only to GPs included on the obstetric list, and who provide MMS to patients on their list for general medical purposes.

2.6.3   Anaesthetic/dental haemorrhage (SFA 29)

In certain cases GPs may be called upon to act as anaesthetists or for the arrest of dental haemorrhage. While in most practices these fees will be infrequent, they can arise at intervals and GPs should be aware of them.

2.6.4   Contraceptive services (SFA 29)

An annual fee is payable under this heading where a GP accepts a patient, gives advice and provides necessary examination, where necessary prescribing drugs or other aids. The fee is also payable where the GP takes steps to determine a method of choice and accepts responsibility for any necessary after-care treatment. An intra-uterine device fee is payable for services given in the 12 months commencing from the date of application to fit such a device.

2.6.5   Temporary residents (SFA 32/33)

Where a GP treats a patient resident in the area on a temporary basis who is not a member of his own list, a fee will be paid:

(a)   where the temporary patient expects to remain in the district for not more than 15 days; or
(b)   where he expects to remain in the district for more than 15 days.

In each of these cases a lower or higher fee, respectively, will be paid. Patients are considered as a temporary resident for this purpose only if they are in the area for more than 24 hours. Certain separate regulations apply with regard to persons resident in holiday camps.

2.6.6   Vaccinations and immunisations (SFA 27)

Fees are payable in respect of adult vaccinations and immunisations, together with those not falling within the ambit of childhood immunisation and pre-school boosters paid as target payments (see **2.5**). These fees are payable to a GP in respect of a patient who is on his own list or that of his partner, who is eligible for treatment as a temporary resident or is in the area for not more than 24 hours.

The regulations for payment of fees under this heading are complex and depend upon treatment given to safeguard against certain conditions from time to time.

While the practitioner is unlikely to become involved in the detailed claiming of these fees, it is essential that he has a working knowledge of the fees for the purpose of advising his client as required.

2.7   Sessional payments

The 1990 GP Contract introduced a number of payments to be made by GPs calculated on a sessional basis, i.e., a fee being paid for each element of work performed or clinic conducted. Not all of these have survived the intervening years without change.

2.7.1   Health promotion (SFA 30)

The 1990 GP Contract introduced a scale of payments for running specified clinics for various aspects of health promotion. These include such clinics as well-man/woman, anti-smoking, alcohol control, diet, exercise, counselling, etc. This list is not exhaustive. A fee of £45 per clinic was paid and there were complex rules governing the number of patients at each clinic, arrangements for partnerships and other matters.

This resulted in a rapid growth of such clinics with, in 1990/91, £50 million being paid to GPs in the UK by way of health promotion clinic fees. This rose until, in the third year of the scheme, £80 million was paid out. To a large degree this was due to the encouragement of the Contract, which gave GPs an opportunity of enhancing their earnings significantly by undertaking clinics of this type.

This caused severe problems for the Health Service as a whole, in that there is ostensibly a pool of money for payment to GPs and, at least in theory, payments in respect of these clinics would result in a reduction of funds available for other earnings.

Eventually, this growth was halted by the imposition of a moratorium on 1 July 1992.

It was subsequently decided to alter the scheme radically and from 1 July 1993 a system of 'bands' was introduced, depending on the level of health promotion work to be carried out by individual practices. There are three such bands in existence, the payment scales being set out in Appendix 2.

At the time of writing, it appears likely that the system of payment for health promotion work will again be amended.

2.7.2 Minor surgery (SFA 42)

A fee, which may vary from year to year, is payable to a practitioner on the HA's minor surgery list, who provides a minor surgery session for patients on his personal list, or on that of his partner or another member of his group. A practitioner is eligible for no more than three such payments in any quarter. Proportionate arrangements are made for doctors in partnerships.

2.7.3 Training of medical students (SFA 40)

A GP who assists university departments of general practice by involving himself in the teaching and education of undergraduate medical students, by giving them experience of general practice in his own practice, is eligible for a fee based on the number of students involved and the time spent by each practice.

The above three items are allocated for statistical and assessment purposes under the general heading of 'sessional fees', and for any purposes of comparison (see **2.11**) they should be combined together for that purpose.

2.8   The dispensing practice

Some rural practices have been allowed to maintain the facility for dispensing drugs to patients on their own lists. Recent statistics show that this involves some 3,650 GPs throughout the UK representing about 11 per cent of doctors in NHS practices. This dispensing facility leads to a number of accounting problems and those advising practices which fall into this category should be aware of them.

The general rule is that in order to qualify as a dispensing practice and be accepted under the scheme, patients to whom the dispensing facility is made available should reside no less than one mile from the nearest pharmacist. To a large degree this limits dispensing practices to rural and a few suburban areas.

Some practices, particularly those on the periphery of urban areas, may well find that they are allowed to provide dispensing facilities for only some of the patients on their lists, depending on their location.

Detailed regulations for the calculation of reimbursements to dispensing doctors are contained in paragraph 44 of the SFA. This lays down that these payments will be calculated under six separate headings.

(a)   The basic price, calculated in accordance with the tariff currently in force. From this price there will be deducted an average figure for estimated discount, which is discussed below.
(b)   An on-cost allowance of 10.5 per cent of the basic price before the deduction of such discount.
(c)   A container allowance of 3.8p per prescription.
(d)   A dispensing fee, which is on a sliding scale, according to the number of scrips issued per month.
(e)   An addition in respect of value added tax, at the rate currently in force.
(f)   Any exceptional expenses provided for by the drug tariff.

2.8.1   Profitability

Many dispensing practices are highly profitable and provide a greatly enhanced level of earnings to their partners. Exactly how much this profit is depends to a large degree on the efficiency with which the facility is conducted, but subject to this the level of profit can also depend on:

(a)   *The turnover of stock.* A quick turnover of drugs means that the practice is not required to have large amounts of capital held up for lengthy periods, although inevitably there will come a time when some drugs are obsolete and may well have to be discarded. Some dispensing practices are able to control this by means of a stock control computer program which allows for re-ordering when stocks reach a certain level. Some well-organised practices manage to maintain a stock turnover average period of four weeks.
(b)   *Discounts which can be obtained from pharmaceutical suppliers.* The supply of drugs of this nature is highly competitive and there are generous discounts available to those practices which find it possible to take advantage of them.

On the other hand, partners in a dispensing practice will almost certainly be required to contribute a higher level of capital (see **5.8**) than those in a similar but non-dispensing practice. The stock of drugs which is required to be carried at any time, even if kept to a reasonably low level, together with the fact that drug refunds are received up to three months in arrears, means that the current assets of the practice are likely to be running at a particularly high level and the higher earnings of the partners, to some degree, represent a return on this higher investment in the practice capital.

2.8.2 Payments by HA

Almost certainly the dispensing practice will find that drug refunds are made several months in arrears. In some cases this may well be three months, although in the majority of cases payments on account are obtained. Nevertheless, even these payments on account may well be one or two months in arrears, so that at any given date the practice is carrying a substantial amount of capital represented by monies due to it. The practice should try and ensure that those payments on account are received regularly and at as high a level as can be negotiated. Apart from this there is little they can do to encourage prompt payment and the partners must accept that carrying relatively high levels of working capital is one of the obligations of running a dispensing practice.

2.8.3 Superannuation

As we have seen, part of the remuneration of the dispensing GP will be in the form of a dispensing fee for each scrip submitted. These dispensing fees are fully superannuable and will be subject to deductions at the standard rate of 6 per cent – or higher if any of the doctors are buying added years (see **9.9.1**).

It is essential that these superannuation deductions are identified and shown, as with other similar deductions from fees and allowances, as part of the charge to each individual doctor through his own current account. The practice should ensure that proper elections are submitted to the HA in order to ensure that these contributions are allocated in partnership ratios (see **9.5**).

2.8.4 Stock on hand

At any given date, there will be a significant stock of drugs on hand. The size of this will depend on the size of the practice and the extent of the dispensing operation. At each annual account date, i.e., the date in the year to which the practice makes up its annual accounts, such stock should be properly valued and shown in the accounts at that value.

Some practices employ specialist valuers who come to the surgery shortly after close of business on the account date to count and check the drugs on hand. These can, if necessary, be valued and the calculations made at a later date. The stock on hand should include VAT at the rate in force which would be paid on these drugs when they were bought. Other practices prefer to have such valuations taken by the doctors and staff, if necessary paying overtime in respect of the additional work entailed.

The valuation should otherwise be made on the standard basis of cost or market value, whichever is the lower. If, therefore, these drugs have been bought at a specially discounted rate, which may well be less than their true value, it is this rate which should be taken into account when the drugs are valued for that purpose. Drugs which have no value, or which have been given free by representatives, should not be included in the valuation. It is common for some drugs to become obsolete from time to time and these again should be excluded.

It cannot be emphasised too strongly how necessary it is that this value is taken and included in the practice accounts. If, as occasionally occurs, a nominal value is included, or even worse the stock ignored totally, the profits of the practice will have effectively been understated and if the Inland Revenue identify this, they will be within their rights in re-assessing the tax, possibly for several years previously. This is obviously a situation that a practice would wish to avoid at all costs.

2.8.5 Private prescriptions

Some dispensing practices find it necessary to supply patients with drugs which are outside the 'limited list' of those upon which NHS refunds are made. This list consists of drugs which the Department of Health feels, for reasons of cost or public policy, are those which it is prepared to finance from public funds. Nevertheless, there is no bar on a GP prescribing drugs outside these lists, to the extent that the patient is prepared to pay for them.

Fees paid for these private prescriptions are part of the income of the practice but should, in order to provide a true illustration of profit, be included in any calculation of profit from the dispensing operation (see Figure 2.3).

It should be noted that where a practice is registered for VAT, it should add VAT at the current rate to the cost of these private prescriptions (see **7.11.4**).

2.8.6 Prescribing doctors

Apart from this, GPs in non-dispensing practices can, under SFA 44.5, claim a refund and fee under similar arrangements to those outlined

31

Figure 2.3 *Dispensing practice trading account: year ended 30 September 1995*

	1995		1994	
Cost of goods sold	£	£	£	£
Stock at 1 October 1994		8,245		7,342
Purchases during year		84,474		82,928
		92,719		90,270
Less stock at 30 September 1995		8,766		8,245
Cost of drugs dispensed (Note 13)		83,953		82,025
Proceeds				
Refunds (including VAT, etc.)	109,598		104,650	
Dispensing fees	5,346		4,985	
Private prescriptions	2,473		2,268	
		117,417		111,903
Dispensing profit for the year		33,464		29,878
Percentage profit return		28.5%		26.7%

It will be seen that the practice has improved its profitability from its dispensing facility, both in terms of actual profit realised and the percentage return. This may well have come about through increased efficiency; improved stock control; higher discounts available, or a selection of all three.

---

above. This applies normally to the supply of vaccines, anaesthetics, injections, family planning devices, etc.

A dispensing practitioner may supply a prescription to a patient, with that patient's consent, rather than supply it from his own dispensary. In that case, no remuneration will be paid to that dispensing GP.

2.9 The training practice (SFA 38)

Some doctors are approved to employ GP trainees during their vocational training period. Only those GPs who have undergone a three-year vocational training period are allowed to join practices as principals and those young doctors who propose to become partners in general practice must therefore be able to supply evidence that they have fulfilled these conditions.

It is normal for the trainer to be one of the doctors in a partnership. Some larger practices may have more than one of their partners as trainers. The trainer will receive a trainee supervision grant as recompense for the work involved, while the practice will receive reimbursement from the HA for the trainee's salary and other payments made on his behalf. The accountant should be aware of the position and ensure that the accounting entries are correctly shown.

It is important that steps are taken to ensure that the refund received from the HA matches the amount paid to the trainee. Ideally, in the final accounts these two figures should match. In legal and taxation terms, the trainee is an employee of the trainer (or his partnership), who is legally required to account to the Inland Revenue for tax under the PAYE regulations and Class 1 National Insurance contributions.

Some HAs will only calculate the trainee refund on a quarterly basis. In these cases, the practice with an eye on successful cash flow should ensure that monthly payments on account are received.

2.9.1 Income tax

The practice should operate PAYE on the employee's salary, including London weighting where appropriate and any other increments which may apply, e.g., the trainee car allowance (see below) as well as any amount which might be paid to the trainee from time to time over and above his normal salary.

This tax need not be applied to refunds of actual expenditure, such as telephone charges, removal expenses, and Defence Society subscriptions.

For taxation of trainee car allowance see **7.13**.

2.9.2 National Insurance

The trainee salary is fully chargeable to Class 1 NIC under the normal rules in force and using tables supplied to the employer. These should be applied at the contracted-out rate, but see **7.13** for separate NIC rules applying to the trainee car allowance.

2.9.3 Superannuation

It will be found that on the HA quarterly remittance statement there is deducted an amount of 6 per cent of the trainee's salary in respect of his superannuation contributions. More may be deducted if the trainee is buying added years. Care must be taken by the practice to ensure that these are recovered from the trainee's salary before payment, otherwise the trainer and his practice will be out of pocket.

Care should be taken to see that superannuation is deducted from the gross pay before the PAYE tax is calculated, but on the other hand it is not deductible when calculating Class 1 NIC.

2.9.4   The trainee supervision grant

As has been seen, this is paid to the trainer as part of his remuneration for his services as a trainer.

Care must be taken to see that this is allocated in accordance with the policy of the partnership. In some practices, this may be retained by the trainer personally; in most cases it will be aggregated with partnership profits for division.

Whichever means is adopted, this must be shown clearly in the partnership deed and allocated accordingly in the annual accounts.

Superannuation at the trainer's own rate (standard plus added years if applicable) will be deducted from the supervision grant on payment by the HA and this should be charged in the partnership current accounts to the trainer concerned, unless an election has been made to the HA for this to be allocated in partnership ratios.

Where, for instance, a partner/trainer not making any added years' contribution receives the trainee supervision grant for the 1996/97 year, this would be £4,925 and superannuation at 6 per cent would be payable, working out at £274.20.

2.9.5   Other payments and refunds

From time to time various payments will be made to the trainer by way of refund from the HA in respect of payments made by the trainee. It follows that these should be passed on to whoever has made the original payment. For instance, payments will be made in part reimbursement of Defence Society subscriptions and if these were originally paid by the trainee they should be passed on to him. It follows that if those reimbursements are made, the trainee can claim tax relief only on the net amount paid after deduction of the refund.

Removal expenses may well have originally been paid by the trainee and should be paid over to him. No tax is chargeable if these are genuine reimbursements.

Similarly, with regard to refunds of telephone rentals, if the original bills were paid by the practice then the refund should be paid into the partnership account and vice versa.

2.10   Non-NHS earnings

While the typical general practice will derive the vast majority of its income from various sources within the NHS, as we have seen, it will not, however, confine its activities exclusively to work for NHS patients. Depending to a large degree on the policy of the practice, many practices will derive a significant level of income from these non-NHS sources or indeed from other sources within the Health Service, such as clinical assistant posts at local hospitals.

Most practices will receive a substantial level of income from fees for insurance reports and medical examinations, where patients take out life policies and the GP is required to make a report for this.

In addition, income will occasionally be received in the form of cremation fees. It is essential that these are paid into practice funds and properly recorded. There is a danger that the Inland Revenue may well pick this up by other means and if it is found that the practice has not properly returned this income for tax purposes it could well find itself ultimately subject to an in-depth Inland Revenue enquiry, which it is preferable to avoid at all costs. See also Chapter 6.

Some practices will obtain lucrative appointments at local hospitals, nursing homes, schools, etc., and these are a valuable source of additional income for the practice. Many practices, particularly those in more prosperous areas, may derive an appreciable level of income from private patients' fees, but again this largely depends on the policy of different practices.

A further useful source of fees can be as a medical officer to a company or business house. If at all possible this should be organised on a retainer basis, so that a regular source of income is received. This is an aid to ensuring an even cash flow.

In addition, all practices will receive a regular, if modest, level of income in the form of sundry cash fees from patients for signing certificates, passport applications and the like. Again, it is essential that these are all paid into practice funds and properly recorded for tax purposes and the accountant would be well advised to go to some pains in ensuring that, so far as possible, this is done.

One problem which particularly affects partnerships is deciding whether fees from non-NHS sources are to be paid into practice funds or retained by the individual doctors. While this depends on the policy of the partnership, nevertheless it is invariably found that those partnerships with a tradition of financial discipline make sure that all fees from medical sources are paid into practice funds and divided between the partners in the shares in which they share practice profits. This policy is not only a great deal more equitable but also tends to minimise disputes in partnerships.

It will be found at times that partnerships will introduce differential means of allocation of profits from non-NHS services. The practitioner should ensure that, either by reference to the partnership deed or otherwise, he is aware of any such arrangements and design his accounts accordingly. See also letters of representation (**4.10** and Appendix 10).

2.11　The use of statistics

Medical practices have easy access to all manner of statistics which the doctors, their manager and professional advisers can use to judge the profitability and efficiency of the practice. In many cases the practitioner can make use of these statistics in advising his clients and evaluating their performance.

2.11.1　Expenditure levels

By the averaging process, and for superannuation purposes, the Department of Health considers that expenses of a medical practice are running at about 35 per cent of gross income. This is in fact well below actual averages; when one bears in mind that it takes into account any items paid personally by the partners, such as motor car expenses, house expenses, spouses' salaries, etc. the percentage is in fact unduly low. It is to the doctor's advantage that this be maximised if at all possible, and this can only be done by the presentation of accounts which are drawn up in such a manner as to maximise the income and expenses of the practice (see **2.2**, Review Body award).

2.11.2　Proportions of NHS income

Figures currently available suggest that at the present time, average proportions of NHS income received by a typical medical practice, up to the 1994/95 year would be as shown in Figure 2.4.

2.11.3　Item of service fees

Several figures are available to give averages of item of service fees achieved by medical practices in recent years. One of these (see Figure 2.5) gives the average earnings of item of services fees per patient. This information is extremely valuable in attempting to judge the results of a practice.

Figure 2.4

	%
Practice allowances	17
Capitation fees	63
Item of service fees	16
Sessional fees	4
	100

Figure 2.5 *Income per patient in 1994/95*

	England £	Wales £	Scotland £	Northern Ireland £
Night visits	1.26	1.96	1.78	2.16
Temporary residents	0.36	0.47	0.37	0.22
Contraceptive services	1.00	0.87	0.87	0.68
Emergency treatment	0.05	0.06	0.08	0.05
Maternity services	1.47	1.31	1.27	1.50
Vaccinations	0.58	0.37	0.36	0.24
	4.72	5.04	4.73	4.85

2.11.4   Gross and net incomes

It is possible to evaluate further the financial efficiency of the practice by comparing gross and net income levels, both upon a 'per partner' and 'per patient' basis. This is done by extracting figures from those published regularly in respect of intended average remuneration levels. These figures are already available up to March 1997 but, where year ends other than March are used, as is increasingly the case, these must be apportioned accordingly. A practice wishing to test itself against these statistics must therefore take into account its gross income from all fees and allowances (excluding refunds and income from non-HA sources), dividing this between the number of partners or the total list size as necessary.

To arrive at the figure of net remuneration, for comparison purposes, it is necessary to take all achieved income from NHS sources including refunds, and deduct from these the total expenditure of the practice,

Figure 2.6 *Income per patient 1994/95*

	England £	Wales £	Scotland £	Northern Ireland £
Health promotion	1.46	1.49	1.23	1.35
Minor surgery	0.53	0.59	0.65	0.52
Child health surveillance	0.51	0.47	0.46	0.67
New registrations	0.41	0.37	0.35	0.23

except where any expenses are specifically allocated against non-NHS income sources. This should then be divided between the number of full-time partners, this being normally defined as those who are receiving the full rate of basic practice allowance.

In making judgements of this nature one must be careful to distinguish between those averages which express the intended remuneration level in any year and those which have actually been achieved.

2.11.5 Other statistics

Figures are available (see Figure 2.6) which show average returns from various other income sources (year to March 1995).

2.11.6 Average list sizes

The number of patients on the lists of medical practices (and upon which their entitlement to fees from capitation-based sources is based) varies considerably. It will be found that in many partnerships personal lists are not equal, in that for various internal reasons some doctors may have more patients on their list than others. Nevertheless, for the purposes of finance and evaluation this can safely be ignored and judgements made upon the average list size.

The latest information is that the average number of patients on doctors' lists (per principal) is as follows, divided according to various parts of the UK:

(a) England   1,877
(b) Scotland   1,513
(c) Northern Ireland   1,734
(d) Wales   1,744

Figure 2.7 shows a typical table of statistics used to evaluate the performance of a medical practice. It will be seen from this that the

Figure 2.7 *The Southgate Medical Centre statistics: year ended 30 June 1995*

	National average year ended 30 June 1995 £	Actual 1995 £	1994 £
1. Total list size	11,592	14,076	13,668
2. Average number of full-time partners	–	6	6
3. Average patients per partner (5)	1,932	2,346	2,378
	Intended		
4. Gross NHS income (excluding reimbursements)			
per full partner (4)	63,122	65,746	62,489
per patient	33.37	28.02	27.43
5. Net NHS income			
per full partner	41,249	42,483	39,476
per patient	21.80	18.11	17.3
6. Allocation of gross NHS income	%	%	%
Practice allowances	17	18	20
Capitation fees	63	65	66
Sessional fees	4	3	2
Item of service fees	16	14	12
	100	100	100
7. Item of service income (£/p per patient, compared with 1994/95 national average)	£	£	£
Night visits	1.26	0.74	0.32
Temporary residents	0.36	0.25	0.24
Contraceptive services	1.00	0.95	0.75
Emergency treatment and INT	0.05	0.02	0.02
Maternity	1.47	1.45	1.35
Vaccinations and immunisations	0.58	0.51	0.40
	4.72	3.92	3.08
8. Ancillary staff reimbursements		68.5%	71.4%

Notes:
(1) Figures for illustration only and do not refer to known practice.
(2) See also section **2.11**.
(3) Calculation of (4): Gross income per patient: $65,746 \times 6 = £394,476 \div 14,076 = £28.02$.
(4) Average list size $14,076 \div 6 = 2,346$.

average patient list size of this practice for the final year for which accounts have been prepared is 2,346. It will be seen also that there are six full-time partners in the practice. This may not always be the case due to retirement, partners being absent for part of the year or working part-time. An average should be calculated which takes this into account.

If, for instance, there is a five-partner practice, from which a partner retired halfway through the year and was not replaced, for the purpose of these statistics, the practice would have had four partners.

Generally speaking, the criterion used for judgement of this type is whether or not, and to what extent, the partners are receiving the basic practice allowance. Average total list size will be calculated by totalling the partnership list sizes shown in the four quarterly HA statements for the year and dividing by four.

2.11.7   Case study

It will be seen from this that a number of useful facts become apparent which can be used to advise the practice on their future policy for management decisions and, if necessary, to institute remedial action.

(a)   The practice is one of a constant six full-time partners, with the average patient list at 2,346, being some 20 per cent above average. Even this shows an increase from the previous year.

(b)   This high patient list size is to some degree responsible for the high level of gross income at £65,746, although when averaged out on a 'per patient' basis, this, at £28.02, is below the intended remuneration level.

(c)   Net achieved NHS remuneration, after deduction of all known partnership expenses, at £42,483 'per partner' is again above intended average, although, again largely due to high list size, the 'per patient' figure is well below average.

(d)   It will be seen from the allocation of gross NHS income that the high list sizes are reflected in the above average income from capitation-based sources. Item of service fees continue to be below average.

(e)   A look at item of service income reveals that, despite an impressive rise from the previous year, this continues to be well below known averages. Although some fees, notably maternity and contraceptive services, are above average, the return from night visits, again despite a significant improvement, is still extremely low and this in itself accounts for the low return from fees of this nature. The partners should discuss whether or not it is possible for them to increase their income from this source, presumably also saving on deputising costs if they are not receiving the higher night visit fee (see **2.3**) for seeing their own patients.

(f) The return from ancillary staff reimbursements, at 68.5 per cent, has fallen from 71.4 per cent achieved in the previous year. Enquiries should be made into this fall, which may well be due to the imposition of cash limiting and a strict budget being applied (see **2.4**).

2.11.8   Keeping up to date

These statistics can and do change, certainly on an annual basis but occasionally at more frequent intervals. The actual average returns from item of service fees, for instance, are published up to four or five months after the end of the financial year to be covered and there is inevitably a time lag before evaluations can be made on that basis.

Practitioners should, therefore, ensure that they keep abreast of information published from time to time in medical journals and similar sources.

2.12   Abatement rule (SFA 51.16.19)

We have seen that NHS GPs are perfectly free to enhance their earnings by income from outside sources. We have also seen that they can obtain direct refunds in respect of certain expenditure paid out in connection with their practices. These refunds will be predominantly concerned with surgery rent and rates, and staffing costs.

There is a clear conflict between these two principles where practices derive a significant level of non-NHS earnings from premises and staff, refunds for which are wholly or partly funded by the NHS. This private income, if it exceeds 10 per cent of gross practice 'receipts', could well result in these refunds being reduced (or abated). This abatement will be to the amount of 10 per cent where income from these private sources represents more than 10 per cent total gross receipts of the practice. Refunds will be abated by 20 per cent where over 20 per cent but not more than 30 per cent of income derives from private work.

It should be noted that for the purpose of this rule, private income is defined as all professional income received from other than public sources. It therefore includes private fees received from NHS as well as private patients, but excludes income from NHS hospitals, health authorities and government departments.

There is ambiguity in the SFA where this clearly refers to total gross 'receipts'. It is, for this purpose, assumed that this figure includes all amounts received by direct refunds, which, elsewhere in the SFA are

41

specifically instructed to be included with practice income. This has, however, never been exactly defined. It should be noted that where more than one practice surgery is in use, one of which is not accepted for the purpose of the rent and rates scheme, the level at which abatement will apply is increased to 15 per cent.

This is not a situation which is regularly seen, although the practitioner should be aware of it and be able to advise his clients as and when it occurs. By definition, problems of this type usually arise with practices in more prosperous areas, which are likely to attract a greater incidence of private patients, and where doctors as a matter of policy have no objection to taking on patients of that type.

In practice, abatement is relatively easy to avoid; the practice should so arrange its affairs that any work performed of this nature is dealt with away from the main surgery premises, either at the private houses of the partners concerned or, in the case of outside appointments, at the premises of the organisation involved. If possible, no use should be made of staff who qualify for the ancillary staff refund. The accounts should be designed so as to distinguish between practice earnings originating from NHS-financed and non-NHS-financed premises.

2.13   Goodwill

Yet another area in which general practice differs from other professional partnerships is in the prohibition of the sale and purchase of goodwill by GPs in NHS practices.

When the NHS, in its present form, came into being in 1948, GPs – who were then mostly in private practice – had the goodwill in those practices bought out by the government. As recently as the mid-1970s those doctors were finding that they were being paid interest on that purchase consideration, which was eventually repaid in full shortly afterwards. It is reasonable to assume that few – if any – of those doctors are still practising.

This bar on the sale and purchase of goodwill in those practices – or indeed any practices which have subsequently been set up – has been enshrined in legislation, currently s54 and Sch 10, National Health Service Act 1977.

In such circumstances, a transaction in goodwill can involve either an actual sale or a deemed disposal brought about, for instance, by the selling of practice assets at a price above current market value. Those practices which may find themselves involved in such a transaction and wish to obtain clearance before going ahead can do so by application to the Medical Practices Committee, First Floor, Eileen House, 80–94 Newington Causeway, London SE1 6EF.

It should be noted that this bar on the sale of goodwill does not apply either to doctors in private medical practice or to dentists, whether inside or outside the NHS. For the effect of the goodwill rule on the valuation of surgery premises, see **3.9**.

2.14 Part-time working

General practice as a profession tends to attract some doctors who for some reason wish to give less than a full commitment to their practice.

A high proportion of GPs are women, who may well leave work to raise a family and then wish to return, but with family responsibilities in mind do not wish to work on a full-time basis. Some GPs take partial retirement (see **9.14**) and return to practice, usually with a reduced commitment. In addition, some doctors choose to pursue other interests; they may be interested in becoming involved in research work, writing, etc. and find it impossible to combine their chosen activity with that of a full-time GP.

2.14.1 Part-time practice

Where at least one member of a partnership is in full-time practice, partners may be engaged on a part-time basis, which is dictated by the elements of availability and fractional pay as compared with that of the highest paid partner.

Thus, Figure 2.8 shows the hours required to be worked in a week and the fraction of a highest partner share which applies to each category of part-time working.

Figure 2.8		
Hours	*Fractional share*	*% of highest partner*
26 or more	full-time	one-third
19–26	75% shares	one-quarter
13–18	50%	one-fifth

If the practitioner's personal or average patient list is smaller than the appropriate limit then that list will dictate the amount of the BPA to be paid; if the list is greater, the notional list size will apply. An identical fraction will apply to the amount of BPA to be paid, as compared with that of a full-time practitioner.

It must be emphasised that the status of a part-time practitioner relates purely to their availability for medical work; for consultations, clinics and visits. In all other respects, the GP's obligations are identical with those of a full-time practitioner, in that he must be seen as a partner in every sense of the word, having a share in the management of the practice, etc.

2.14.2 Job sharing

A further recent development is that the status of two doctors sharing a single appointment is now formalised.

The basis of the system is that job sharers will be treated jointly as a single practitioner and, as such, they are eligible for only one full-time BPA. This is an arrangement which gives rather more flexibility than for part-time working. While each GP will normally be available for less than 26 hours in a week, in aggregate they will be available for no less than that time. The difference between job sharers and part-time practitioners rests in the eligibility for the BPA and the additions to it, such as seniority, PGEA, etc. Job sharers, who are jointly eligible for a single BPA, have this calculated by reference to their total list size (or average in a partnership) and their personal list sizes are disregarded.

Job sharing is ideally suited, for instance, to a husband and wife partnership. In these circumstances the manner in which they allocate their hours between themselves is their own decision; so long as the total hours are worked and the contract fulfilled in every way, they can divide their responsibility more or less as they think fit.

It should also be borne in mind that whereas job sharers may well divide their responsibility for clinical duties, their expenses may be more than would have been the case for one full-time practitioner. Some of these expenses may be peculiar to themselves, for instance, each doctor will have to pay their full rate of medical subscriptions and Defence Society contributions. They may well each require a car; and certain administrative expenses, such as stationery and telephone costs, may be higher.

For the accountant drawing up accounts for a partnership in this position, it must be emphasised that each of these individual doctors, for financial purposes, is a partner; how they divide their profits is their own decision but the accounts should reflect this and it should be perfectly evident exactly how such profits have been divided on the agreed basis. Where a partnership consists purely of a husband and wife, again it must be treated as a partnership in every sense of the word, both for accountancy and taxation purposes.

2.15   Computer grants and reimbursements (SFA 58)

GPs are able to obtain grants towards the costs of computer systems or in some cases partial refunds of expenditure. Broadly speaking, the items of expenditure available for assistance under this scheme are for:

(a)   purchasing or upgrading a computer system (hardware and software);
(b)   leasing a computer system where the practice is responsible for leasing costs;
(c)   upgrading a practice computer system (hardware and software);
(d)   maintaining a practice computer system (hardware and software) under a formal maintenance contract;
(e)   the initial staff costs of setting up the system.

Where this applies, in calculating the amount due, HAs will deduct any income received from this source.

The computer reimbursement scheme falls within the ambit of that expenditure which is subject to cash limiting in the hands of HAs. To a larger degree, therefore, these grants by individual HAs will depend on adequate funds being available.

The scale of computer reimbursements depends on the list size of a practitioner and is set out in Figure 2.9.

Practitioners preparing accounts for practices receiving reimbursements of this nature should take care to ensure that these are properly shown in the accounts, being advised to bear in mind the distinction between reimbursements of a revenue nature and those of a capital nature.

For the computer reimbursement scheme for fundholding practices see **8.16**.

2.16   Payments during sickness and confinement (SFA 48/49)

Doctors who are absent from their practice due to sickness or maternity leave will, subject to certain conditions, be entitled to receive special and additional payments, over and above their continued entitlement to their share of practice profits, with the intention of reimbursing the partner concerned, in whole or in part, for the cost of a locum or other deputy from outside the practice, who has been engaged to look after patients during their absence.

Figure 2.9 *Computer cost reimbursement: maximum payments according to list size of a practitioner, restricted principal, partnership or group practice*

	A Systems Purchase/1 Upgrading £	B Systems Leasehold/2 Upgrading £	C Maintenance 3 £	D Staff 4 £
List size				
1–2,000	1,800	450	270	490
2,001–4,000	2,410	600	360	600
4,001–6,000	2,900	720	440	770
6,001–8,000	3,400	850	510	840
8,001–10,000	4,200	1,050	630	900
10,001–12,000	5,500	1,370	830	970
12,001–14,000	6,000	1,500	900	1,030
14,001–16,000	6,500	1,620	980	1,090
16,001–18,000	7,000	1,750	1,050	1,160
18,001–20,000 or more	7,500	1,870	1,130	1,240

NB All payments include VAT.

1. Maximum amount payable for computer systems purchased and upgrades purchased for the duration of the scheme (see also SFA paras 58.8 and 58.14)
2. Maximum annual payment for the duration of the scheme.
3. Maximum annual payment for the duration of the scheme.
4. Once-only payment for first-year staff costs incurred in transferring clinical records within the practice onto a computer.

There are complex arrangements for eligibility in respect of age, length of service and number of patients on the practice list.

It is emphasised that these payments are applicable only to NHS principals, i.e., those entitled to the basic practice allowance.

When accounts are prepared the practitioner must exercise extreme care in identifying such locum payments as are:

(a) applicable to the practice in general and which they would have paid out in any event; and
(b) those locum payments which directly arise from the absence of a partner for these reasons.

This is considered in more detail in the section on practice accounts (**6.4.1**).

2.17   The doctors' retainer scheme (SFA 39)

As an incentive to encourage those doctors who for some reason have left the profession (for instance, doctors who have left to raise families) to return to practice, the doctors' retainer scheme was introduced to enable practices to be paid a modest allowance to defray the cost of engaging such doctors.

The fee paid under the doctors' retainer scheme changes from time to time but payments will be made by the HA up to a maximum fee currently in force. The fee quoted is for a notional half-day of 3.5 hours.

Practitioners preparing accounts for doctors receiving such a fee should ensure that this is shown under the general heading 'reimbursements' in the annual accounts. The actual amount paid to the retained doctor should be shown as such under 'payments to retained doctors'.

It is not uncommon for such doctors to be paid an amount in excess of the actual fee for the 3.5 hours weekly, to take account of extra hours worked. These should be properly regarded as locum fees.

Practitioners should also ensure that the correct rules are observed with regard to the taxation of such doctors. If it is shown that a genuine employment exists, with a fee or salary being paid on an annual, weekly or monthly basis, then this is prima facie evidence of employment and the normal rules of PAYE/NIC should apply.

2.18   GP co-operatives

A feature of the last year or so in general practice has been the setting up of a number of co-operative arrangements, which enable GPs to control their out of hours working in a manner which may not have previously been possible. This has also been encouraged by the setting-up of the development fund for funding out of hours work (see **2.6.1**).

Practices will normally pay to their local co-operatives fees as follows:

- an annual retainer;
- a monthly fee; and
- night visit fees, which will be retained by the co-operative.

For accountancy purposes, the first two items should be shown in the accounts under the general heading of 'co-operative expenses'. Night visit fees will be shown on the HA statement as having been received by the practice and paid out to the co-operative. It is essential that these are 'grossed up' in accordance with accepted principles.

47

On the other side of the coin, those doctors who work for the co-operative will find that a fee is paid to their practice. It is a matter of practice policy as to whether this fee is pooled with partnership earnings or retained by the individual doctors. If the latter applies, it should properly be included with practice income and shown as a prior share of the profits in the annual accounts (see Chapter 6).

Chapter 3 – The ownership of surgeries

The practitioner will, at times, inevitably find himself drawn into advising his surgery-owning clients on the financial aspects of surgery ownership, including the potential taxation advantages. It goes without saying that he should have a sound working knowledge of the topic.

We have seen (**2.4**) how GPs can obtain refunds of much of the expenditure connected with the provision for surgery premises, including rent paid to the owners of the building. In an increasing number of cases, however, practices will actually own their own premises: because no rent is paid out to other parties it follows that none can be refunded.

This does not mean that these surgery premises are provided without charge to the NHS, nor that the doctors cannot receive some element of financial recognition for use of their privately owned surgeries in the Health Service. This is very much the case and this section looks at the various financial aspects of surgery ownership by GPs, the manner in which this can be developed to their ultimate advantage and considers in some detail the provisions of the cost rent scheme.

The allied questions of surgery-owning partnerships (**5.7**) and taxation (**7.4**) are dealt with separately.

3.1   Principles and practice

The type and standard of accommodation provided by practices for their own use as surgery premises can come in many forms; on the one hand the established building which has been in the hands of the practice almost since time immemorial, to the house in an urban area acquired for conversion to medical use, or at the top end of the scale the new purpose-built surgery, developed under the cost rent scheme at significant capital outlay on a green field site (see Figure 3.1). It is the manner in which these are catered for in financial terms which is of greatest concern to the adviser dealing with GP clients.

One common feature of all these surgery ownerships is that they will attract an allowance, in the form of the notional or cost rent allowance.

Figure 3.1 *Differing categories of surgery premises*

NHS in practice ownership	%
Health centres (publicly owned)	16
Rented surgeries	21
In practice ownership	
Converted properties	33
Purpose-built	30
	100

This will be paid under certain rules to the practice on a regular basis and we shall look separately at each of these.

Whichever of these is paid, it is, for all intents and purposes, the income of the practice; it should be included with the partnership profits for allocation between the partners; it should be treated as assessable to Schedule D tax, again divided in appropriate ratios. These allowances are paid to GPs by virtue of their contract of engagement with the NHS; conditions and rules for payment are set down in the Red Book (SFA para 51). As we shall see, subject to logical variations, they are merely another component of the GP's practice income.

3.2   The notional rent allowance

The purpose of the scheme for direct payment of rent and rates for GPs is to reimburse practitioners for the rent, rates and other costs of providing practice accommodation by reference to the amount each practitioner pays or is deemed to pay. Premises are only acceptable under the scheme where the HA is satisfied that the accommodation provided is adequate and falls within certain parameters, including ease of access, treatment and consulting facilities, adequate waiting areas and security.

It is by no means unknown for partnerships to own two or more surgeries, or indeed to have rented and owned accommodation simultaneously.

Where a GP practices from his own house, and this is more normal in the case of sole practitioners, payment of any rent allowances and refunds in respect of rates and similar items will relate only to that part of the residence used for practice purposes. In such situations, the HA will determine the amount of the notional rent payable as advised by the District Valuer, who will provide an assessment of the current rental value of that part of the premises used as practice accommodation. This applies whether the property in question is owned or leased.

Where surgery premises are occupied by the practice but for some reason fall outside the ambit of the cost rent scheme (see below) a notional rent allowance will be paid to the doctor(s) occupying the surgery. The amount of this allowance (both in respect of separate premises or those forming part of a residence) is determined following an assessment by the District Valuer as to the current market rent which might reasonably be expected to be paid for the accommodation. This amount, when agreed, is paid in full to the practice concerned, usually at quarterly or monthly intervals. For the benefit of the cash flow of the practice, it is better if arrangements are made for payments to be made regularly at the end of each month.

These notional rent assessments are revalued at triennial intervals, again by the District Valuer. If a practice is not satisfied with the amount of the new assessment, it has a right of appeal to the Secretary of State. This is frequently exercised and until very recently there was reason to believe that the vast majority of such appeals were successful, to a greater or lesser degree.

These arrangements for revaluation of notional rent assessments have been brought into much sharper focus in recent years, due to the increasing likelihood of the District Valuer reducing such an assessment, taking into consideration the fall in rental values as a result of the property recession in the early 1990s. This view has been contested as a result of a provision of SFA paragraph 51, Schedule 4, which provides that as a basis for making this assessment 'an assumption will be made that the building is held on a fifteen year lease provided for upward only reviews every three years'.

Very largely as a result of this, a number of appeals have been lodged against these reduced assessments (see also **3.9**).

The interpretation of SFA 51.4 and the determination of such appeals still largely remains unsettled. It is understood that some appeals have been settled by retaining the status quo, i.e., neither an increase nor reduction, but these decisions are by no means binding and any practice finding itself in the somewhat invidious position of having its notional rent allowance reduced is strongly advised to appeal against this decision.

In practice, those surgeries which attract a notional rent allowance will normally be those which have been held and used by the practice for many years, together with those which have been developed under the cost rent scheme during more recent years and where the doctors have felt it to their advantage to opt for the notional rent basis at one of their triennial opportunities to do so.

3.3   Outline of the cost rent scheme

It has been said, with some truth, that the cost rent scheme for development of GP surgeries offers an investment opportunity unique in UK business life, inside or outside the National Health Service. With the scheme offering, if used to its best advantage, the prospect of GPs acquiring a share in a valuable capital asset, without any significant capital outlay and with, effectively, an additional income to cover the interest charges of loans raised for the development, this is a comment with which few would argue.

The cost rent scheme proper, introduced in the mid-1970s, has already played a major role in providing new and improved surgery facilities for NHS patients. It is perhaps surprising that, even so, some GPs have felt unable to take advantage of this, frequently being inhibited by the apparently large costs involved.

It is fair to say that the popularity of the scheme has somewhat waned in recent years, beyond its high point of attraction in the mid-1980s, when practices were able to take advantage of this opportunity, virtually without let or hindrance, and many projects which came to fruition at that time have brought tremendous financial advantages for those GPs fortunate enough to have shared in the development at that time. However, see also **3.8** below on negative equity.

While the scheme still retains its inherent advantages, nevertheless it has become somewhat less attractive in more recent years, primarily due to the difficulty in many practices of obtaining funding from their HA due to the imposition of cash limiting procedures. It is by no means unusual to find practices asked to wait several years before funding will be available for their project and in virtually all cases HAs have only a very limited amount of money available to be used for this purpose.

In addition, the effective reduction in cost rent limits in recent years has resulted in practices being less likely to recover the whole of their interest costs.

What, then, are the financial benefits of the cost rent scheme which make it so attractive? These can be fairly summarised:

(a)   acquisition of a valuable asset over a period of years without significant capital outlay;

(b)   interest and possibly an element of capital repayment being covered by receipt of the cost rent allowance;

(c)   the likelihood of tax-free capital appreciation to retirement (but this possibility has been modified in recent years by considerations of negative equity);
(d)   the possibility of increasing level of income over the years; and
(e)   significant taxation benefits.

3.4   Establishment of cost limits

In order to qualify under this scheme, a project must fall within one of the following headings:

- the erection of entirely new premises;
- the acquisition of a building for substantial modification;
- the extension or improvement of existing premises.

The essential feature of the scheme is that the initial cost rent allowance is based upon the total cost of developing the new surgery, or the cost of modification in other cases. To this total a percentage factor is applied, resulting in the term 'cost rent'. For instance, if the total cost of the project is £900,000 and there is a 7 per cent rate of cost rent in force at the time, the annual reimbursement will be £63,000.

The determination of the total agreed cost of the project (which is not limitless) is by negotiation with the HA, using cost rent limits in force at the time (see below). To that agreed total is applied the percentage rate in force at the time.

3.4.1   Calculating the total cost

There are four major components in determining the cost of a development under the cost rent scheme.

The cost of acquiring the land
This would normally be included in the calculation of total cost on the basis of the actual cost to the practice. Where a District Valuer's valuation is very much less and it is impossible to reconcile the two through negotiation, it is the District Valuer's figure which will be used.

In practice, many such projects are developed using land already owned by some form of public body, which is also subject to the District Valuer's valuation and it is unlikely therefore that a conflict will arise.

The total building costs
These are limited to certain cost rent limits which depend on the limits published from time to time. The responsibility for ensuring that building costs do not exceed those figures largely rests with the architect, upon whom the final responsibility lies to design a building which will not only

be acceptable as a development of a place to work but will also be financially viable. Cost rent limits in force at the time of writing are set out in Appendix 13. To these building limits are applied certain area cost factors, which are discussed more fully below.

Professional and architects' fees
These will normally be 11.5 per cent of the building costs, plus VAT. Within this is included all fees paid to architects and allied professionals such as surveyors, engineers and the like.

The cost of raising finance
The major component here will be the cost of bridging finance which, for a major project, possibly where the development lasts over several years, is likely to be high. There can also be included under this heading any additional cost of raising finance, such as accountants' and surveyors' fees, although this is very much subject to negotiation with the HA.

As we have seen, the total amount which the GP can spend on the development of his surgery is limited in a number of ways, including the total building costs. In practice, a major point of decision in these projects usually arrives when tenders are invited for building costs, only for it to be found that these are a great deal higher than originally estimated. By that time, of course, the practice may well have expended an appreciable amount of money to date; architects' and surveyors' fees will have been paid, the land may have been bought, planning permission obtained and the like. The project may well have passed the point of no return. If all else fails, and GPs seek to go ahead with the project, they may well be left in the position of having to finance this either through their own resources or by higher loan finance, whilst only obtaining cost rent reimbursement up to the prescribed limits.

3.4.2   Area bands and factors

For many years, a chief factor in determining building costs was the area in which a development was to take place. For instance, in a rural practice, the cost would be likely to be a great deal lower than in a large urban area. In a move to counteract this apparent inequity, a system was introduced from 1 May 1993 by which a factor is given for each FHSA area. These factors are then applied to the cost rent limits and it will be seen, generally speaking, that higher factors apply in areas of high building costs. A full list of these cost limit location factors is set out in Appendix 14.

Once all this information is available, the total cost of the project has been established and the method of reimbursement arranged, it should be possible to make a reasonable calculation of the likely return in terms of cost rent. A typical calculation is set out in Figure 3.2.

Figure 3.2 *Showing calculation of cost rent allowance on typical surgery development project (development after 1 April 1995 in (say) Avon)*

			£
1.	Site (cost or District Valuer's valuation, whichever the lower)		150,000
2.	Building cost (subject to cost rent limits), say	575,000	
	Adjust: factor for Avon HA (0.96)		552,000
			702,000
3.	VAT @ 17.5% on £552,000 (see **7.11**)		96,600
4.	Architects, etc. fees (b)	63,480	
	VAT (17.5%)	11,109	
			74,589
5.	Bridging interest (say)		46,811
			920,000
	Cost rent reimbursement at variable rate (say, 7.75%)		71,300

(a) Figures do not relate to any actual project.
(b) Architects' fees at 11.5% of building cost (£552,000) plus VAT.

3.5   Fixed and variable rates

Two rates are available for practices developing surgeries under this scheme, a variable and a fixed rate. The variable rate of reimbursement is reviewed annually and normally changes from 1 April each year. This will change only at annual intervals as necessary. If the practice opts for a fixed rate of reimbursement, this will remain constant until the practice chooses to vary the method of reimbursement by applying for a change to notional rent basis.

This option is available to practices at triennial intervals, in the same way that notional rent might be updated. Once a practice opts for the change it cannot go back to the cost rent basis. In practice, the variable rate of reimbursement will normally apply to all such projects except where the GPs are financing the scheme wholly or mainly through their own private resources, or the GPs have chosen to finance the scheme with a loan bearing a fixed rate of interest.

In some cases GPs will choose to finance their development through a fixed rate loan, but carrying the option to switch to a variable rate at some agreed future date. In these cases, the fixed rate of reimbursement will apply until the option is exercised, when the variable rate will come into operation. This rule allows GPs to enter such arrangements without the insecurity of knowing that if they do exercise the option at some future date, and at a time of high or rising interest rates, they will not be penalised through being required to pay a higher floating rate of interest to the finance house concerned while receiving a lower rate of fixed cost rent. It is frequently found that fixed rate borrowing is only available on such a project where other, and possibly unacceptable conditions are imposed; for instance, the practice may be required to take out a succession of endowment or pension policies which they would not otherwise require and which may merely increase their total outgoings.

3.6   Financing the project

It is, rather sadly, a misconception that the cost rent reimbursement is a refund of interest charges. This is not the case; if one were to imagine a situation where the doctors in the practice were of sufficient means to fund the project from their own resources, they would still receive the cost rent allowance under the formula as set out above but they would, of course, have no interest charges to pay if they had not funded the project through loan finance.

The practice will receive the cost rent reimbursement as outlined above; where they go for the money is entirely up to them and they must, with proper advice, look at the sources currently available and select the one most suitable for their needs.

In most of these projects, it goes without saying that there are few GPs who have the resources to fund the project from their own free capital; in the vast majority of cases loans will be taken out, in many cases for 100 per cent of the total cost of project and the GPs will effectively have to finance this from the proceeds of the cost rent allowance or, if this is insufficient, from their own residual earnings.

The initial borrowing requirement will be to provide bridging finance during the development period. Practices are well advised to open a separate loan account with their bank and to pay all charges appropriate to the project out of that account. This will naturally result in an increasing overdraft, upon which the interest will be aggregated, i.e., 'rolled up' up to the date of final completion. Where funds are being advanced from an outside source, i.e., the GP Finance Corporation, it will normally be possible to draw down instalments of the loan so that the bank bridging loan is kept at a relatively low level.

So far as the final source of borrowing is concerned, the problem facing the GP is not so much how to find the loan finance, as how to select the best option from the numerous ones which are available. Factors which should be taken into consideration when evaluing sources of finance are:

(a) the rate of interest available;
(b) conditions for repayment (20/25-year terms are normally available);
(c) whether conditions are imposed concerning collateral life assurance or pension policies;
(d) whether capital repayment holidays will be available;
(e) option of variation from fixed/floating rates.

The lending institution must be able to satisfy itself that the practice will be able to service and repay the loan on the agreed terms. Where, for instance, the cost rent reimbursement appears to be lower than the total cost of servicing the loan, then the GPs will have to finance the shortfall from their own earnings. In a high earning practice this should cause few problems provided that the net cost is kept within reasonable bounds. Less remunerative practices may, for that reason, find greater difficulties in obtaining loan finance where the project is not completely viable on its own and they are in a less advantageous situation when negotiating over conditions to be imposed. Whatever the size of the practice, it is essential that any potential surplus or deficit is estimated at the outset. This will have to be taken into consideration by each individual GP when assessing his own particular need.

Many finance houses will do their utmost to persuade GPs to enter into some sort of endowment-linked mortgage. Whilst each case must be considered on its merits, it is usually found, particularly in a partnership, that such a means of repayment is unsuitable. In a partnership, problems arise where at some future date a surgery-owning partner seeks to leave the practice and it is necessary to value the accumulated premiums on the endowment policy. Conversely, a new partner buying in will find that he must take over a share of the existing loan, but again problems may well arise over the valuation of the endowment policy.

Similarly, with collateral pension policies, these are really only effective where it is possible to obtain a full measure of tax relief on the pension premiums. In the case of GPs, in order for this to be allowed in any event, it will be necessary for the GP to renounce the tax relief on his NHS pension contributions (see **9.15.2**), which again merely increases the total cost.

In the majority of circumstances, it will be found that the economy offered by a normal repayment mortgage will be to the benefit of the practice concerned.

Some finance houses are prepared to offer capital repayment holidays, whereby there is a moratorium on repayments of capital for, say, the first six years of the loan. These are superficially attractive; the period of six years is designed as the period after which a practice might reasonably be expected to convert to notional rent basis, with the additional income this generates.

There are many and varied packages of loan facilities available to GPs developing surgeries. Interest rates are competitive and the adviser may well wish to see his clients negotiating initially on the basis of an interest rate of 1 per cent over base. This depends on the security offered, the financial viability of the project and the economic circumstances at the time.

3.6.1   What will it cost?

Naturally, a question that the GP is likely to ask is what the effect will be on his own pocket. Not an unreasonable question and one to which he is entitled to have an answer.

When all the information is available it will be possible to put this together and to prepare a statement which will give some idea of any likely shortfall or surplus on the project. Only then will it be possible for GPs to evaluate this in the light of whether they wish to go ahead with the project.

Figure 3.3 shows a simplified but typical situation which might arise.

Figure 3.3 *What will it cost?*

		£
Total cost (see Figure 3.2)		920,000
Cost rent allowance (7.75% variable)		71,300
Loan repayments:		
Annual interest (say 8%)	(3)	73,600
Total annual shortfall		2,300
Per (5) partners		460

(1) Assuming building erected within cost rent limits.
(2) The illustration ignores the effect of taxation.
(3) Assumed 1.5% over bank base rate on 100% loan finance.
(4) This shows a typical situation where the proceeds from the cost rent allowance (£71,300) are slightly less than on the loan finance.
(5) Assumes capital repayment 'holiday' requires no capital repayments during early years.

Carrying on from Figure 3.2, we see the practice with a potential cost rent allowance of £71,300, which has been unable to borrow funds at 7.5 per cent and is obliged to do so at 8 per cent. The shortfall is therefore £2,300 per annum or £460 per partner. In a high-earning practice one would not expect this to be any undue problem, particularly bearing in mind the potential for increases through option for notional rent basis in future years.

It has been assumed for this purpose that the practice has opted for a capital repayment holiday, possibly for up to six years when they might reasonably expect the rent allowance to have increased to such an amount as will cover both the interest charges and a reasonable amount of the capital repayments.

3.7   The sale and leaseback scheme

Introduced in the 1980s, with the intention of catering for those practices which found themselves in difficulty when shares of the surgery were required to be bought and sold between partners, the sale and leaseback scheme has existed in various manifestations ever since.

As with any other similar development, the principle of the scheme is that the practice develops a surgery, going through all the processes required for the cost rent scheme and with the same limiting factors applying, then sells it to a third party, after which the practice becomes a tenant and reclaims the rent from the HA.

Some practices have gone down this route and have been extremely satisfied. On the other hand, the scheme avoids the major fiscal advantages of the cost rent scheme proper, i.e., a regular and increasing source of income, possibly tax-free capital appreciation.

If and when such a transfer is effected, there is no guarantee that the rent to be refunded will be equivalent to the charge made by the new owners. HAs are now subject to all manner of restrictions and will only pay the rent reimbursement to the extent they are satisfied, in conjunction with the District Valuer, that this is a fair market rent for the property in question. It is perfectly possible for practices to receive less in rent refund than they pay out to the new owners.

The situation may well now have changed somewhat as a result of the property recession which makes schemes of this nature, where there is no guarantee of long-term capital growth, seem more attractive.

The practitioner who finds himself advising doctors in this position would be well advised to tread warily; each case must be considered on its merits and the wishes of the clients taken into consideration.

3.8 Negative equity

It is frequently said that the economic recession of the late 1980s and early 1990s has scarcely affected general practice, or indeed the medical profession at large. There is some truth in this: GPs are working within certain limits which are regularly becoming more stringent; the principal, in practice, has a regular source of income; it is highly unlikely that his business will go to the wall and any effect is likely to be minimal – certainly when compared to the rest of the trading community.

Where GPs have, however, been adversely affected in recent years is as a result of the downturn in the property market. As we have seen, many GPs own their own surgeries and these are invariably developed on the basis of a 100 per cent mortgage, so that in the early years of ownership there is little if any equity remaining in the building. Classically, equity has tended to build up over the years as a result of upward revaluations of the property and gradual repayments of the principal loan.

For medical practices, negative equity is not of recent origin, nor is the recession in the property market. Many GPs have had to live with negative equity, certainly in the early years of their ownership, due to high building costs which they have frequently been unable to recover in terms of cost rent income. Also it has regularly been found that the building value shortly after completion is worth a great deal less than the cost of development and in many cases also less than the amount outstanding on the surgery loan.

Usually such surgeries were initially valued for insurance purposes. There has always been a problem with regard to retiring partners who again normally found it beneficial not to join in such a development if it took place within a few years of their pending retirement. In most cases, however, practices, particularly those with a relatively high level of income and comprised of partners not nearing retirement, were able to weather this problem without too much difficulty. Provided there were no partnership changes pending and they were able to fund the cost of servicing the loan without undue difficulty, they could fairly confidently wait for a few years in the reasonable expectation that property values would increase over the relatively short term so that the negative equity was extinguished.

In those cases, it became common for a clause to be inserted in the partnership deed to the effect that a partner retiring or leaving the

practice within a specified period, say five years, would be protected in
that his share of the property would never be sold at less than cost. This
gave him an assurance; it encouraged doctors in their fifties to join in the
development in the knowledge that they would not find themselves with a
substantial debt when they left the practice. They may well not have
increased their equity but at least it could not fall lower than zero.

Doubts have recently been expressed over the legality of such clauses and
the extent to which these represent a hidden sale of goodwill (see **2.13**).

This also raised problems for incoming partners which are largely tied up
with the methods of valuation and will be dealt with under that heading
(**3.9**).

To a large degree GPs have a real advantage over the householder or the
conventional businessman who finds himself in a parallel situation. A GP
can reasonably expect to receive a direct reimbursement for his ownership of the surgery, in the form of the notional or cost rent allowance.
With an element of good fortune and depending on the date of
development, this allowance may well pay the whole of the interest on his
bank loan and even some element of the capital repayment. This alone
means that, even in a property recession, a GP is unlikely to have any
undue problem in servicing this loan out of income.

3.8.1   Existing surgeries

Figure 3.4 shows the position of an inner-city practice which has owned its
surgery for some years, having been developed in 1987 at a total cost of
£1.5 million. This was revalued on the retirement of Dr A in 1988 at £1.6
million and has been shown as such in successive balance sheets, being
owned only by Drs B and C. They are receiving cost rent and servicing the
loan interest out of this reimbursement. However, the senior partner, Dr
B, announces his intention to retire at the end of December 1996 and to
sell his share in the surgery to Dr D on the same date. The partners have
obtained a professional valuation and found that the current value of the
surgery is £850,000.

What is already an extremely difficult situation is made even more
problematical in that Dr D, who joined as a junior partner on 1 January
1994, is to reach parity after three years, i.e., on 1 January 1996, from
which date he was given an option to buy an appropriate share of the
surgery. In view of the valuation and the outstanding loan he does not feel
able to buy a share of the property. Because of the requirement for him to
take over obligation for part of the outstanding surgery loan he is not now
intending to go ahead with this purchase so that the ownership will

Figure 3.4 *Negative equity: existing surgery*

Drs B, C & D
Surgery developed 1986/87
Completed 1 June 1987

	Original finance 1987	1988	1996
	£'000	£'000	£'000
At cost	1,500		
Valuation			
31 December 1989		1,600	
31 December 1996			850
Loan finance	1,500	1,400	1,200
Positive equity, 1989		200	
Negative equity, 1996			(350)

devolve only on Dr C, who himself is due to retire in some three or four years.

Although there was no clause in the partnership deed, Dr C agreed that Dr B would be paid out on the basis of the amount outstanding under the loan, which gave him nil equity. Dr C therefore finds himself saddled with an outstanding loan. While the interest is covered by the rent allowance, he has a continuing problem in meeting the capital repayments.

Dr C finds himself in a classic 'catch 22' situation; whichever way he turns he is likely to lose money. So long as he continues to practise, his situation is barely sustainable; he is able to make interest payments on the loan out of the cost rent income, but he must meet the capital repayments out of his own free income and on that basis his only hope for improvement is that in a few years he may be able to opt for notional rent basis with a consequent increase in reimbursement. Even this, however, is far from certain.

With some three years before a decision has to be made, his main alternatives appear to be:

(a)   to keep his options open, hoping the property market picks up in the meantime;

(b) to agree to defer his own retirement. But he is now aged 57, and intends to retire at 60 and has already made plans for his eventual retirement home;

(c) to retire but to charge an enhanced rent to the practice. This assumes that the then partners will wish to continue to practice from that surgery and indeed, unless they are able and willing to pay a higher rent and the HA will make the appropriate refund, they may well decline to do so. To continue to own a business asset for 12 months after the date of his retirement could also bring a possible loss of CGT retirement relief, but this is a somewhat academic concept if there is no capital gain in any event;

(d) to sell the building for what he can get, accept his loss, repay the mortgage and meet the deficit out of his own free estate. This could, perhaps, be the most disastrous option of all; it may well mean that Dr C will lose all the retirement benefits he has worked to build up and it is the sort of problem which practitioners are now finding themselves asked to advise upon.

It goes without saying that each case should be considered on its merits and a decision arrived at only after careful thought and the examination of all possible options.

3.8.2 Ownership by trust

Some practices have sought to avoid this problem by transferring the property into some form of trust, so that the building is owned by the practice in perpetuity, rather than shares being held by the individual partners. For practices which already have such a problem, it may well be too late for this to be an effective solution, although practices whose surgeries are at the planning stage may well feel they should enter into such an arrangement.

While this obviates such fiscal advantages as are due to the GPs, nevertheless it caters for those practices which feel that finance is a secondary consideration and whose main intention is to provide adequate surgery accommodation for their patients.

3.9 Basis of valuation

For many years the accepted basis for valuation of doctors' surgeries is that this is to be based upon continuing use of the building as a doctor's surgery. Indeed, in many cases, there is little alternative; particularly where land is purchased from a local authority or health body, it is common for there to be a restrictive covenant on the land so that it cannot be used in any event for other purposes.

This principle has, however, not served doctors particularly well during the recession in property values. As we have seen in the previous section, general practices are now experiencing unacceptable problems which in themselves result directly from the basis used for the valuation of the surgery.

The principle which until now has been in force has been called into question, with some justification.

It is now being suggested that rather than using this method, the surgery should be valued upon the upgraded capital value of the notional/cost rent allowance, using a factor of some 7.5 per cent (or surveyors' recommendation).

In practice, this basis is more likely to apply to notional rents, which are in themselves subject to the vagaries of the property market. Variable rate cost rent allowances are geared to a specified factor each year and in those cases the value projected by either method is unlikely to be materially different. In the case of a practice receiving a notional rent of, say, £75,000 per annum, this would give an upgraded valuation of £1 million, depending of course upon the size and location of the surgery, and is likely to be a great deal higher than that produced by a conventional valuation. At first sight this would seem to present no undue problems; provided the doctors were in agreement over buying and selling shares there is no reason why the transaction should not go through on that basis. However, in medical practice, as in so many other areas, different regulations prevail and there are reasons why this cannot be done.

We have seen (**2.13**) that the sale and purchase of goodwill in NHS medical practices, whether on an actual or constructive basis, is illegal and doctors found entering into such agreements can find themselves answering for their actions before the Medical Practitioners' Committee, which has a number of sanctions available to it.

In this case, it has been held that if doctors knowingly take part in such a transaction, where shares of property were changing hands at a value knowingly above the actual market value, then this would be considered as a constructive sale of goodwill and would not be allowed to take place. This puts all the parties to such a situation in an extremely invidious position, not least the young partner entering general practice and wishing to buy his share of the surgery.

At the time of writing, recent cases passing through the courts suggest that the law on the subject may be amended, but this is by no means certain.

The problem of valuations of surgery premises is a very real one and, it is felt, one that could well cause concern and disputes in practices for the foreseeable future. As a help in determining realistic valuations, the Royal Institution of Chartered Surveyors has recently (January 1996) issued guidelines to its members involved in such work. These guidelines came into operation from 1 February 1996.

3.9.1   The incoming partner

We have already seen (**3.8**) the situation which may apply when an outgoing partner leaves the practice, with the benefit of an agreement to the effect that his share of the surgery will be deemed to have been sold to him at a value based upon original cost.

On most such occasions, an outgoing partner will be replaced by a new partner who has the opportunity of buying into the surgery at the earliest convenient date. For many reasons it has been considered standard practice for such a new partner to buy direct from the outgoing partner without involving the continuing partners.

This now appears, to all intents and purposes, impracticable. The new partner may well not be prepared to buy in on the same valuation as that which the outgoing partner sold; he knows perfectly well that if the outgoing partner has been paid out on the basis of his share of the original cost of the surgery at, say, £600,000, when the current valuation is £400,000 he may well not be prepared to do so.

Even if he is prepared to do so and both he and the continuing partners are in agreement, they could well fall foul of the 'goodwill' rule and for this reason many young partners in practices are finding it all but impossible to acquire a share of a surgery. This is a problem which, it is suggested, will only be resolved once the property market begins a significant upturn and GPs can once again look upon their surgery with some assurance as a potential 'nest egg' on retirement.

3.10   Improvement grants (SFA 56)

All GPs offering restricted general medical services, provided their list size exceeds certain modest criteria, can obtain grants under specified conditions towards the cost of improving medical practice premises and facilities. These improvement grants can only be obtained where prior approval of the HA has been received. Where this is granted, the GP will be required to complete the works within a specified period. Normally grants will be to the amount of one-third (33.3 per cent) of the cost of the work, although at the discretion of the HA this may rise up to two-thirds. In practice, the two-thirds limit will only be given where surgeries are in development areas.

Projects which are likely to be eligible for the grant include the provision of new rooms within or adjacent to the building; improved access facility; additions to and improvement of toilet and washing facilities; improved lighting ventilation and heating installation and extension to telephone facilities. It can also be extended to provision of car and pram parking accommodation, installation of double glazing and security systems and work required by statute for fire precautions.

From the point of view of the accountant acting for a practice applying for such a grant, it should be borne in mind that the cost of the work involved cannot qualify both for grant aid and tax relief. The claim to be completed when application is made includes a declaration that no part of the cost will be claimed for tax purposes. Where, for instance, grant is obtained on a cost which would normally be included for capital allowances, such as the installation of a telephone switchboard, central heating, double glazing, etc., it is the cost which qualifies for grant (not the actual grant itself) which must be deducted in making a capital allowances claim.

Practitioners advising GPs should take into account all the circumstances at the time, such as the rate of capital allowances claimable, the marginal rate of tax of the doctors making the claim and each case should be considered on its merits. Having said that, in the majority of cases it will be found that it will be preferable to claim the grant as an initial payment and forego subsequent tax relief, particularly where the GPs are able to negotiate an improvement grant in excess of the one-third minimum.

In some circumstances it will be found that improvement grants will be payable on expenditure which would otherwise be treated for normal accounting purposes as of a revenue nature and would otherwise represent a perfectly legitimate deduction before arriving at assessable practice profits. In those cases, it will be necessary to add back the charge in the accounts and to deduct the improvement grant when preparing the tax computation.

It should be noted that this restriction applies only to the actual cost of the works qualifying for grant. If the practice borrows money for that purpose no such restriction applies to the claiming of tax relief on that interest.

From 1 June 1995, the minimum cost acceptable for a grant is £643, plus VAT. Where premises have not previously been used as a practice, the maximum grant per doctor is £5,875, plus VAT with an overall limit for each project of £20,522 plus VAT.

Certain revised rates of grant apply to practices situated within the London limitations zone. See the tax computation at Figure 7.1 (para **7.3.2**).

Chapter 4 – Acting for doctors

It is no secret that doctors – particularly GPs – can be awkward and demanding clients. Invariably highly educated people, as well as high net worth individuals, they are a boon to any accountancy practice. It is unlikely that they will go out of business; the practice itself (but not necessarily the surgery – see **3.8**) is not subject to the same economic trends as the normal business community and it is highly unlikely that a practice will cease to exist.

Fees will invariably be paid reasonably promptly and the incidence of bad debts is likely to be extremely low.

All trades and professions have their own characteristics when it comes to dealing with accounts. However, perhaps only with general medical practitioners are their finances so arcane and complex that it is really only an expert in the field who is able to act adequately for GPs and to whom they feel they can fully relate. The accountant who proposes to act for GPs, not having acquired the necessary expertise, will almost certainly be quickly found out.

It is a frequently heard comment in the accounting profession that life would be extremely easy were it not for clients. A whimsical remark perhaps, and invariably said tongue in cheek, but for those acting for GPs it can carry a great deal more poignancy than with most other clients.

The GP may have a rather touching belief that, unlike in his own profession, the accountant is expert in all fields. He may be blissfully unaware that such a speciality exists, that all accountants are expert in GP finance and in appointing a professional adviser he has no need to look beyond the bounds of fee levels and, possibly, proximity.

Woe betide the accountant, however, who – and such replies are by no means unknown – responds 'what is the cost rent scheme?'; 'what are leave advances?', or – even worse – 'what is the "Red Book"?' At the best he will have lost a number of brownie points and, in the fullness of time, possibly the client also.

The purpose of this chapter is to explore ways in which the professional adviser can act for his client more efficiently; how he can try and ensure that work is produced at a minimum cost and, hopefully, an acceptable recovery rate in his own office, so enhancing his own reputation and financial well-being.

It is not the purpose of this book to lay down means by which this can be done, or even interfere with firms' existing policies. Rather, it should be read in the context of both experience gained to date and hopefully at the end of the day of producing a system which is efficient, useful and productive.

4.1 Acquiring a speciality

There are numerous specialities within the accounting profession, only one of which is work for GPs in the National Health Service. With the arcane nature of the finances, it is, above all, necessary that an individual or firm who seeks to act for doctors in a serious and professional manner should go to such lengths as are both reasonable and economic to acquire such a level of acknowledged speciality and repute which will both attract and retain clients.

Indeed, GPs, some of whom change accountants with some regularity, are now being strongly advised through their own journals and otherwise, to ensure that accountants acting for them are specialists in that field and GPs are being advised that when such a post is being filled, at an interview, questions should be asked which will ensure that the successful firm can clearly display such a record of experience and speciality. This is, of course, not easy to come by; it is something of a 'catch 22' situation where accountants cannot acquire this expertise unless they have sufficient clients to justify it, yet without this speciality they are unlikely to be able to attract those clients.

Firms who therefore wish to jump onto this bandwagon should make certain that they have the facility to obtain the necessary literature; access to the Red Book and specialist medical journals and that the appropriate training courses are attended. A level of internal training is also necessary to guarantee that, for instance, more junior staff are aware of the level of advice they will be required to give to clients at a rather more basic level.

All this of course places a practitioner who has no known experience in work for GPs in a somewhat difficult position when approached by such a client with a view to acting for him. He can, of course, decline to accept the assignment, advising the doctor to seek out one of his more specialist colleagues. On the other hand, he may feel that it is worthwhile acquiring such a speciality, with all that this implies. Whether this would be financially viable, if only one client is acted for, must remain somewhat doubtful.

The formation of AISMA (see Preface) has greatly aided the work of specialist accountants in the fields of training and dissemination of information.

4.2 Internal organisation

Firms will already have adequate systems set up for dealing with unincorporated clients and the necessary taxation work which this engenders. It is not the intention of this book to try to change those systems in any way, although it may well be that in view of the unusual situations which apply to acting for GPs, these can be adapted in order to cater for this specialist activity. Those firms which have already established an expertise in this area have felt able to concentrate the work involved within a single office in groups of specialists at various grades, who will deal with the whole of the work for the GPs in that office.

Those firms which are unable to justify a separate group or department dedicated to this work, may well feel that they should, nevertheless, concentrate whatever work there is within a select group of individuals, hoping that this will grow over a period and that the expertise will be there when required.

Again, those firms which are organised on such a basis may well accept that they should allocate one partner/manager to this work who will become experienced not only in overseeing and supervising the technical quality of the work, but also in the preparation of advice to his clients.

GPs tend not to be great respecters of persons; they are less inclined to be impressed by the status of the individual within his organisation than the ease with which he can converse and advise them on their specialist affairs. These two concepts may not necessarily go together.

4.3 Working papers

It is essential – and this is by no means peculiar to doctors – that a well-organised working papers file is prepared for each year of work. To cater for the rather specialist needs of GPs as clients, it is suggested that a specially designed index be used and sections be allocated according to the requirements of these clients. A specimen master index for a GP's working papers file is shown in Appendix 6.

The file should be prepared by the staff accountant dealing with the accounts preparation work and it should be made available, with the draft accounts, or for review (see **4.6**) before these are sent to clients for approval. Such a file should have a 'trail', which is easy to follow and backs up the figures shown in the accounts. An acceptable system of indexing and cross-referencing (the details of which have no place in this book) is essential in order that queries might be answered and the accuracy of the accounts is shown.

The working papers file should include, as well as the routine schedules from which the accounts are prepared, the following:

(a) completed letter of representation (see **4.10** and Appendix 10);
(b) draft accounts (or signed copies if applicable) (Chapter 6);
(c) taxation computations and allocation of liability between partners (Chapter 7);
(d) copies of quarterly HA schedules;
(e) details of assets purchased/sold/depreciated;
(f) outstanding debtors, including provision for HA fees and allowances (see **6.3.12**);
(g) outstanding creditors, including full amounts payable to drug suppliers (see **6.3.14**);
(h) calculation of drug stock valuation, with certificate signed by client or valuer (see **6.3.9**);
(i) details of transactions on capital and property capital accounts (see **5.8**) showing allocations between partners;
(j) full profit-sharing ratios during current and succeeding years (see **5.3**).

4.4   Planning the work

It is highly desirable that before the work is put in hand a significant level of planning is undertaken. Much of the work can be done before the actual work of the accounts preparation commences and sound planning will go a long way to ensure a timely, accurate and economic operation.

GPs tend to prepare their accounts to one of the major quarter-ends, i.e., June, September, December or March, with a greater emphasis in recent years towards June year ends for tax planning reasons. Try and make sure that all such work is identified some few weeks before the end of that quarter. The work can then be allocated to individuals within the office who can organise their own timetables to ensure that time is available when required.

A further decision to be made is exactly where the work is to be performed. Some accountants prefer to do this at the client's surgery, while others prefer to do the work within their own office. Experience has shown that such work will be done more quickly and efficiently at the client's premises, largely because:

(a) staff are able to work in a more concentrated manner upon one client without the interruption that usually goes with working in their own office;

(b) staff are available to meet the partners at the outset of the work in order to discuss their personal affairs such as completion of expenses claims (see **7.6**);

(c) queries can be taken up and answered on the premises without the need for lengthy subsequent telephone calls and correspondence;

(d) the system of working may obviate the necessity for the client's books to be taken from his premises, which frequently causes annoyance, particularly if these are not returned for a lengthy period.

Having taken this decision, to some degree in agreement with the client, a 'year-end' letter can then be sent to the client explaining exactly the type of information required, the manner in which this is to be set out and confirming arrangements for the visit. A specimen of a year-end letter is set out in Appendix 11.

When this has been sent, arrangements can be made for the visit to take place. It will then be normal to write a letter of confirmation, specifying the members of staff who will attend and asking for certain required facilities to be made available to them.

At this stage also, time can be booked and diary notes arranged during which eventual reviews can take place (see **4.6**).

Where it is decided that no visit will be made but the work will be done in the practitioner's own office, again it should be possible to identify when the records are expected to arrive, so that time can be set aside.

Before the work is put in hand, it will be necessary to work through the previous year's working papers file, highlighting any matters which may have been set aside for consideration in the following year, looking at any points of advice which were given in order that these might be followed up and to see if any recommendations for improvements in the system have been carried out.

4.5   Progressing the work

Having – hopefully – planned successfully, we can now put the work in hand as already arranged with the clients. Having briefed our client's staff for what we require, we would reasonably expect that we would be presented with a properly written-up balanced reconciled set of accounting records, drawn up in the way we require, which will enable us to deal with the work promptly and efficiently.

When we arrive at the client's premises we should try and ensure that all the information is available to us, and it is not a bad idea to check this at the outset. If anything is missing we should ask for this as soon as we can. A copy should be taken of the records produced and seen.

The client will presumably keep some form of petty cash record and initially one member of staff should work on this, producing an analysis and summary for the year which can be used as an aid to posting when the time arrives.

Hopefully the client's staff, as we have asked, will produce a summary of the cash book, properly analysed and mathematically correct. We should try and check that the balance in the cash book agrees with the balance on the bank statements at the same date and that the client has provided an accurate bank reconciliation.

It is suggested that, if this is made available, then a test check is made of the, say, the first month and last two months' bank entries, so that we can satisfy ourselves that the final balance is correct. Enquire into any long outstanding cheques and, if necessary, these should be written off. Once this is completed it will be possible to prepare a brief bank summary, which will prove the agreement of the bank account with which the detailed receipts and payments summaries should agree:

	£	£
Balance at bank, b/f 1.7.95	3,968.42	
Receipts, per summary	458,624.75	
Payments per summary		454,627.45
Balance at bank, 30.6.96		7,965.72
	462,593.17	462,592.17

Such a statement should be prepared for each bank account and building society account which has been in existence during the year. Ensure that one is prepared for every such account upon which a balance was shown at the previous year end, or which has been opened during the year of account.

We can then go on to prepare our statements of summaries of receipts and payments. That for the receipts should be extracted from the analysis columns of the cash book, with sub-analyses being prepared as necessary.

This summary should in its final form show details of income received from every individual source, including analyses of HA income, non-NHS income, refunds and the like. Deductions should be shown in respect of superannuation, leave advance repayments, interest payments, NHS levies and any other deductions made in the NHS statements.

It is usual and beneficial to prepare a sub-analysis of the HA income which in itself represents an analysis and summary of the four (or more at times) HA statements received during the year. This total should then be reconciled to the total of the NHS receipts column in the cash book. The total of the receipts summary should agree with the receipts total in the bank account summary.

We can then proceed to prepare a similar statement for payments, which again should be analysed so as to tally with the headings which will ultimately find their way into the final accounts.

Once this has been completed it will then be possible to proceed to the preparation of a trial balance prior to the completion of the final accounts. Into this final trial balance we should introduce the following information:

- opening balances;
- petty cash transactions;
- bank account transactions.

Where necessary, journals should be used when transfers between accounts are necessary.

It will then be possible to adjust the accounts for closing adjustments, debtors and creditors, stock on hand, etc. and from these a final statement of accounts can be extracted.

Once these accounts are available it is suggested that they be sent for review (see **4.6**), in accordance with the policies of the firm involved.

When these accounts have been reviewed and they are at such a stage that they can be sent to the client, copies can be sent to the practice with an invitation for the partners to sign them as correct. It is suggested that a top copy be sent first which will ultimately bear the signature of all partners, together with one further copy for each partner to retain until the final accounts are submitted.

Some partnerships prefer at this stage to meet their accountant in order to run through the draft accounts and to provide such explanations as the partners might require.

Once the accounts have been returned duly signed, final copies can be made, the accountant's report can be signed and final copies circulated to individual partners. It may be necessary at this stage to include final adjustments for tax reserves and other items which might not have been apparent when the draft accounts are sent. Where necessary alterations are made between the draft accounts and the final accounts being issued, these should always be explained to the client.

4.6 Reviewing files

As we have seen, an essential process during the production of the accounts is the independent reviewing of files within the office concerned. Some firms require these to be reviewed by two people, and possibly a separate taxation review. Generally speaking, the more reviews that are carried out the less likelihood there is of incorrect accounts being sent to the client but, nevertheless, reviews are expensive and it is a constant problem to find a happy medium between the process of minimising errors and the charging of additional time to the job.

Where the work is unduly simple, say with the accounts of a small single-handed practitioner, it may be possible to dispense with one or more of these reviews, so long as this is carried out by an individual experienced and specialised in the type of work involved.

Where a review has taken place, the job should not be progressed further until any review points have been settled to the reviewer's satisfaction. In a large office it may be beneficial to book a reviewing time well in advance, in order to minimise delays.

4.7 Permanent files

It is equally essential that for each medical client there is retained a permanent file which should be divided into sections and include, *inter alia*, details of the client's operation and location, names and addresses and details of partners, previous years' signed accounts, partnership deeds and the like.

It is important that this permanent file is kept up to date and reviewed (see **4.6**) at least annually when the accounts file is reviewed.

4.8 The charging of fees

If one were to ask the average GP what he most required from his accountant, a truthful answer would probably be that he would prefer not to pay any tax at all and that he expected his accountant to do his work for nothing. To those of us who live in the real world this is not a practical possibility, yet it is precisely the charging of fees which may well lead the accountant into most disputes with his GP client and which he must do his utmost to resolve.

In recent years, fee resistance among GPs has risen to a uniquely high level. Surveys taken from time to time show that this is a major point of concern. Articles published on a fairly regular basis in the medical press show this to be a matter of great interest to GPs (not to say medical journalists), with extracts from specialist accountants displaying huge differences in levels of fees quoted.

The limitation on GPs' pay rises in recent years (see **2.2**) means that GPs, if they are to show any real increase in their net disposal income, must look at means of cutting costs and introducing such economies as they can. It is scarcely surprising that one of their main targets is that of the accountancy fee. The market has become increasingly competitive in recent years and the abiding danger is such that due to pressure on income and profits GPs will be reduced to choosing the cheapest service available, regardless of the speciality and quality of work.

The accountant on the other hand, is in an equally impossible position. On the one hand his salary costs and overheads are increasing at what might appear to be quite an alarming rate, whilst he is constantly trying to trim his fees in order to meet his clients' requirements. All firms have their own policies and philosophy as regards charging fees and it is not the purpose of this book to discuss that to any great degree, still less to quote fee levels. In any event, the constant public quotation of fees puts accountants in an invidious position; seldom do those quotations specify exactly what fees are covered (do they include personal taxation fees and VAT?), nor do they take account of regional differences which can be quite wide.

4.8.1 Fee budgeting

While GPs may well express discontent at fees in general, what appears to cause most annoyance – often with some justification – is where the fees cannot be foreseen, and they see themselves as giving the accountant virtually a blank cheque to charge what he will. To counteract this, it is highly desirable that a properly organised fee budgeting system is put in place, with the client advised in advance of the amount he will be required to pay in a year for a specified service. The quoted fee should also specify whether, or to what extent, this includes work on the personal affairs of the individual partners and that it is exclusive of VAT. The likelihood is that the practice will be unable to recover the VAT charged as it is not registered (see **7.11**) so this is merely an added cost, but nevertheless the fact must be spelt out clearly to the client.

So far as the accounts preparation process is concerned, the biggest single determining factor is the level and quality of records provided by the client. The accountant who wishes to avoid problems of this nature would be well advised to go to considerable lengths to ensure that the client produces records in the manner he requires and which will enable him to do the work in the least possible time and at the minimum cost. Where, however, this does not apply and the accountant is given a rudimentary set of records, possibly having to prepare accounts without any formal books at all, this should be clearly laid down; the cost of the additional work should be specified so that the client is in no doubt as to how much this is likely to cost him.

Where taxation work is undertaken, again it is necessary for this to be budgeted in advance. Some accountants, with the agreement and encouragement of their clients, prefer to bill an 'all-in fee', which will be charged as agreed.

Whatever policy is used and however fees are submitted and paid, this must be clearly set down in the letter of engagement agreed between the parties when the work is first undertaken (see **4.9**).

For accountants acting for particularly large partnerships, where the charge is likely to be substantial, there is pressure to remove work in progress and pass the charge on to the client at fairly regular intervals. Again, this depends on the policy of the firm involved, but a system in use which applies to accounts preparation essentially is for fees to be billed as follows:

(a) 50 per cent of the previous year's fee on commencement of the work;

(b) 80 per cent of the budgeted fee for the year (less that invoiced under (a)) on presentation of the draft accounts for agreement; and

(c) a final invoice for the full budgeted amount, taking into account the cumulative fee in (b) above.

At times, the accountant will be asked to perform other assignments for his client which fall outside the routine compliance work covered by his normal budget. This work could take several forms, including:

- advice on cost rent schemes (see **3.3** *et seq.*);
- pension and retirement planning (see Chapter 9);
- advice on accounting systems;
- computer advice;
- advice on partnership deeds (see **5.6**)
- business planning;
- partnership changes (see **5.2**); and
- GP fundholding (see Chapter 8).

Where this is done, a fee should be agreed before the work is commenced and a scale of payment agreed at the same time. Care should be taken to record separately additional time spent on such projects and a separate bill should be rendered in accordance with the timescale agreed.

Equally important is to determine exactly how fees are to be settled. Payment by monthly standing order tends to be popular with some GPs in that it enables them to plan their cash flow rather more easily. If such a system is in force, however, the practitioner should ensure that the rate of payment is reviewed at regular intervals, in order to avoid large outstanding balances building up.

4.9   Action on new clients

From time to time new GP clients will be attracted and every effort should be made to create a sound early impression. Such a reputation earned at this early stage could last for many years and may well outweigh any problems caused by minor crises in the succeeding years, which would otherwise have created discontent.

In the early days of such a relationship there is invariably a 'honeymoon' period, during which it is as well to lay down the guidelines of the future relationship. The client may well have had a difficult relationship with his previous accountant (which is why he changed in the first place) and again it is possible by a show of efficiency to make it clear to the client that he has made the right decision in changing and that his choice of new advisers was correct.

The decision to change accountants and the process of selecting a successor is invariably one of some controversy within a general practice.

Not all the doctors may be in favour; some may prefer other firms and the new accountant will invariably feel it necessary to justify his appointment.

This goodwill will not last for ever; it must be earned and retained. This can best be done by an efficient approach to the new client, making sure that letters are answered promptly and accurately and that cordial relationships are established with all the partners at an early date. It is always a good idea to take some trouble to make an impression particularly with the junior partners as they are likely to be in the practice for many years.

Do not forget the practice manager; she has an important role to play in the practice and again it is necessary to ensure that her goodwill is maintained.

The first point of contact between the accountant and the potential new client will probably be a request for an interview and discussion. It is of great benefit if this is arranged on the client's premises, so that the books of account can be examined and some idea of procedures obtained. Try to ensure that all the partners and the practice manager attend the meeting. There is nothing worse than making a good impression on all the partners who attend the meeting only to find that two of those who were not present have dissented from a decision and have brought influence to bear against an appointment.

Try also to ensure that there are available for examination at the meeting at least the last set of partnership accounts, and the partnership deed. It is even better if the accountant can be given an opportunity to examine these before the meeting.

After the meeting, point out that the discussion and any fee estimates will be confirmed in a formal tender document. It helps to impress clients if this can be sent off within a day or two of the meeting. With the use of modern word processors this should present no undue difficulty.

Assuming the engagement is made as envisaged, a letter of appointment will be received from the client, to which a reply should be sent in acceptance. At this stage it should be ascertained whether the accountant is to act both for the partnership and the individual partners. If he is not to act for all the partners he should take steps to find out the names of those other accountants (see also **4.12**).

Simultaneously, a formal letter should be written to the outgoing accountants asking for their professional clearance and for certain other documents and information which will be necessary in order to put the work in hand. This should include such items as the last set of accounts, lists of debtors and creditors, outstanding loans, bank reconciliation, etc. It may be preferable, particularly where all the partners are not to become personal clients, if a separate letter is written in respect of each of those doctors requesting production of expenses claims, copy tax returns, etc.

Once this clearance has been obtained, a formal letter of engagement can then be prepared and sent to the client requesting signature. It is as well to obtain the signature of all the partners on this. A sample letter of engagement is set out in Appendix 9.

Such a document should set out, *inter alia*:

(a) the fact that an audit is not to be performed (see **1.5**);
(b) the nature and extent of the work to be performed;
(c) any additional (non-compliance) services available;
(d) the manner in which fees will be charged and paid (see **4.8**);
(e) an outline of the 'nominated partner' system (see **4.11**);
(f) the obligations of the accountant and rights of the client under the Financial Services Act.

It is suggested that such a letter of engagement should not be sent to the client for signature until clearance has been received from the outgoing accountant.

Every effort should be made to obtain such information as is required from the outgoing accountant at the earliest possible time. In particular, where the engagement comes immediately before the client's year end, every step should be taken to ensure that this does not inhibit or delay the work for the client. Otherwise he may well doubt the wisdom of the change he has made!

4.10   Letters of representation

General practices are not incorporated businesses; they have no Memorandum and Articles of Association to govern the external and internal working of the business. Nevertheless, the accountant should be able to obtain authority for the work he is doing, the manner in which it is to be done and, particularly, how the accounts are to be designed and profit allocated between the partners.

In a well-organised partnership, this authority will normally come in the form of a partnership deed (see **5.6**). In many cases, however, it will be found that the partnership deed, if it exists at all, is out of date, or it may well be invalid due to subsequent partnership changes or indeed that the partners between themselves have agreed to vary certain provisions in the deed.

A reading of the partnership deed should be an essential preliminary to putting the work in hand. This will give the accountant knowledge of exactly how the partnership finances are organised. Where this does not apply, however, it is highly desirable if a letter of representation is prepared and sent to the client for signature. A sample letter of representation is set out in Appendix 10.

It is emphasised that it will inherently aid the accounts process if this letter of representation is sent out as soon as possible within the progress of the work. It is perfectly possible that the partners have decided to make certain arrangements affecting the organisation of their finances about which they have not felt it necessary to advise their accountant. There is nothing worse than drawing up a set of accounts, sending them to the client for approval, only then to be forcibly reminded that there have been changes during the year which have not been effected in those accounts. This may well not be the fault of the accountant, but nevertheless it is difficult to persuade a client to pay for the cost of amending those accounts!

All this can – in most cases – be avoided by the early supply of a letter of representation, which sets out exactly the financial arrangements to be taken into account, having this signed by the clients, preferably before the accounts are finally drawn up and the profit allocated between the partners. This can save a great deal of valuable time and cost.

4.11   Nominated partners

In some practices several partners have adopted the habit of approaching their accountants separately on all manner of topics affecting the partnership accounts and finances. It is often found that the accountant is answering identical questions from different partners. One hopes that they will all receive identical answers! This, needless to say, is both wasteful and expensive. It is best solved by having the partners agree among themselves that one of their number will act as a correspondent or 'nominated' partner. That doctor will then be responsible for all correspondence and communication with the accountants; all negotiations upon partnership matters will be carried on through him and he will have the responsibility of ensuring his partners are kept aware of the position.

In order to clarify this, it is often a good idea to have a brief note signed by all the partners to confirm the arrangement. A specimen letter showing nomination of such a partner is set out in Appendix 12.

4.12   The partnership and personal accountant

One decision which each partner in a practice will be required to make is whether he wishes his personal taxation and financial affairs to be dealt with by the partnership accountant or by another accountant of his choice. Where changes in partnership accountants take place, it is not uncommon for GPs to wish to stay with their own accountant, whether or not he has previously been the partnership accountant. While in some ways their loyalty can be commended, nevertheless having separate accountants acting in this capacity causes many problems and is best avoided if at all possible.

The basic duties which a personal accountant will provide for his client are the submission and agreement of his annual income tax return and expenses claim. From this will come further work of a compliance nature, such as the checking and approval of personal assessment notices, negotiating on expenses with the Inland Revenue and the like. In addition, he may well be asked to provide advice on other areas, such as pensions, retirement and estate planning.

It is as well also to give a quotation of fees for this compliance work, particularly where the doctor as a personal client is to be billed separately.

Experience tends to show that where the same accountant acts for both the partnership and the individual partners, matters run a great deal more efficiently. Having separate accountants involved in the practice tends to encourage additional correspondence, telephone calls and the like, rather than having the information available in files in the same office.

Where partners feel they prefer to be advised separately, their wishes must be respected and every assistance given to them and their accountants, as required. It is, however, necessary not to overstep the mark between advice to the partnership and that of a personal nature. It is often difficult to identify this. Indeed, a personal accountant would have every right to complain were he to find that the partnership accountant was advising his client on matters of a personal nature, such as retirement and pensions, loan finance and the like, without his knowledge and approval.

Where changes of accountants take place, this is a matter which should be discussed with the partners before a final decision is taken.

4.13   Avoiding problems

There is no easy way to avoid problems arising in work for GP clients. Doctors are highly intelligent individuals who, although they may not immediately show a great deal of interest in finance and accounts, once this is aroused can be exacting and demanding clients, who are perfectly capable of asking searching questions which the accountant will ignore or answer inadequately at his peril.

At the end of the day the same applies as with any other client. If the work provided is unprofessional or substandard in any way, then this will inevitably be discovered and will rebound on the firm responsible.

Some relief will be gained from the introduction of new rules for assessment of partnerships, which will at least obviate the necessity of the completion of continuation elections, with all the lengthy explanations which these have required over the years.

It is, however, suggested that in a number of respects the practitioner may be able to alleviate his problems with clients by adhering to a number of principles, listed below. Whilst it cannot be guaranteed that if all these are complied with then one's troubles will be at an end, nevertheless, experience has shown that they will at least tend to work in the right direction:

(i)   Always try and forecast future tax liabilities. One of the things which annoys a GP is receiving unexpected tax demands, possibly for large amounts, which he has not foreseen and for which he has not budgeted.

(ii)   So far as accountancy fees are concerned, make a forecast at the start of the year and stick to it. If this results in a higher time charge than has been envisaged, through no fault of the client, then it is suggested that he should not be called upon to pay the cost. He may well do so, but his time as a client may be limited.

(iii)   Present a timetable for completion and presentation of the accounts. If, for any reason, it is not found to be possible to adhere to the dates given, then the client should be advised accordingly.

(iv)   Try and give proactive advice where possible. Obviously this has to be tempered with the cost of providing such advice, but it will almost certainly help to cement relationships with the client. He may well ignore it, but at least you cannot be accused of not keeping him informed.

(v)   Let the client know when you are submitting the accounts to the Inland Revenue and when they have been agreed.

(vi)   Always complete forms 64–8. When copy assessments are received, try to submit, where appropriate, early appeals and advise the client accordingly.

(vii)   Make sure the partnership capital is properly organised. Discuss capital requirements with the incoming partner, as it is unlikely his partners will do so.

(viii) Where large differences arise on the partners' current accounts (see **5.11**) the inevitable balancing of these is again likely to give rise to an element of dissent. Try and analyse exactly how these differences have come about and how they might be avoided in the future.

(ix) Acknowledge letters promptly and return telephone calls with the minimum of delay.

(x) Acquire a speciality in the field – and make sure all the clients are aware of this.

(xi) Capitalise on the 'honeymoon' period with new clients.

(xii) Try and build up a rapport with the younger partners. They may well be the most difficult and ask the most searching questions but, properly handled, they are likely to remain clients for the next 20 or 30 years.

Chapter 5 – The GP partnership

Those accountants with GP clients will not need reminding that a high proportion of the problems they encounter will derive from their work for partnerships. Such matters as how the partnership capital is to be contributed, the organisation of profit-sharing ratios, the equalisation of current accounts and finance on partnership changes are all matters which can cause great concern and confusion among GPs.

Of the 34,000 (latest statistics 1994: 34,430, including trainees and assistants – 1996 Review Body report) GPs in the United Kingdom some 81 per cent practice as members of groups or partnerships. Groups, which are normally defined as one or more sole practitioners practising together but who remain separate profit centres, form only a small part of this. It is evident therefore that the vast majority of GP clients will be members of partnerships or indeed the partnerships themselves and it is the problems these entail which are the subject of this chapter.

5.1   How the partnership is organised

The modern sizeable GP partnership is by most definitions a business of some repute and standing. It is now by no means unusual to find a practice with a turnover in excess of £1 million – and probably a great deal higher if a dispensing facility is also available (see **2.8**). A practice in the GP fundholding scheme (see Chapter 8) could simultaneously be managing funds as a separate entity far in excess of that amount.

Gone are the days when a typical medical practice operated as a 'cottage industry', with little business input and a minimum of staff. The modern GP partnership operates much as any other business partnership, such as that of the solicitor, accountant or architect. Bound by a properly drawn-up partnership deed, the partners will meet regularly to discuss common problems, delegate the whole or a major part of the management of the practice to a properly qualified practice manager and operate to a common policy, agreed by discussion and negotiation.

It is not unusual to find doctors who prefer to remain in sole practice; they may at some time have had an unfortunate experience in partnership which has affected their outlook, or they may see a partnership as limiting their independence. In some cases, and rather sadly, their doubts can be justified. From time to time one comes across partnerships which split up; in some cases through genuine differences of opinion within the partnership, but more likely due to a lack of business acumen and the absence of a true philosophy of partnership. These divisions can at times take place with a high level of acrimony. Many GPs who find themselves in partnership nevertheless prefer to, in effect, run their own separate practice, jealously guarding their independence and probably with little contact, either in the practice or outside, with their fellow partners.

Ideally, what all GP partnerships should have in common is that they are made up of a number of doctors combining together, hopefully to their mutual advantage, who all pull in the same direction with a common purpose. Unfortunately, this does not always apply.

Unquestionably, the major advantages of partnerships lie in the pooling of resources. There is a tremendous economy of scale which finds its greatest benefits in the larger partnerships. A typical example of this is in the field of accountancy fees in which the larger partnerships, with more partners to bear the cost, will find that this works out on a 'per capita' basis at far less than those for their colleagues in sole practice or in a smaller partnership.

Those larger practices will find little difficulty in operating their own rotas for out of hours duties, with a consequent benefit to their night visit fee income and limitation on the cost of deputising services.

Many doctors feel they wish to preserve and control the succession to their practice. A sole practitioner who seeks to retire has no such opportunity available to him. If he retires from practice, the vacancy will merely be advertised by the FHSA and a new doctor appointed after interview. On the other hand, a partnership has the absolute right to introduce new partners into their practice, the choice being their own, subject of course to that doctor's qualifications and experience being acceptable to the NHS authorities.

5.1.1 Pooling of income

Probably in no other field is the difference between GPs and other professional partnerships so evident as in the policies for pooling professional income.

In, say, professional accountancy or a legal practice, it will be taken as read that all the earnings of the partners would be pooled with partnership income for division in agreed ratios. Many medical practices, however, find it difficult for some reason to operate in that manner and insist on the partners personally retaining some of their medical earnings, probably from such items as private patients, cremation certificates, insurance reports, etc. It need hardly be said that this can give rise to a number of practical problems, not least of these being the responsibility of those partners to return that income separately for taxation purposes and to be responsible for the settlement of tax liabilities which then arise. Any lack of accuracy in returning this income can lead to Inland Revenue enquiries which are – to put it mildly – best avoided at all costs. The introduction of self-assessment makes this even more important.

Whatever the policy of the GP partnership, however, this should be enshrined in the partnership deed (see **5.6**) or, if a deed is not in existence or is incomplete, in a letter of representation (see **4.10**). Whilst this is in the last analysis the policy of the partners, nevertheless it is found invariably that those partnerships with the greater tradition of financial discipline insist on all medical earnings by the partners being paid into partnership funds and divided accordingly. This is by far the better course of action and is worth pursuing at regular intervals.

This is a topic which has caused great discussion in some medical partnerships and it is often found that the retention of medical earnings by some or all of the partners is a major source of dissent. At times it has even been the immediate cause of the break-up of partnerships.

5.2   Partnership changes

Most GP partnerships are dynamic and change with some regularity. There are a number of reasons for this: the practice allowances system which rewards partnerships in the form of the BPA for each principal in the practice (see **2.2**); the fact that in most partnerships there will be a regular succession of partners retiring on age grounds at maybe, four- or five-year intervals; and the fact that GPs are appointed as partners from the outset, with probably no more than an initial interview (see **5.1**).

Most partnerships conventionally replace a partner who retires, and one frequently comes across a practice which wishes to increase the number of partners usually due to expansion, but at times for other reasons.

The manner in which GP partners are appointed, which is in contrast to that employed in other professions, is a major reason for this relatively high number of partnership changes. A new GP may well commence as a partner on a term of probation, probably six months, after which he can part company with the practice, and frequently does. It is by no means unusual to come across partnerships which have five or six physical changes of personnel within a single 12-month period.

The professional adviser will, hopefully, be kept aware by his clients of pending partnership changes, as and when these occur. He may well be asked to advise on the calculation of future profit-sharing ratios and he will almost certainly be asked to advise upon the capital requirements of incoming partners. (Taxation on partnership changes can be complex and is covered in detail in **7.3**.)

If at all possible, careful forward planning should be ensured so that any change can be made as smoothly as possible. In a conventional retirement situation where the senior partner announces he is to retire, say, a year hence, plans can be made, and new partners interviewed and appointed well in advance so that, hopefully, the retiring partner will depart on one day and the new partner join on the following.

In the case of a death in service, however, this may well not apply. A death by its very nature is likely to be sudden and it will not have been possible to embark upon any scheme of long-term planning. This may well mean that the GPs' earnings are reduced for a significant period; not only will they have lost the BPA for the deceased partner but also in order to run their practice satisfactorily, they may well have to engage expensive locums until a new appointment is made.

Experience tends to show that this is likely to be an expensive period for the continuing partners, who not only have an increased workload and clinical responsibility but also may well be rewarded rather less satisfactorily for their efforts. It is a situation which should be kept for as brief a period as possible.

In the event of a partnership change, one of the initial duties for either the practice or its accountant will be to organise the new profit-sharing ratios and we shall now see how this can be done.

5.3   Organising the profit-sharing ratios

As we have seen, it is fairly standard (but no means universal) practice to engage a new partner on a share of the profits rising to parity over three years. While this may well be usual practice, one does come across partnerships which, as a matter of tradition, appoint partners in order to achieve parity over a greatly reduced period. Some partners may well not be young doctors fresh from their training contract but could be more experienced doctors, who have either been in a previous partnership or who have occupied a high position in the hospital service. It is right and proper that these doctors should be required to serve less than a full period before rising to parity.

It is highly desirable that the practitioner is involved in this process from an early stage. It may well be that the practice has previous experience in this and is fully aware of the ratios that will apply. Nevertheless, the accountant will have to manage such changes as are required to the partnership tax liability – arranging for a continuation election and all that goes with it. He may well also be asked to allocate the ratios and particularly to estimate what effect the partnership change will have upon the earnings of the continuing partners.

Example

Drs Truman, Bass & Partners is a practice of five parity partners with a total list size of 12,000 patients. They feel they can no longer cope with the workload this entails and have been successful in applying to the HA and LMC for an appointment of an additional (sixth) partner.

They are, however, having second thoughts in that, while they are pleased to reduce their workload, they are less than happy at the prospect of reduced income and they feel that with an additional partner their profits will be diluted.

The last year for which completed accounts are available is to 30 June 1996 which showed a total partnership profit of £197,964, or £39,593 per partner. They are contemplating making the additional appointment from 1 July 1997. All the partners receive seniority awards and/or PGEA which they retain themselves and this is not included in that figure.

They have asked their professional advisers to prepare a schedule (see Figure 5.1) indicating what might be their likely earnings over the period of the new partner's progress to parity. They have agreed that this period will be over three years and have specified that they propose to pay the new partner an income equivalent to £24,000 p.a. for the first year, with an option for conversion to percentage basis if this is beneficial to him. It is to be assumed that partnership profits will rise by 3% in both the 1996/97 and 1997/98 years and by 5% in succeeding years. The partnership has paid out £15,000 in locum fees which they feel they will be able to save by the introduction of an

---

additional partner. They will also attract the BPA for this sixth partner.

A specimen of such a schedule is shown in Figure 5.1.

From this a number of points will be apparent:

(a) the additional BPA and saving in locum fees are likely to bring about a significant increase in partnership profits which will then rise at a more modest rate as a result of anticipated pay increases;

(b) the new partner will commence with a share of the profits at 10.3% or £24,000 p.a., whichever is the greater, for one year. He will then progress by two equal and intermediate stages of 12.42% and 14.54% to final parity at one-sixth (16.66%) of the profits on 1 July 1999.

The saving in expenses has resulted in significantly more income for the continuing partners and shows a steady profit increase over this period. There is little cause, therefore, for them to be concerned at a possible fall in income levels, although it may well be that their annual profit increases will be less than had they not recruited an additional partner.

In addition to this, all partners will receive seniority/PGEA at their appropriate rates.

Ratios have been adjusted where necessary to a limit of two decimal places.

See Figure 5.1 for a worked example.

5.4   'Fixed-share' partners

The term 'salaried partner' is still in common usage in other professions. In medical partnerships, however, the term has fallen into disrepute and it is strongly recommended that it is not used when describing a partner whose remuneration level is fixed at an agreed sum per annum and is not dependent upon the level of profitability of the practice.

Of far more common usage is the term 'fixed-share' partner. It may well be thought that these two terms are virtually interchangeable but it is generally accepted that the term 'salaried' has such unfortunate connotations as regards possible taxation consequences that it is best avoided.

Figure 5.1. *Drs Truman, Bass & Partners: illustration of future shares of profit*

On the introduction of a new partner from 1 July 1997 at an initial remuneration of £24,000 rising to parity over three years (assuming annual profit increases of 5% p.a.)

	Current earnings	
	£	£
Profits per accounts to 30 June 1996		197,964
Add: Projected saving in locum fees	15,000	
Additional BPA (1995/96 rate)	6,912	
		21,912
		219,876
Add: Projected increase: 1996/97 (3%)	6,596	
1997/98 (3%)	6,794	
		13,390
		233,266
(say)		233,000
		233,000

	First year from 1 July 1997		Second year from 1 July 1998		Third year from 1 July 1999		Fourth year from 1 July 2000	
	%	£	%	£	%	£	%	£
Dr Truman	17.94	41,800	17.52	42,853	17.09	43,906	16.67	44,958
Dr Bass	17.94	41,800	17.52	42,853	17.09	43,906	16.67	44,958
Dr Whitbread	17.94	41,800	17.52	42,853	17.09	43,906	16.67	44,958
Dr Young	17.94	41,800	17.51	42,853	17.09	43,906	16.67	44,958
Dr Webster	17.94	41,800	17.51	42,853	17.10	43,906	16.67	44,958
New Partner	10.30	24,000	12.42	30,385	14.54	37,350	16.67	44,958
	100.00	233,000	100.00	244,650	100.00	256,880	100.00	269,748

The appointments column in the *British Medical Journal* is headed with a standard sentence to the effect that advertisers are requested not to show their vacancies as 'salaried partnership'. The criterion as to whether or not a doctor is a partner in a practice is whether or not he receives the basic practice allowance. Whilst no assurances can be given, this has, at times, been negotiated with local Inspectors of Taxes and no objections have been raised to this type of treatment. As a principal in general practice, a doctor cannot simultaneously be that and an employee, and again this point has been made to Inspectors of Taxes with some success.

It must be emphasised that when accounts are drawn up the partner in question should be treated as such; his name should appear with the other partners and his share of the profits should be shown as an appropriation of profit rather than a charge in the income and expenditure account. It is strongly stressed that nothing must be done to jeopardise the position of this partner who, properly advised, will obtain all the advantages which Schedule D status brings with it.

If he were to be treated as an employee of the practice, not only would he be subject to PAYE/Class 1 NIC but he would also receive more stringent judgement on any claims for practice expenses. From the practice's viewpoint, they would be liable to the employer's share of Class 1 NIC which they would be unable to recover as with an ancillary staff member.

A doctor who joins an NHS medical partnership, in whatever capacity, can basically have only one of two possible statuses; he is either a partner or he is an employee, with all that these terms imply. One does at times come across situations where doctors are held to be engaged in some form of 'intermediate status': as a locum, a consultant, an associate or an assistant. If, as is invariably the case, he is engaged with a fixed annual income, unless he is a partner in every sense of the word and qualifies for the basic practice allowance, that individual will be an employee and must be treated as such. He exhibits all the characteristics of Schedule E status and a practice seeking to pay such a doctor on the assurance that he will be responsible for his own tax, could well be treading on dangerous ground. This situation is best avoided at all costs wherever possible.

5.5 Prior shares of profit

Yet another aspect in which GP partnerships differ from many other businesses is the manner in which they choose to retain certain items of income for individual partners before profits are allocated in prescribed ratios. To a large degree this applies to seniority awards and post graduate education allowance, although there are an appreciable number of practices which prefer as a matter of policy to pay these into partnership funds and merely distribute them in agreed ratios.

However, there will be other items which some partnerships decide to allocate to individual partners:

- night visit fees (see **2.6.1**);
- surgery income (see **5.7**).

While these are the most frequently seen examples of this, some partnerships will make their own policy as to other items of income which are to be allocated on that basis.

By whatever means this is done, it is essential that these prior shares of profit are identified; preferably by inclusion in the partnership deed but otherwise by obtaining authority via a letter of representation (see **4.10**). When preparing the accounts, it is essential that these prior shares are isolated from the residual shares of profit which are to be allocated in partnership ratios. This will be evident from the accounts set out in Appendix 1.

5.6   Partnership deeds

It is a rather surprising statistic – but nevertheless true – that no more than 50 per cent of GP partnerships have a current and valid partnership deed in existence. This surprising figure may be due to a number of factors: the partners believe there is no prospect of them disagreeing; by a rather false economy they wish to save the cost of preparing the deed; or, in some cases, they are quite unable to reach agreement as to its content. Just as one can lead a horse to water, one cannot make it drink, and in the same way the practitioner advising his GP clients should take whatever steps he can to make sure that a deed is executed, although there are obvious limits to his powers of persuasion and if the partners have set their face against it, his influence is limited.

In order to safeguard his own position, however, the accountant should, if no deed is in existence, if one has been executed some years ago but is no longer valid, or if clauses to the current deed have been superseded, for his own protection apart from anything else, invite his client to sign a letter of representation (see **4.10** and Appendix 10). This will set down the manner in which the partnership finances are to be conducted and will serve as his authority for drawing up the accounts with the intentions of the partners in mind.

If a partnership has no valid deed in existence, in the event of dispute they will have no alternative but to fall back on the provisions of the Partnership Act 1890, which may be contrary to their wishes.

Appendix 4 sets out a sample partnership agreement. Let us, however, look at a number of requirements which should be shown in a deed for any GP partnership. These are clauses which are of a financial nature but, nevertheless, whatever the policy of the partnership is, it must be expressed as such in the deed. References are to clauses and sections in the specimen deed shown in Appendix 4.

(a) Profit-sharing ratios. These should be set out clearly showing the ratios to apply up to the parity of a recently admitted partner (Clause 6 (1): Schedule II).

(b) Definition of capital. There should be clearly set out what represents the capital of the partnership, how this is invested and the manner in which the partners are to contribute to this. Where possible, amounts involved and contribution dates should be shown (Clause 5: Schedule I).

(c) The requirements of surgery ownership. Where the partnership owns a surgery this should be shown clearly in the deed with the names of the property-owning partners. It should also be stated that those partners will receive the cost/notional rent allowance and be responsible for servicing surgery loans (Schedule I).

(d) Provision for proper accounts to be kept (Clause 8(1)).

(e) Definition of income. It should be clearly laid down exactly what represents partnership income and what does not; whether the partners are to retain their seniority/PGEA or whether this is to be pooled in partnership income; whether they are to be allowed to retain legacies from patients; if there are any exemptions and that, if partners are to be allowed to retain an amount of medical income, this should be clearly defined here (Clause 6 (2)).

(f) Definition of partnership expenses. Which expenses are the liability of the partnership and which of the individual partners should be stated. Expenses which historically in medical partnerships may well vary between the two are:
(i)   motor car expenses (Clause 11);
(ii) medical subscriptions;
(iii) spouse's salaries and pension contributions;
(iv) private telephone bills.
While the decision on how these are charged rests with the partnership, whatever their policy is should be clearly shown as such in the deed (Clauses 11/12).

(g) That each partner should own a house or reside within or immediately adjacent to the practice area. This clause can at times be beneficial in negotiating tax relief on house expenses (see **7.6.4**).

(h) Provisions for payments during the sickness of a partner (Clause 14).

(i) Provisions for retirement of a partner. How payments are to be made; how the capital is to be valued; whether interest is to be paid. Similarly, provisions on the death of a partner (Clauses 20–23: Schedule III).

(j) Arrangements for annual accounts, accountant, etc. (Clause 8).

(k) Provisions for continuation election on partnership change, with indemnity clause, but only up to 1996/97 (Schedule III, para 8).

It is emphasised that it will be the partnership's solicitor who will be responsible for drawing up the deed. The accountant does, however, have a significant role in that he should ensure that he is given the opportunity of perusing the deed while in draft form, so that he can satisfy himself that the financial clauses are in order and in accordance with the intentions of the partners. He should make sure that once the deed has been signed by the partners and witnessed, he retains a copy of this on his permanent file (see **4.7**) for future reference.

As we have seen, partnerships can change at regular intervals. It would clearly be uneconomic to have a full partnership deed, which is a lengthy document, prepared on each of those occasions. It is normal, therefore, so long as the principal clauses and philosophy of the partnership do not vary, for a supplemental deed of partnership to be executed when a new partner joins. In practice, this is unlikely to be done during the probationary period of an incoming partner and may well be left until his appointment is confirmed.

5.7   The surgery-owning partnership

We have looked (Chapter 3) at the principles by which surgeries are owned and financed by GPs. These principles, broadly speaking, apply regardless of the type of practice; they would in most cases equally apply where surgeries are being developed by sole practices. By definition, however, the vast majority of GP surgeries will be owned by partnerships. These partnerships can take many forms, as can the manner in which the surgery ownership is divided between some or all of the partners involved.

In some cases, the arrangement will be relatively simple in that the surgery will be owned by all the partners in the practice who may well, for example, be five equal partners. So long as the partnership remains stable, this is a relatively simple situation and will present few of the difficulties both to the partners and advisers which other types of ownership might cause. In the majority of cases, however, this will not apply; some of the partners may be partially retired GPs who have taken 24-hour retirement (see **9.14**); GPs who are working their way up to parity (see **5.2**) or part-time doctors (see **2.14**) who may have no intention of remaining in the partnership on a long-term basis and may choose not to buy into a share of the surgery.

In thankfully only a few other cases will one come across situations where a senior GP, for whatever reason, has not sold shares of the surgery to incoming partners, so that inevitably – and over a period of years – this results in one doctor owning the building. This is a situation to be avoided at all costs: the problem which will arise when the only surgery-owning partner seeks to retire and realise his investment in the surgery can create all manner of difficulties which could previously have been avoided by careful planning.

These situations normally occur for one of two reasons. The partner concerned is unwilling to allow his more junior colleagues to become involved in what he sees as a lucrative proposition, not only looking forward to capital appreciation on retirement but also a gradually increasing source of income in the form of the notional rent allowance (see **3.2**). In some cases, however, the situation arises from successive junior partners joining the practice who may well feel, in the circum-stances at the time, that they are unwilling to embark on the responsi-bilities of ownership and the financial penalties which might perhaps ensue.

Part of the planning and advice which the experienced practitioner will give to his clients is how to avoid situations like this arising by, in an ideal world, ensuring that the surgery is owned, if not by all of the partners in a sizeable practice, then by the majority, or at the very least by all the full-time parity partners.

It follows that accounts prepared for GP partnerships should be designed so that they give the partners, or any other interested parties, full information concerning surgery ownership so that it can be seen at a glance:

(a)   how the equity in the surgery building is held by the partners; and
(b)   how the income from the rent allowances and cost of servicing loans are dealt with so that these are allocated between the partners in surgery-owning ratios. The accounts illustrated in Appendix 1 show how this can be done (see also **6.3.5**).

The income from the cost or notional rent allowance will be received by the practice and allocated between the partners in owning ratios. Where changes in ownership have taken place during the year, this allowance should be allocated so that the income of each partner reflects their proportionate share of ownership during the year of account. Similarly, where, for example, an incoming partner takes over responsibility for the overall partnership loan from an outgoing partner, the interest charges should be allocated on an identical basis. The rent allowance in effect represents the return by the surgery-owning partners on their investment and it is clearly equitable that they should receive this, without any benefit to non-surgery-owning partners.

In a partnership where not all the partners own the surgery, it is at times postulated that the non-surgery-owning partners should pay a fixed rent to the surgery-owning partners. Proposals of this type should be discouraged at all costs.

As we have seen, GPs are entitled to claim a refund or allowance for the rent of the premises from which they practice. Unfortunately, what at first sight may appear to be an acceptable ploy to obtain extra funds from the HA, will not work in that manner. If such a payment of rent were to be made, firstly, it might inhibit the tax position of the owning partners and could well have an effect on a future claim for CGT retirement relief. In addition, when this comes to the attention of the HA, they will merely deduct the rent received from the non-surgery-owning partners from the rent allowance, so that the surgery-owning partners would in effect be no better off.

A typical situation, which could apply in a surgery-owning partnership where changes in both surgery-owning and profit-sharing ratios take place during the year is illustrated in Figure 5.2.

Figure 5.2

	Surgery		Practice	
	To 31.12.95	To 30.6.96	To 30.9.95	To 30.6.96
	%	%	%	%
Dr U	20	–	17	10
Dr V	20	20	17	18
Dr W	20	20	17	18
Dr X	20	20	17	18
Dr Y	20	20	17	18
Dr Z	–	20	15	18

In this practice, Dr U took a 24-hour retirement from 1 October 1995, when his share of the practice profits reduced from 17 per cent to 10 per cent and Dr Z achieved parity at 18 per cent. On 1 January 1996, Dr U sold his 20 per cent share in the surgery premises to Dr Z, who from that date became entitled to an equivalent share of the rent allowance.

5.7.1 Retiring partners

From time to time partners will leave the practice, for whatever reason, but upon normal retirement age, they will leave owning a share of the building. Where this applies, the partnership deed should be read carefully so that the expressed wishes of the partners are implemented. It is, in fact, rare for outgoing partners to be paid for their share of the surgery immediately on retirement. More frequently, there will be a time interval between retirement and sale of a share of the building, although for reasons concerned with retirement relief for CGT, this should not normally be extended in excess of one year. There are currently reasons concerning negative equity (see **3.8**) why variations in this practice may occur. The retention of shares of surgery premises after retirement can again cause practical difficulties arising from the manner in which the consequent income is to be taxed. This is considered under **7.3**.

5.7.2 Property capital accounts

If accounts are being drawn up for a six-doctor practice, of whom four own equal shares in the surgery at the accounting year end, and the surgery has recently been revalued with a new up value of £800,000 the accounts, summarised in Figure 5.3, should show the following entries:

Figure 5.3

Surgery premises	£
As valued (cost value)	800,000

Represented by:

Property capital accounts	£
Dr A	200,000
Dr B	200,000
Dr C	200,000
Dr D	200,000
	800,000

There are no property capital accounts for Dr E and Dr F, who have no shares in the property ownership. It is assumed that a previous surgery loan account has been transferred into the names of the individual partners (see **7.5.1**).

5.8   Organising the capital structure

There are few topics in the field of GP accountancy, particularly concerning partnerships, which cause more concern and controversy, particularly with younger partners, than the matter of the introduction of capital into medical partnerships, how this is organised and by exactly what means it should be contributed by an incoming partner.

Needless to say, the task of the professional adviser can be a great deal easier if he has the authority of a signed partnership deed (see **5.6** and Appendix 4) to back up his advice, but if not it is suggested that a letter of representation (see **4.10**) would serve much the same purpose. The manner in which the capital of a practice is organised, however, can be of great benefit to the partners; it can assist them in future planning to ensure that equity is served between them and in appropriate cases it can give significant taxation advantages (see **7.5**).

The capital in the majority of medical partnerships can be fairly easily allocated under three headings:

(a)   *Surgery capital*, representing the partners' interest in the equity in the surgery building. As we have seen, this should be allocated by means of property capital accounts, between the partners owning the building.

(b)   *Other (or fixed asset) capital*, representing the partners' investment in the non-building fixed assets, i.e., the fixtures and fittings, medical equipment, computers, partnership-owned vehicles (if any) and the like. These represent the assets from which the partners earn their general practice income and it is right and proper that these are held in the same proportions as those in which the partners share the practice profits.

(c)   *Working capital*, represented effectively by the net current assets in the practice. Again, it is appropriate that these should be owned by the partners in profit-sharing ratios.

Let us now look at a typical balance sheet of a medical practice (in summary form), using the property ownership figures set out in Figure 5.3.

Figure 5.4 shows the situation of a highly-capitalised dispensing practice, with total net assets of some £925,000; how this is allocated between the various types of capital and how this has been financed by the partners.

It is normal in such cases to provide a supporting note to the accounts by which the various components of capital are allocated between the

Figure 5.4 *Drs A, B, C, D, E & F: Balance Sheet: 30 June 1996 (Summary)*

	£	£
Surgery premises (as valued)		800,000
Fixed assets (at book value)		45,000
Current assets		
Stock of dispensing drugs	56,742	
Sundry debtors	35,469	
Balance at bank	16,442	
	108,653	
Less: Sundry creditors	28,484	
Net current assets		80,169
Net assets		925,169
Financed by		
Property capital accounts		800,000
Fixed asset capital accounts		45,000
Current accounts		80,169
		925,169

partners and we can now look at how this can be done, using the principles set out above. The allocation of the property capital accounts is as set out in Figure 5.5.

It will be seen that these are allocated between the partners in exactly their profit-sharing ratios at the year end. In practice, this will require

Figure 5.5 *Fixed asset capital accounts*

		£
Dr A	(10%)	4,500
Dr B	(19%)	8,550
Dr C	(19%)	8,550
Dr D	(19%)	8,550
Dr E	(19%)	8,550
Dr F	(14%)	6,300
		45,000

adjustment to the accounts and will normally be reflected by means of adjustments through the partners' current accounts (see Figure 5.6), which are intended to reflect the extent to which partners have invested in fixed assets (less depreciation) during the year out of current earnings.

If there had been a surgery loan in existence, then this would have been shown as a deduction in the balance sheet, with the property capital accounts being reduced accordingly.

Figure 5.6 *Current accounts*

	£
Dr A	16,964
Dr B	13,982
Dr C	12,847
Dr D	14,963
Dr E	12,369
Dr F	9,044
	80,169

The question of partners' current accounts and how these should be equalised is dealt with separately in **5.11**.

This system of balancing off certain net assets against specific types of capital contributed by the partners serves a limited purpose and is popular with some partnerships which are able to see exactly how – and to what extent – each partner has contributed. It does, however, have a number of drawbacks: the balances on the partners' current accounts cannot effectively be fully withdrawn as, although they effectively represent undrawn profits of the partners, probably accumulated over a number of years, part of this is required to be retained in the practice. It will be seen that while the partners' current account balances total £80,169 there is a balance at the bank of only £16,442. There is plainly, therefore, insufficient cash available to make a full distribution to the partners. The majority of this capital is tied up in stock of drugs and debtors, which are a running item and can reasonably be expected to recur from year to year.

5.8.1 Fixed capital accounts

The system now used by a number of partnerships, therefore, is to vary the system somewhat so that there are fixed capital accounts which are intended to represent the combined investment of the partners both in the book value of the fixed assets and in the net current assets. In order to implement such a system it is first necessary to calculate the amount of this required fixed capital (see Figure 5.7).

Figure 5.7 *Calculation of fixed capital requirement*

	£	£
Fixed assets		45,000
Working capital		
Stock of drugs	56,742	
Debtors	35,469	
	92,211	
Creditors	28,484	
		63,727
Estimated cash requirement		6,273
		115,000

If we then apply this new principle to a revised balance sheet, this will look rather different, as can be seen in Figure 5.8.

Figure 5.8 *Revised balance sheet: 30 June 1996 (Summary)*

	£
Net assets, as shown (Figure 5.4)	925,169
Financed by	
Property capital accounts	800,000
Fixed capital accounts	115,000
Current accounts	10,164
	925,169

The detailed allocation of these will become, using identical ratios:

Fixed capital accounts	£
Dr A	11,500
Dr B	21,850
Dr C	21,850
Dr D	21,850
Dr E	21,850
Dr F	16,100
	115,000

It will be seen that the fixed capital accounts are allocated between the partners in exactly their profit-sharing ratios at the year end. In practice, this will require adjustment to the accounts and will normally be reflected by means of adjustment through the partners' current accounts, which is intended to reflect the extent to which partners have invested in fixed assets (less depreciation) during the year out of current earnings (see Figure 5.9).

Figure 5.9

Current accounts	£
Dr A	9,964
Dr B	682
Dr C	(453)
Dr D	1,663
Dr E	(931)
Dr F	(756)
	10,169

It will be seen from this that we have accomplished two purposes:

(a) The balances on the fixed capital accounts more exactly represent the partners' true investment in the non-surgery capital, both fixed assets and working, of the partnership.

(b) The balances on the partners' current accounts now more exactly represent the undrawn profits of the partners, which can be withdrawn by them. There are sufficient funds in the bank to enable this to be done, and once these withdrawals have been made, this will then allow the partners to start the new accounting year with accurate balances. The three partners whose balances are currently overdrawn should be invited to repay these amounts to the partnership.

This system also facilitates transactions in respect of incoming and outgoing partners. The retiring partner has a more exact idea of the amount of capital which will accrue to him and he will be more able to plan his financial strategy in retirement accordingly. The new partner will be in a position to be given more accurate information concerning the amount of capital he will be required to contribute to the partnership and the dates for this. In preparing this calculation of fixed partnership capital, the imponderable figure is that of the estimated cash requirement. This will largely be a question of judgement, which can be extracted from the accounts of the partnership and is intended to represent that amount which should remain in the partnership bank account from one month end (when most of the GPs' finance transactions will take place) to the next, without the account going into overdraft.

5.9   The outgoing partner

We have looked at several aspects of partnership capital insofar as this affects the outgoing partner. It is essential that where partners retire from a practice, the financial arrangements following their departure are organised in order to comply with the provisions of the partnership deed. This should lay down, *inter alia*, exactly how and when an outgoing partner will be paid for his share of the capital; the basis upon which valuations will be made; the dates of payment and, possibly, any interest to be paid to an outgoing partner during this intervening period.

Partners leave practices for a number of reasons – they may well leave due to a dispute in the partnership or purely because they reach retiring age. In the larger partnerships it is common for partners to retire, more or less on a scale of age, every few years and it is helpful if a policy and procedure can be adopted with which each of the partners is happy and which will naturally follow on as each successive partner retires.

Where partners leave through normal retirement, this can usually be organised well in advance; so that, say, Dr A retires on 31 March and a new partner, Dr F, commences on 1 April.

However, where partners die in service, this is a very much more difficult situation, with one pair of hands suddenly disappearing from the scene; the practice has to carry on and the remaining partners must somehow cater for all the patients. It is unlikely that they will wish merely to absorb his workload (although this might be feasible within a very large partnership) and it is more likely that they will seek to engage locum cover. This could be expensive and, with the loss of the practice allowances for the deceased partner, this may well be something of a financial setback for the practice. Although there is one less partner with whom the profits have to be shared, nevertheless experience tends to show that more often than not the continuing partners will be at a financial disadvantage and every step must be taken to see that the vacancy is filled without undue delay.

5.10   The incoming partner

To some degree, the transactions affecting the outgoing partner apply in reverse to the incoming partner. He will at some time be required to

103

contribute capital to the practice, although it is unlikely that he will immediately be a parity partner, and any capital contribution (apart from the surgery) will merely be required at this lower ratio.

It is normal for the incoming partner to be invited to contribute capital into the partnership, based upon an agreed scale, or to a fixed capital account (see **5.8.1**) but again this will simply be in line with his starting ratio. It would be unusual to expect him to contribute this capital before he had at least served his probationary period and it was reasonably certain that he would become an equity partner on a permanent basis. In addition, it would be usual to delay the new partner buying into the surgery, possibly until it was clear that he would stay but in some practices this is delayed until a junior partner achieves parity. There are advantages in a new partner buying his share of the surgery directly from an outgoing partner, without involving the continuing partners in any way. This means that a straight transaction can be arranged between the two of them and it would normally be in the outgoing partner's interest for this to be done within one year, in order to avoid any possible loss of CGT retirement relief.

All valuations given to an incoming partner for purchase of practice assets must be fair and reasonable, in accordance with current market values and agreed between both parties. Any efforts to sell these at inflated prices will fall foul of the restriction on sale and purchase of goodwill (see **2.13**) and are illegal.

We have seen (**5.3**) how shares of profit can be organised when a new partner joins the practice. Again, it is normal for this to be done on the basis of a rise to parity in three years, possibly during the first year enjoying the option of a percentage ratio or fixed share, whichever is the greater. This has two attractions: if the new partner is buying a house in the practice area it will give him an element of security when applying for a mortgage and, at least in theory, the opportunity to share in the practice profits at an early date, which will encourage him to try and increase the practice income by attracting work from outside sources.

It is highly desirable that an income tax reserve is instituted for an incoming partner, even when no such reserve is kept for the remainder of the partners (tax reserves are discussed more fully in **5.12**), but this is especially important in the case of an incoming partner who may not stay with the practice for a lengthy period, and if he departs, possibly with some bad feeling, the prospect of his being persuaded to pay an outstanding tax liability could well be somewhat remote. However, this situation will alter following the full introduction of self-assessment in 1997/98 (see **5.12.2**).

The incoming partner may not find this a particularly popular source of action, but may well see reason if it is explained that this is being done to safeguard the continuing partners; at some date in the future he will be a senior partner and would hope that his advisers would protect him in a similar way.

5.11   Current accounts

We have examined the question of capital contributions into the partnership and discussed the rationale of this, hopefully in a manner which can be explained to incoming partners who find themselves in this position.

While the principles of introduction of capital as applied to readily distinguishable assets can be explained with little difficulty, the question of current accounts, representing the undrawn profits of the partners, is perhaps rather less easy to accept. However, this is made a great deal more plausible if, following the introduction of the fixed asset capital account system (see **5.8**), the balances on the partners' current accounts at the end of each year are their own to withdraw.

Put at its simplest, partners' current accounts are their bank accounts with the practice; on the one hand they are credited with their profits and any other prior charges to which they are entitled (see **5.5**); on the other hand there is set against this such items as drawings and payments made on their behalf such as superannuation, added years, National Insurance, income tax and, possibly, private payments.

Inevitably, in the majority of cases it will be virtually impossible to calculate drawings so accurately that it will not be necessary to adjust these following completion and agreement of the annual accounts.

If possible, and where funds allow, it may be preferable to try and organise a situation so that all of the partners are able to withdraw funds, of greater or lesser amounts, which will give a similar picture.

Figure 5.9, however, shows a situation where fixed capital accounts have been created, leaving smaller balances on some of the partners' current accounts which they are able to withdraw and if this system is operated, this obviates the need for other adjustments.

5.12   Drawings and tax reserves

As we have seen, the accurate calculation of drawings is the major factor in determining the final balances on the partners' current accounts which, in turn, will require equalising by some means or other during the ensuing period. It is essential that these calculations are done as accurately and consistently as possible, not only to maintain fairness between the partners but also to avoid the situation arising where substantial adjustments are required at the end of each year.

In many professional partnerships this is not an unduly serious problem; drawings in all probability can be made in accordance with strict profit-sharing ratios with no further adjustments required. In medical practice, however, this rarely applies; in a typical partnership one will find partners not only with differing shares of profit but also with differing levels of income from seniority, PGEA, shares of surgery ownership, etc. On the other hand, they will have payments made on their behalf in respect of such items as superannuation, possible purchases of added years (see **9.9.1**), National Insurance, income tax, and possibly some private payments. The complexity of this means that there must be in force some fairly sophisticated method of calculating drawings so that they reflect with some accuracy the level of disposable income, not only for the partnership but also for the individual partners, between whom this can vary widely.

Partners, particularly those new into general practice, frequently regard the monthly amounts they withdraw from the partnership as a 'salary' rather than merely a payment to them on account of their profits. This is a notion it is wise to counter at the outset.

There are many systems of calculating drawings. Whatever system is used it is essential that it is operated properly and calculations made accurately:

(a)   The simplest system of all is one where available funds are divided, normally monthly, between the partners in their current ratios. This may just work in a stable partnership where all the doctors are on parity and where payments on their behalf are minimal. Such a practice will probably have partners paying their own tax privately and be responsible for their own National Insurance, etc. These practices are few and far between. Were this system to be used in any complex partnership, this would inevitably give rise to large differences at the year end, the effects of which we have seen.

(b)   The system perhaps most widely used in partnerships is the 'quarter-end' system, under which payments on account equal to their ratios are made to the partners at the end of each month, with adjustments being made quarterly when the HA statement is available and when adjustments for such items as superannuation, leave advance repayments and the like can be seen. In some ways this is the best system of all, provided it is carried out in house and that all possible adjustments are made. If this is done accurately, the likelihood is that required adjustments at the end of each year will be within the limits of tolerance.

(c) Many partnerships, however, prefer to operate systems of equalised drawings, which are derived from a statement not unlike a cash flow projection under which a forecast is made of likely profits and outgoings during an ensuing year, these being adjusted in such a manner as will provide an equal monthly amount to be paid to each partner.

This is a system which has a number of obvious advantages, not least of these being that the partners have the assurance of a regular amount being paid into their bank account at the end of each month which allows them a great deal more certainty in their personal budgeting. Provided that all proper adjustments have been made, this regular monthly withdrawal can be paid to the partners' personal bank accounts by standing order each month, obviating the need for a regular drawing of cheques.

The preparation of such an equalised drawing system would normally be done by the partnership accountant, who should have the required information available to him and will be in a position to calculate the tax reserve to be operated during any given period.

Example

Drs A, B, C and D are equal partners in a practice, with Dr C and Dr D having ratios of 23% and 17% respectively, and Dr A and Dr B on 30% each. The partners have differing rates of seniority and PGEA, which they retain; Drs A and B only own the surgery premises which is estimated to receive an annual rent allowance of £8,000. The profits for the last completed year of the accounts to 30 June 1995 were £123,810, excluding separately allocated items and it is assumed that this profit will increase by 5% over the ensuing year. Drs A and B both receive seniority awards at the top rate while all partners will be entitled to a post graduate education allowance.

The partners pay a total of £9,000 in superannuation contributions, Drs A and B pay £900 and £400 respectively by way of added years; Drs B and C pay £30 and £40 respectively in superannuation and outside appointments; the same partners pay £50 and £80 respectively in Class 1 NIC on those appointments. All four partners pay Class 2 NIC contributions at the rate of £5.55 per week, and have

107

taken the leave advance at the 1996/97 rate. They are to contribute to the tax reserve in a proportion to £5,200; £4,800; £4,000 and £3,500 and Dr B pays private loan repayments to the GP Finance Corporation of £800. We are asked to prepare a schedule showing the calculation of equalised drawings for the year to 31 March 1997. Figure 5.10 shows how these projected equalised drawings can be calculated. It will be seen that this is reduced to an exact monthly amount, it being normal to reduce this to the nearest round figure (say £10). All figures are shown for illustration purposes.

Figure 5.10 *Drs A, B, C and D: Calculation of equalised drawings year 1996/97*

	Total £	Dr A (30%) £	Dr B (30%) £	Dr C (23%) £	Dr D (17%) £
Estimated profit					
(£123,810+5%)	130,000	39,000	39,000	29,900	22,100
Seniority awards	9,330	4,665	4,665	–	–
Post graduate education					
allowance	8,400	2,100	2,100	2,100	2,100
Surgery rent allowance	8,000	4,000	4,000	–	–
Total income (1)	155,730	49,765	49,765	32,000	24,200
Deductions					
Superannuation (est)	8,000	2,400	2,400	1,840	1,360
Added years	1,300	900	400	–	–
On outside appointments	70	–	30	40	–
National Insurance					
Class 1 (appointments) (est)	130	–	50	80	–
Class 2 (direct debit)	1,152	288	288	288	288
Repayment of leave advance	5,300	1,325	1,325	1,325	1,325
Repayment of loans (GPFC)	800	–	800	–	–
	16,752	4,913	5,293	3,573	2,973
Income tax reserve 1996/97	17,500	5,200	4,800	4,000	3,500
Total outgoings (2)	34,252	10,113	10,093	7,573	6,473
Net (1–2)	121,478	39,652	39,672	24,427	17,727
Monthly (divided by 12)	10,123	3,304	3,306	2,036	1,477
(but say) . . .	10,100	3,300	3,300	2,030	1,470

Where projections of this nature are prepared by the practitioner, care should be taken to ensure that all possible information is included. For instance, if it is known that a partner will become entitled to a higher rate of seniority during the year, then this must be taken into account. The drawings must be kept under review at fairly regular intervals so that if any radical changes become apparent during the year, these can be amended without undue delay. If this is not done, it will to a large degree cancel out the advantages of the system and result in significant differences between the partners at the end of the year.

Schedules of this nature can be organised without difficulty using a computer spreadsheet system which will ensure that changes can be made quickly and accurately.

A major factor in any such drawings calculation will be the amount of the income tax reserve and this again can vary due to unforeseen factors during the year. We will therefore now look at ways by which these reserves can be implemented and the rationale behind this.

5.12.1   Income tax reserve accounts

There are numerous ways by which income tax liabilities can be reserved by GP partnerships. The practitioner would be well advised to recommend to his clients ways and means by which such transfers can be effected, for two major reasons:

(a)   It eases the cash flow both of the practice and the individual partners. The transfer of funds into a separate account means that they are always available when the half-yearly income tax demands fall due and partners will not be asked to write out fairly large cheques at six-monthly intervals. This can, at times, cause some difficulty where partners have not been sufficiently prudent to set aside sums for that purpose.

(b)   It safeguards the continuing partners against a partner leaving the practice with a liability behind him. Although rarely seen, nevertheless this is a danger which should always be insured against and, with partners having joint and several liability for their tax assessments, all partnerships would be well advised to set money aside for this purpose.

This can, at the most basic level, be done by transferring funds into a separate tax reserve account each year, probably held on deposit at a bank or building society. This system in itself works reasonably well, with funds being available when required and takes a great deal of worry away from partners when demands fall due. However, this system does have its drawbacks. Setting aside large amounts in a separate interest-bearing account merely excludes those amounts from the working capital of the partnership and means that this money is not available for use when required. Again, the system is not popular with, usually, junior partners, who may well have a bank overdraft on which they are paying interest at a high rate, obtaining no tax relief and who not unnaturally feel aggrieved at the thought of these fairly substantial amounts sitting in a bank account earning very much less interest.

This can be counteracted to some degree by including those reserves within the accounts, and transferring amounts from the partners' current accounts each year which will effectively reserve the liability of all the partners up to the account date. While steps must still be taken to ensure that funds are available as and when demands fall due, nevertheless this system means that the partners can have the use of the money in the meantime and it can, in fact, count as part of the working capital of the practice during this period.

Where an income tax reserve is prepared, in whatever form, this cannot be isolated within a single year. Almost inevitably adjustments will take place in respect of earlier years, possibly concerning partners' individual tax relief for loan interest, superannuation, etc. which will result in retrospective adjustments to their tax liability. All these must be properly adjusted through the tax reserve account, using normal accountancy principles.

5.12.2 Tax reserves: future policy

The introduction of self-assessment and its consequences upon the manner in which partnership taxation is assessed have a bearing on the way in which these tax reserve accounts will be organised in the future.

As we have seen, a major reason for holding funds in such accounts is the security of knowing that money is available to meet possible tax liabilities of a partner who has left the partnership. Under self-assessment however, no assessments will be issued on the partnership but rather on individual partners. It will not, therefore, be necessary to hold funds for that purpose.

The obvious final result of a partner not having sufficient funds held privately to meet his tax liability is that he would ultimately be preceded against by the Inland Revenue or, in the last analysis, made bankrupt. Whether this is an acceptable situation for his continuing partners is another matter and this could well lead to the dissolution of a partnership.

This is a matter which is integral to all partnerships, whether or not they have previously held tax reserve accounts. This should be discussed with the partners and a decision made, according to their own aspirations and preferences.

Chapter 6 – General practitioner accounts: principles and practice

6.1 Introduction

The major function which the accountant will provide for his GP client, apart from the determination and settlement of his tax liability, will be the preparation of his annual accounts.

The typical GP may, at times, speculate upon whether he needs accounts and whether or not he can do without them. Does he really need to pay what he sees as a fairly handsome (or possible extortionate!) fee each year to a professional accountant for drawing up his accounts? He is not required by law to have his accounts audited, so can he prepare them himself and dispense with accountants entirely?

This is, of course, a highly fallacious view. A GP or his partnership needs accounts for a number of purposes, none of which will be properly fulfilled without the drawing-up each year of a proper set of accounts to a high professional standard:

(a)   to agree the practice's assessable profits with the Inland Revenue (see Chapter 7);
(b)   to determine the tax liability of the practice, partnership and individual partners;
(c)   to support any applications for loan finance, particularly in connection with cost rent schemes (see **3.6**);
(d)   as an aid to future budgeting and forecasting;
(e)   to assist in the economic management of the practice, particularly with a view to increasing profitability;
(f)   to maintain equity between the partners, including establishment of capital requirements (see **5.8**);
(g)   accounts are likely to be required under the terms of the partnership deed (see Appendix 4: Clause 8.2).

The preparation of a full set of partnership accounts is therefore essential to the efficient, financially aware and properly managed general practice.

Whilst it is right and proper for a GP to seek to reduce his accounting fees, the avenue by which this might be done invariably lies in the area of improving his own accounting records rather than in reducing the level of work performed by professional advisers.

Appendix 1 shows a specimen set of GP partnership accounts. These are drawn up in such a form that they will include most of the features which will be found in the accounts of a typical partnership. Not all of the entries will be necessary; for instance, not every practice has a dispensing or fundholding facility; only rarely will they require use of a retired partner's account and some stable partnerships may well go for some years without a partnership change. Nevertheless, the example shown should act as a base upon which the practitioner can design the accounts to the requirements of his particular client.

It should be emphasised that these accounts are intended purely by way of illustration; it is accepted that many firms will have, and wish to maintain, their house style and this is perfectly acceptable so long, of course, that the various principles outlined below are adhered to.

The accounts illustrated are those of a GP partnership. Despite the vast majority of GPs practising in partnerships, there are still a number of sole practitioners who will also require annual accounts prepared. It is suggested that in those cases the accounts are prepared on a similar but abbreviated basis, omitting all those features which are peculiar to partnerships.

6.2   Choice of year ends

Although essentially concerned with tax planning, it is as well in this section to mention the question of accounting year ends. It is becoming generally accepted now that 30 June is the most beneficial year end for use in practices of this nature. This is because all NHS/HA income is geared to a quarterly basis and it is a great deal easier if accounts are prepared to a conventional quarter end, i.e., March, June, September and December. As June happens to be the earliest such quarter end within the tax year, it has become more or less accepted wisdom that accounts should be prepared to that basis, so long as there is no tax disadvantage in changing. With this in mind, the accounts are illustrated to a June year end.

The pending introduction of the current year basis of assessment may well affect choice of year ends, with each case being considered on its merits.

This question of accounting year ends is a matter of some dissension between the GPs' negotiating body, the General Management Services Committee of the BMA, and the accountancy profession. Left to themselves the GMSC would much prefer accounts to be drawn up to a year end within the first quarter of the year because that is the only year end which is used for the purpose of the 'sampling' process for determining the GPs' annual pay award (see **2.2**). However, this is in direct conflict with the advice frequently given by GP accountants.

There are many computer programs in existence which have been developed by separate accountancy firms, some of these specially designed to produce accounts in a suitable format for GPs and their partnerships. Such programs, so long as they are suitably designed and cater for the various principles essential in GP accounts, can result in significant savings to the practitioner in preparing these accounts, which again will be a factor in the constant attrition between chargeable time and fees.

There are, however, a number of principles which should be taken into account when preparing and drafting GPs' accounts, which have become apparent over the years.

6.3   Several major principles

Set out below are several separate principles which it is suggested are mandatory in the preparation of accounts of this type. While the style and presentation may vary somewhat according to the preferences and house style of the practitioner concerned, nevertheless it is suggested that accounts prepared without taking these principles into account will not give the GP the level of service he requires. (References in bold are to text elsewhere in this book; page and note references are to the accounts set out in Appendix 1.)

6.3.1   Grossing-up (2.2)

In preparing these accounts, at all times the principle of 'grossing-up' directly reimbursed expenses has been complied with. If, for instance, we refer to note 1.5 (page 208) we see that we set out the principles from the SFA used in preparing these accounts. In note 10 (page 211) we see the gross amount of reimbursements received, which should, unless there are any good reasons to the contrary (see **2.4**) exactly balance with the matching items of expenditure shown in note 14 (pages 212–3).

6.3.2   Partnership changes (5.2)

We have seen that in some partnerships the incidence of changes in partners tends to be extremely frequent. It follows naturally that the larger the practice the more frequent these changes are likely to be, although where choice is possible a practice would be well advised to gear its changes to the practice year end. This is not always possible, particularly where doctors wish to plan their retirement, or obviously in the case of unforeseen deaths.

Where changes occur within a year, it is not considered acceptable practice to prepare a separate set of accounts for each change in partnership. With the likelihood of five or six changes in such a year, the prospect of preparing a separate account for a period of a few months, or even days, is not a serious possibility, on the grounds of practicality apart from the cost involved.

It is therefore conventional practice to prepare a single set of accounts to the standard partnership accounting year end, regardless of the changes that have taken place during that period and to divide the profits on an agreed basis.

Having determined this, we must then look at exactly the means by which such profits are to be allocated between the separate periods involved. The policy which is to be utilised in preparing these accounts should be established from the outset. It should be discussed with the partners of the practice and the alternatives made clear to them. Where this policy is not set down in a partnership deed it should be included in a letter of representation (see Appendix 10).

For many years it was accepted wisdom that where such changes took place, the income, expenditure and consequent profits were to be divided on the basis of actual earnings and expenses within each separate profit-sharing period during a single accounting year. While this, at least on the face of it, gave accurate allocation of those profits, as a process it was both time-consuming and expensive. This was a subject upon which specialist accountants held lengthy debates but invariably decided that their professional responsibility led them to prepare accounts on an accurate basis, although the possible alternative of time apportionment was always available.

To a larger degree this policy was triggered by the fact that doctors' earnings in a partnership were very largely dependent on the number of partners and, with the basic and other practice allowances accounting for some 36 per cent of a typical GP's income, the alternative time apportionment basis could well have produced inaccurate figures of apportioned profits, which would have resulted in one (normally the incoming) partner suffering.

This debate was, to a large degree, settled with the introduction of the 1990 GP Contract, bringing with it a reduction in the proportion of practice allowances to an estimated 17 per cent of a GP's income. This therefore reduced the possible distortion between profits earned in separate profit-sharing periods and it has now become more or less accepted practice to divide profits on a time apportionment basis.

If we refer to the illustration set out in Figure 5.2 (see page 96), with a change in profit-sharing ratios after three months of the accounting year, the allocation of profits (assuming distributable profits of £329,460 after allowance for prior charges on profits) on the time apportionment basis would look something like this (see Figure 6.1):

Figure 6.1

	£
Period 1 July to 30 September 1995 (3 mths)	82,365
Period 1 October 1995 to 30 June 1996 (9 mths)	247,095
	329,460

It is considered adequate that, where breaks occur at the end of calendar months, then apportionment on a monthly basis will be adequate. Where, however, a break takes place mid-month, e.g., on 15 October, then the apportionment should be made on a daily basis.

Nevertheless, some practices may insist on profits being allocated on an actual and, theoretically, more accurate basis. Where this is done, it is suggested that the likely additional costs of the work are outlined to the partners.

As a 'halfway house' it would, with the agreement of the clients, be acceptable to allocate the income on an actual basis but the expenses on a time apportionment basis. While this would again result in a far greater time input than allocation purely on a time apportionment basis, in certain cases it might be an acceptable option.

6.3.3   Prior shares (see 5.5)

It is important that where partners are entitled, as will be the case in virtually all partnerships, to retain prior charges on profits, these are clearly set out in the accounts and the partners are well aware of exactly how much has been credited to them before profits are allocated in agreed ratios.

The manner in which this is shown is set out in note 2 (see page 208). It will be seen that this caters for four separate elements of prior shares:

- night visit fees;
- seniority awards;
- post graduate education allowance;
- surgery income.

6.3.4   Profit allocation (see 5.3)

All profits will be allocated on some ratios agreed between the partners from time to time, and possibly from period to period within a single accounting year. In Figure 6.2 we can see how profits for each period can be determined. When the total profit for each such period has been calculated, this must then be divided between the partners in agreed ratios. The manner in which this is done is set out in note 3 on page 209.

It is emphasised that in all cases it must be perfectly apparent to partners or others reading the accounts exactly how the profits have been allocated and each figure shown must agree exactly with the proportion which the profit-sharing ratio bears to the total profit. Exactly how this is done, using the figures set out in Figure 6.1, is shown in Figure 6.2.

Figure 6.2

		Period to 30 September 1995		*Period from 1 October 1995*	*Total*
	(%)	*£*	*(%)*	*£*	*£*
Dr U	(17)	12,982	10	24,710	37,692
Dr V	(17)	12,982	18	40,877	53,859
Dr W	(17)	12,982	18	40,877	53,859
Dr X	(17)	12,982	18	40,877	53,859
Dr Y	(17)	12,982	18	40,877	53,859
Dr Z	(15)	11,455	18	40,877	52,332
Dr T	(fixed share)	6,000		18,000	24,000
		82,365		247,095	329,460

The ratios are as shown in Figure 5.2 (see page 96), except that it has been assumed the practice has a 'fixed-share' partner (see **5.4**), earning £24,000 per annum.

It is normal to allocate to the nearest pound. In practice, to these shares of profit will be added any income from prior shares, surgery income, etc.

6.3.5 Surgery ownership (see 5.7)

As we have seen, a large proportion of GP partnerships hold the surgery in different shares to those in which practice profits are divided. This must be clearly evident from the accounts, both as regards capital and income.

Note 2 on page 208 has a column so that, where applicable, this surgery net income can be divided into separate ratios and is effectively a prior charge on profits. Note 17 on page 214 shows the receipts from the rent allowance, which after deduction of interest charges leaves the net surgery income to be divided among the surgery-owning partners.

In some cases, particularly in the early years of ownership, there may be a deficit on this note (resulting from the interest charges exceeding the rent allowance) and it is this deficit which must be used as a 'reverse' prior charge. We have seen (**5.7**) and (**5.8**) how the partners' investment in the equity of the surgery should be shown in the accounts. It will be seen that specimen property capital accounts are shown in note 22 on page 217 and these are reconciled to the equity in the building.

6.3.6 Capital grants

From time to time, practices receive grants to set against sums expended by way of purchases of capital equipment. Fundholding practices will receive grants of this nature (see **8.7** and **8.10**), while computer-owning practices will receive reimbursements towards the cost of installation (see **2.15**). These grants are offset against the cost in note 19 on page 215.

Where such grants are received in defrayment of revenue expenditure, these must be shown as a credit in the reimbursements (note 10 on page 211) of the accounts.

6.3.7 Fundholding (see Chapter 8)

Accounts for fundholding practices must show clearly in accordance with the 'grossing-up' principle (see **2.4**), that the disbursement and refund of the management allowance is shown on both sides of the accounts, where appropriate by cross-reference to a note (note 16 on page 214) from which will be clear exactly the type of expenditure paid and refunded. The balance on the fundholding bank account should not be included in the balance sheet as it is not a practice asset, neither should any account be taken in the practice accounts of any charges or interest, paid or credited, on that account.

6.3.8 Dispensing practices

It is recommended, as an aid to the clients, that a memorandum 'trading' account is shown within the annual accounts so that there will be apparent the amount of profit realised on this facility during the year. An example of such an account is set out in Figure 2.3 (see page 32). We should remember to include in this account any amounts received by way of fees from private prescriptions. However, this does not preclude the requirement to include gross costs and total refunds on both sides of the account.

6.3.9 Stock on hand

Particularly where large amounts of drugs are held, a proper stocktaking should be carried out at the end of each accounting year, valued with the addition of VAT, and this will form the basis of the figure included in the annual accounts. This will also be adjusted through the dispensing trading account (see Figure 2.3).

Where, particularly in a non-dispensing practice, the value of drugs is not material, say, under £200, it will, with the agreement of the clients, be acceptable to include an estimate, although this must be done on a realistic basis.

It is always advisable to invite the client to sign a brief form of certificate, confirming the agreed value and that it is inclusive of VAT.

6.3.10 Superannuation (see Chapter 9)

Superannuation contributions by the partners are not an expense of running the practice, but rather of providing a pension for the GP on his eventual retirement. As such, these contributions should not be shown as an expense in the annual accounts but should be charged to individual partners through their respective current accounts.

Section **9.6** looks at the manner in which tax relief is granted on these contributions.

6.3.11 Personal expenses claims (see 7.6)

These should be made up to the same year end as the practice accounts. Although not an integral part of the accounts as they apply to each individual partner, nevertheless it is normal practice to include such claims in the package of accounts sent to the partners. In many cases a partner will receive only a copy of his own practice expenses claims so that the details of claims made by other partners are confidential to them.

6.3.12 Debtors

The accounts to be prepared are on an earnings basis (see note 1.1 on page 208) and do not merely show receipts and payments during the accounting year.

118

It is therefore important that account be taken of all outstanding items at each year end.

This principle manifests itself particularly in the requirement to provide as accurately as is reasonably possible for outstanding NHS fees and allowances, as well as the various outstanding refunds.

Many NHS fees are paid substantially in arrears. Certainly, most items of service fees will be paid one quarter in arrears, although practice may well vary between one HA and another. In other cases target payments and sessional fees may well be paid in arrears and this should be considered carefully before the accounts are completed.

It is often good practice to discuss this with the practice manager and to try and ensure that information is given during the accounts preparation process which will enable accurate provisions to be included in the accounts.

6.3.13   Pre-payments

In order to arrive at an accurate assessment of the profits, account should be taken of all items paid wholly or partly in advance. An adjustment to the appropriate expenditure account should be made. Items of expenditure to which this is likely to apply are:

- insurance premiums;
- equipment hire/rental;
- maintenance contracts;
- rates/water, etc.

6.3.14   Creditors

In most practices creditors will be of a routine nature, e.g., accountancy fees, PAYE/NIC due and normal outstanding accounts. In a dispensing practice care must be taken to see that all fees for drug supplies have been invoiced and the correct balance taken at the year end.

Some practices buy drugs from more than one supplier and the balance due to each at the year end should be ascertained.

6.4   Potential problems

Having looked at the various principles which are to be used in preparing the accounts, let us now look at a number of problems which can arise in this work and consider means by which they might be solved.

6.4.1 Locum and maternity leave (see 2.16)

In a typical larger GP partnership, by the law of averages, rarely a year will go by without at least one partner being away for part of the year due to sickness or maternity leave.

From the accountant's point of view, problems arise here in identifying the policy of the partners with regard to the payment of locum fees and receipt of any HA allowances, by whom these are paid and who is entitled to them.

There are several possible permutations as to how these might be dealt with, but the following should be identified:

(a)   The agreed interval between the start of the absence from practice and the time at which the partner becomes responsible for payment of his own locum fees. It is normal to have such an interval which may be anything upwards of four weeks and again this should be shown in a partnership deed or letter of representation.

(b)   Who receives the sickness/maternity allowance. It is natural justice that whoever pays the locum receives the allowance but again the matter should be clarified.

(c)   How the payments are actually made. Are cheques drawn on the partnership account or does the partner responsible draw cheques on his private account?

(d)   When, if at all, the partner involved ceases his entitlement to his agreed share of the practice profits. This is likely to apply only in extremely lengthy absences due to ill health.

It is essential that as soon as it is established whether a doctor has been away from the practice during the year, the policy is established, the nature and source of the payments are identified and the accounts prepared accordingly. Many is the trap which the unwitting accountant has fallen into with regard to such matters.

Where it is known that such a period of absence is about to occur (which is normally the case in maternity leave) it is usually best, and in order to avoid confusion, if those partners responsible for payment of locum fees draw cheques on their own personal accounts. This avoids detailed analyses being made, which can go wrong, in the event of all the locum fees being paid from the partnership account. By the same token, the sickness or maternity allowance for the identical period should be paid over to that partner.

Where such locum fees are paid privately, either personally by the partner or by charging to his current account, they must be included in the personal practice expenses claim of that doctor. Similarly, any receipt of sickness or maternity allowance must be excluded from the accounts and charged to that partner through his partnership income tax allocation.

6.4.2 Current accounts (5.11)

One of the biggest sources of disagreement when accounts are produced to a partnership for agreement can be the differences on the partners' current accounts. We have had a look at this in some detail but suffice it to say here that where drawings are prepared within the practice, any differences between the individual partners' current account balances will normally result, provided adjustments have been made on an annual basis, from errors in drawings calculations. In some cases, partners will want detailed explanation of these differences and why these errors have occurred. It is important that when accepting an assignment the accountant makes it clear whether or not part of his standard terms of reference include looking into such matters and that, if additional work is required, an appropriate fee will result.

6.4.3 Drawings

It is always as well to include within the accounts a schedule of drawings by the partners. It is normal for these to be paid monthly but the presence of such a schedule, where errors can occur, not necessarily through the fault of the accountant, can frequently result in an explanation of apparently different current account balances becoming evident.

6.4.4 Negative equity

It is by no means unusual, particularly in the early years of a surgery ownership, for the outstanding loan at the end of a year to exceed the book value of the surgery premises shown in the balance sheet. This can arise through the addition of rolled-up interest to the loan account which then becomes greater than the book value of the surgery premises in the balance sheet.

It is standard practice for such interest to be included in the income and expenditure account as a charge in the accounts to obtain the consequent tax relief (see **7.4.2**). Where this occurs, it is good practice to include two correcting entries, including this rolled-up interest, in the book value of the surgery premises, and also to increase the current accounts of the surgery-owning partners.

The purpose of this is to cancel out or reduce significantly the negative equity which has resulted for this reason and also to credit the partners'

121

accounts with an amount equivalent to that which their profits have reduced due to the inclusion of this interest as a charge in the accounts. The book entries for this (assuming an accrued interest charge of £25,269.47) will, therefore, be as shown in Figure 6.3.

Figure 6.3

Original entries

		£	£
(a) Loan interest	Dr	25,269.47	
To bank loan account			25,269.47

Being charge of rolled-up interest for the
year consolidated in overall loan balance.

Adjusting entries

		£	£
(b) Surgery premises (asset accounts)	Dr	25,269.47	
To partners' current accounts (property-owning partners only)			25,269.47

Being adjustment of rolled-up interest for
the year now capitalised in book value of
surgery premises.

6.4.5   Tax provisions

We have considered how drawings and tax reserves can be effected in the partnership accounts. In some cases, however, partnerships are amenable to a recommendation that these reserves should actually be built into the accounts, with tax being accrued on a preceding year basis up to the accounting year end concerned. If, therefore, we were preparing accounts up to 30 June 1996, we would provide for the whole of the 1995/96 tax liability, together with one-quarter of that for 1996/97.

This system effectively ensures that sums will not be paid over to partners by way of undistributed profits without taking into account any potential tax liabilities.

If it is apparent that a partnership change will be treated as a cessation for tax purposes, then the taxation provision should be prepared on an actual year basis in order to provide fully for any potential liability.

The preceding year basis tax provision is only adequate so long as the partners continue to take their drawings net of tax so that throughout the year money is retained within the partnership to fund this taxation provision.

In some cases it will be found that partners are opposed to the principle of including tax reserves within the partnership. In these circumstances, a note should be included in the accounts to the effect that the partners are jointly and severally liable for the tax liability of the partnership and are responsible for providing their own shares of the partnership tax liability as and when this falls due.

6.4.6 Business rates (see 2.4.2)

Some care must be taken to see that the payment and refund match, or any reason identified and the difference reconciled.

Where rates are paid early in the year, it may be necessary to adjust the final figure to take account of both a pre-payment and an accrual. If, for instance, a practice making its accounts up to 30 June pays its full rates bill for the year in April and obtains a refund in May, an adjustment of nine months, both for the payment and refund, should be made. While this process will not affect the overall profit, each individual item, expense and refund, will represent a more correct figure than would otherwise be the case.

6.4.7 Trainees' salaries (see 2.9)

As we have seen, training practices will pay out the salaries of their GP trainees and recover the cost from the HA. It is necessary that in the accounts of such a practice these two items are identical, or at least any difference is kept within reasonable bounds.

The biggest reason for such a difference is likely to be that the staff PAYE/NIC payment has been analysed as staff salaries without taking into account that some of it will refer to the trainee. In such a case it will be necessary to identify payments over the year which refer to the trainee and a correcting transfer made.

6.5 Management information

Many practices prefer to obtain more than merely a set of accounts, and feel they would like their accounts to be interpreted in such a way as will offer a high level of management information and advice. Such a review may take the form of a management letter which could, depending on preference, be bound into the accounts booklet. It could well include such items as:

(a)   comments on income and expenditure;
(b)   suggestions for increased profitability;
(c)   highlights of weaknesses and opportunities;

(d)   review of internal accounting systems;
(e)   adjustments to current account balances (see **5.11**);
(f)   projected drawings (see **5.12**);
(g)   projected tax reserve transfers (see **5.12.1**);
(h)   estimates of future tax liabilities.

6.6   Accountant's certificate

Page 204 sets out a form of accountant's certificate, which can be varied to suit the style of individual firms. It should, however, make it clear that no audit has been conducted. Indeed, the practitioner should ensure that he does nothing which might lead either the client or a third party to conclude that an audit was being carried out.

It has been held in a negligence case (not involving a GP) that even the word 'audit' appearing on an accountant's working papers file might be sufficient evidence for that to be assumed. Similarly, junior or other staff engaged upon the work must not, even in conversation, do anything which might involve the improper use of the word 'audit', the consequences of which might not be fully understood by either party.

Chapter 7 – Taxation

7.1 Introduction

There can be little question that the manner in which income tax is assessed and paid and its allocation between partners represents a major share of the financial problems which confront the average medical practice. Fortunate indeed is the practice whose professional advisor completes his accounts in good time, submits them to the Inland Revenue for agreement and advises his clients of any future and present tax liabilities. The advantages and peace of mind which the average medical practice derives from an alert and expert advisor cannot be stressed too strongly.

It is, of course, true that in this GPs are little different from the majority of non-corporate businesses, yet the manner in which GP partnerships are organised (see Chapter 5) and the likelihood of a steady pattern of partnership changes over the year invariably results in computations of tax liabilities and particularly their allocation between partners, being rather more complex than those of other trading partnerships of a similar size.

This situation will scarcely be helped by the radical changes pending in the taxation system. Introduction of the current year basis of assessment, together with self-assessment for individual taxpayers, and the somewhat draconian penalties which will be available to the Revenue, will automatically prove expensive for those GPs who have been in the habit of delaying submission of accounts and returns, possibly for several years.

These pending changes are of a general taxation nature; they do not affect GPs alone and consequently will not be addressed to any great degree in this chapter. Where relevant, suitable comments will be included, but, by and large, the effect on GPs and their partnerships will be no different to other Schedule D taxpayers.

It is often assumed that taxation for GPs is something of a special case, that they are subject to all manner of legislation which does not apply to the rest of the community. This is quite incorrect; the taxation laws for GPs do not differ from those which apply to the rest of the Schedule D taxpaying community. There is only one extra-statutory concession which applies to

GPs and there is very little case law on the subject. Inevitably, therefore, one falls back on common usage and to procedures which have developed over the years and which appear to receive tacit approval. While this may not at first sight appear to be a satisfactory position, nevertheless it does give the practitioner an element of flexibility which may not be apparent were he to be bound by a more structured legislative regime.

The purpose of this chapter is not so much to explore the basic taxation rules as to highlight those which are of special interest to the practitioner specialising in the affairs of GPs; to look at the problems he is likely to encounter and to consider ways by which the client's affairs might be organised to his optimum advantage.

7.2   Partnership taxation and the preceding year basis

Doctors in partnership are treated no differently than any other individuals trading in partnership; assessments are made on the partnership as a whole and the partners are jointly and severally liable (s111 ICTA 1988); they are assessed on the basis of the profits returned in the accounting year ending within the preceding tax year (s60 ICTA 1988); and partnership profits are divided between the partners for tax purposes upon the profit-sharing ratios applicable in the year of assessment and not in the basis period (s277 ICTA 1988). This will apply to partnership changes only up to 5 April 1997.

Where GPs are likely to differ from other more conventional traders in partnership is not in the application of the law but in the matters to be taken into account when judgements are made. Particularly, this is relevant in the case of a change in partnership, and when a decision has to be made as to whether a continuation election (s113 ICTA 1988) is to be submitted to the Revenue.

In the case of many other professional firms, profits can and do vary widely from one year to another, according to trends in the national economy and conditions in the particular trade or profession. In medical partnerships it is rare for such conditions to apply; the likelihood is that profits will increase at a fairly steady – if unexciting – rate over the years, more or less in keeping with both annual increases in GPs' remuneration and the extent to which partners devote their time and energy to the practice. It is rare indeed for profits in a partnership to actually fall within a single year, although in the present economic climate and the likelihood of modest pay increases this is by no means impossible. Nevertheless, in many cases the only real possibility of partnership profits falling by a significant amount is where the practice reduces in size, say from seven to five partners, with a consequent loss of practice allowances and, perhaps, capitation and similar fees if those partners take patients with them.

From time to time partnerships dissolve and again these demergers of partnerships can cause problems to the practitioner seeking the best advice for his clients. While it is not proposed here to go into the detailed conditions for the demergers of partnerships, in medical practices where this occurs it usually manifests itself in a situation where a number of partners, for reasons probably of an internal nature, decide to go their own way.

Example

The partnership of Drs A, B, C, D, E & F, practising in the village of Hogmire, has for some years been in dispute over various matters of finance, clinical policy and the like. Eventually they decide their interests will best be served by dividing the partnership and going their separate ways. Ultimately, Drs A, C and E decide to practise as one partnership, with Drs B D and F as another. They agree to take their own patients and one of the new practices finds separate premises within the same village.

In a situation like this the practitioner would be well advised to seek to have a continuation election accepted by the Revenue. It is likely that the profits of the combined practice will continue to rise and that in their first year the two new practices will together earn rather more than in the concluding year of the original partnership. While each case must be considered on its merits, nevertheless, this is a matter upon which at times Inspectors of Taxes are prepared to allow continuation elections so long as:

(i)   the two succeeding partnerships are in effect a continuation of the original business, dealing with the same patients and practising in roughly the same area; and
(ii) the personnel of the two partnerships remains unchanged.

It is suggested that, while such an election may be submitted, no guarantee should be given to the clients that it will be successful. Indeed, in some cases where HM Inspector of Taxes has indicated that this will be allowed, a new Inspector has chosen to revert to a cessation basis, with significant loss of tax to the clients.

This situation is frequently left to the discretion of individual Inspectors and reference should be made to Inland Revenue Statement of Practice SP 9/86.

A situation such as that outlined above will only be relevant up to 1996/97 following which time self-assessment will ensure that each partner accounts for his own liability only.

7.3   Assessments on partnership changes

As we have seen (Chapter 5), one major feature of GP partnerships is the frequency with which partnership changes can take place. While this is by no means universal, with some practices continuing with the same partners for many years, nevertheless these tend to be the exception rather than the rule, with the majority of partnerships experiencing a regular pattern of such changes, frequently within months or even weeks of one another.

These all lead to tremendous problems for the practitioner dealing with the allocation of the assessment profits, particularly bearing in mind that these must be allocated on the basis of profit-sharing ratios during the year of assessment. To a large degree these difficulties arise from the methods of treatment of:

(a)   seniority awards and other separately allocated items (prior shares; see **5.5**); and

(b)   the equitable allocation of practice expenses.

7.3.1   Allocation of 'prior share' items

On any change in partnership involving the departure of a partner for whatever reason, an immediate problem will arise when allocating the tax assessment for the year of change as to the correct treatment of those items which are allocated separately to those individual partners and not allocated with partnership profits. For instance, a partner retiring on 31 March 1995 may well have earned during his final year of service, a seniority award of £4,665 which is allocated to him and in which his partners have no share. Such a former partner would have no share in the 1995/96 tax assessment, although the seniority award is correctly assessable on the partnership and, had that partner remained in practice, this would have been added to his share of the assessable profits.

While this problem is most likely to involve seniority awards of this nature, it can include any other prior shares (see **5.5**), such as PGEA, night visit fees, surgery income and the like.

7.3.2   Personal practice expenses claims

In a converse manner, an outgoing partner is likely to have incurred personal practice expenses during his final period in the practice and almost certainly will have a properly justified claim (see **7.6**). In the normal scheme of things the expenses allocated to a partner on retirement are likely to be substantial. He may well have a significant claim for his cars, wife's salary and pension scheme, house expense/study allowance and if of comparatively senior years may have been obliged to pay out locum fees in the event of illness. All this may add up to a substantial claim. There is likely to be no dispute except on technical matters over the level of a claim; what is rather more contentious is exactly the means by which this is to be allowed against partnership profits and allocated between the partners; particularly, as we have seen, as the retiring doctor will not be a member of the partnership and, again, can receive no direct relief for his claim, assuming, as will normally be the case, that a continuation election is being submitted.

In such cases a practitioner may well be approached by the retiring partner who, perhaps understandably, feels aggrieved at this apparent loss of tax relief. One must bear in mind, however, that by exactly the same token, just as he loses tax relief on those personal expenses, neither will he effectively pay tax on profits earned during his final period in the practice. Exactly how this is quantified depends entirely on the date of his retirement and the date to which the annual accounts are made up. Retirement was normally highly tax-efficient for a GP under the preceding year basis but is likely to be less so under the current year basis.

A similar but opposite situation applies in the event of a new partner joining the practice. The new partner will, during the basis period, incur no such expenses, which he can set against any income from this practice. He may well have incurred expenses in some previous appointment but these can only be set against his income from such an office. He therefore finds himself in a position, on joining his new partnership, of having no valid claim in that he has no expenses to set against the partnership assessment in his first year of working.

In those circumstances it is normal to allow a notional amount against the assessment of that partner, this being transferred from the expenses of the continuing partners. While by no means perfect, this gives at least some measure of equity and offers the new partner a marginal tax benefit in his early years of practice. Exactly how much the notional claim should be is a matter of judgement; the practitioner must take into account the personal situation of the incoming partner and try to assess what would have been a reasonable claim for the period involved.

It will invariably be found that Inspectors of Taxes are unlikely to raise objections to this course of action, as long as some logical reason for the transfers can be sustained and, most importantly, that there is no alteration in the quantum of the assessment.

Example

Drs Ansell, Boddington, Courage & Flowers are practising as equal partners. They make up their accounts to 30 June annually. For the year ended 30 June 1994 their accounts showed total partnership profits, including separately allocated items, of £197,462. At the same time there was a depreciation charge of £4,965; entertaining expenses of £347 and revenue expenditure on which an improvement grant was received totalling £9,000. There was also deposit interest received of £1,926, together with an improvement grant of £3,000. Expenses claims and capital allowances for the four partners have been negotiated and agreed as follows:

	Personal expenses £	Capital allowances £
Dr Ansell	8,294	2,497
Dr Boddington	4,425	1,346
Dr Courage	3,645	892
Dr Flowers	2,896	435
	19,260	5,170

In addition, capital allowances on partnership assets of £10,964 have been calculated. We are asked to calculate the assessable partnership profits for 1995/96. A computation of adjusted profits is prepared in Figure 7.1.

After these accounts have been submitted to the Inland Revenue and agreed, Dr Ansell announces that he proposes to retire from the practice on 31 March 1995. The partners subsequently announce that they have engaged a new partner, Dr Tetley, who will join with an initial share of the profits of 12%, rising to parity over three years. The other partners' shares will remain equal.

During the year to 30 June 1994, the partners received the following prior charges on profits:

	Seniority £	PGEA £
Dr Ansell	4,665	2,100
Dr Boddington	2,166	2,100
Dr Courage	2,166	2,100
Dr Flowers	2,166	–

Dr Flowers was not entitled to PGEA as he had not attended the necessary number of courses to qualify (see **2.3.3**).

It will now be necessary to re-calculate the 1995/96 assessment showing the amended allocation between the partners. This is shown in Figure 7.2.

It will be seen that:

(a)   Dr Ansell's seniority award and PGEA (total £6,765) have been added to the share of profits for allocation between the partners.

(b)   Separately allocated items are deducted from the overall profit before being added back in separate shares.

(c)   Dr Ansell's personal practice expenses (£8,294) and capital allowances (£2,497) have been re-allocated to the three continuing partners in their respective shares at the date of change, which in this case was equally.

(d)   It should be noted that in the succeeding accounts Dr Ansell will have a further claim for practice expenses in respect of the nine-month period to 31 March 1994. At that date it will be necessary to revalue his assets and calculate the balancing allowance or charge based upon that value.

(e)   There has been deducted from Dr Tetley's share a notional expenses allowance of £1,500, again by adjustments to those of the three continuing partners.

There are other means by which these adjustments on partnership changes can be accounted for, particularly to adjust or overlap prior charge items and practice expenses. It is perfectly acceptable for these prior charges to be regarded as being in the nature of partners' salaries, being restricted through the profit allocation upon the basis of those received or incurred during the year of assessment, rather than the basis

---

Figure 7.1 *Drs Ansell, Boddington, Courage & Flowers: computation of adjusted profits, 1995/96*

(based on accounts for the year ended 30 June 1994)

	£	£
Profit for the year		197,462
Add: Depreciation	4,965	
Entertaining	347	
Expenditure eligible for improvement		
grant (see section **3.10**)	9,000	
	———	14,312
		211,774
Less: Deposit interest	1,926	
Improvement grant (see section **3.10**)	3,000	
	———	4,926
		206,848
Less: Personal practice expenses		
Dr Ansell	8,294	
Dr Boddington	4,425	
Dr Courage	3,645	
Dr Flowers	2,896	
	———	19,260
		187,588
Capital allowances		
Partnership	10,964	
Personal	5,170	
	———	16,134
Adjusted partnership profit, assessable 1995/96		171,454

---

period. This form of allocation is acceptable, although it does tend to result in adjustments to computations having to be prepared a great deal later than the end of the year assessment. This can be both expensive and time-consuming.

These somewhat complex adjustments arise from the principle of dividing profits according to profit-sharing ratios in the year of assessment. With the advent of self-assessment and the ending of partnership assessments this relevance will to a large degree disappear.

Figure 7.2 *Drs Ansell, Boddington, Courage, Flowers & Tetley: income tax computation and allocation of adjusted profits for the year of assessment 1995/96*

	Total £	Total £	Dr Ansell £	Dr Ansell £	Dr Boddington £	Dr Boddington £	Dr Courage £	Dr Courage £	Dr Flowers £	Dr Flowers £	Dr Tetley £	Dr Tetley £
Partnership profit for the year												
(per accounts)		197,462										
Add: Depreciation	4,965											
Entertaining	347											
Eligible for improvement grant	9,000											
Dr Ansell's seniority/PGEA	6,765	21,077										
		218,539										
Less: Bank interest	1,926											
Assessed separately (see below)	15,712											
Improvement grant	3,000	20,638										
		197,901										
Divisible as follows:												
28%: 29%: 28%: 16%						55,412		55,412		55,412		31,665
Allocated separately												
Seniority awards	9,412		4,665		2,166		2,166		415			
Post graduate education allowance	6,300		2,100		2,100		2,100		—			
	15,712											
Less: adjustment for Dr Ansell's seniority/PGEA	6,765		(6,765)									
	8,947		(6,765)			4,266		4,266		415		
		206,848				59,678		59,678		55,827		
Less: personal practice expenses												
Per schedule as agreed	19,260		8,294		4,425		3,645		2,896			
Adjust: for Dr Ansell's expenses	—		(8,294)		2,765		2,765		2,764			
To give Dr Tetley notional year's claim	—				(500)		(500)		(500)		1,500	
						6,690		5,910		5,160		1,500
		187,588				52,988		53,768		50,667		30,165
Capital allowances												
Partnership	10,964				3,070		3,070		3,070			
Personal	5,170		2,497		1,346		892		435			
Adjust: for Dr Ansell's claim			(2,497)		833		832		832		1,754	
		16,134				5,249		4,794		4,337		1,754
		171,454				47,739		48,974		46,330		28,411

7.4 Taxation on surgery ownership

As we have seen, a large number of practices own their surgery premises, either through recent development under the cost rent scheme or a long-term ownership. This is considered at length in Chapter 3 and the manner in which property capital can be organised is discussed in **5.8**.

It must be emphasised that the receipt of the notional or cost rent allowance is part of the earned income of the practice or partnership. It is assessable under Schedule D Case II with the remainder of partnership profits, being a receipt by the GPs under their terms of agreement with the NHS. It is not a rent in the accepted sense of the word and should not be shown in the personal tax returns of the individual partners as such. Rather it should be included in the partnership income tax assessment, assessable with the remainder of partnership profits.

7.4.1 Partnership allocations

It therefore follows that in a surgery-owning partnership, as is likely to be the case, the surgery may well be held in different ratios to those in which partnership profits are shared. A separate allocation of taxable profits must be prepared, using the 'prior charge' principles outlined above. If, for instance, in Figure 7.2, three of the partners had owned the surgery premises, their total income from the rent allowance would have been deducted before arriving at the profit allocation between the partners, which would then be re-allocated between the three surgery-owning partners only. Where those three partners were paying interest on surgery loans, this would be treated in a similar (but reverse) manner.

7.4.2 Relief for interest paid

Virtually all practices will, from time to time, incur interest charges on loans taken out for several purposes. A short-term loan, for instance, may be taken out to buy a computer or some reasonably expensive piece of equipment. This would normally be repaid over, say, two or three years and the interest on such loans would be charged in the income and expenditure account as a normal charge on income.

In other cases, however, GPs will take out long-term loans in order to finance the development of their new surgery (see **3.6**). In those cases, it is likely that the loan will attract interest charges during the period of development which will effectively be 'rolled-up' into the eventual capital of the loan and will not physically be paid out of the free funds of the practice. As we have seen (**3.3**), this bridging interest is a component of the total cost upon which the cost rent income will be calculated.

Nevertheless, there is no reason why this interest should not be allowed for tax purposes, so long as it is included in the partnership accounts as an item of partnership expense and allowed in the normal way for Schedule D purposes. Where the ownership of the surgery has different profit-sharing ratios in force, it will be necessary for an adjustment to be made both in the accounts and the income tax computation to take this into account. This would normally be effected through the prior charge system.

It should be noted that income tax relief on this 'rolled-up' interest cannot be claimed as an annual charge through the personal income tax returns of the individual partners on an actual year basis, as the interest is not actually paid during the year of assessment (s353 ICTA 1988). However, for possible subsequent tax planning opportunities see **7.5.1**.

7.4.3   Capital allowances: new surgery developments

Where a practice is developing a new surgery it will invariably be found that included in the overall building contract are a number of items which might, broadly speaking, fall under the heading of plant and machinery and upon which capital allowances can be claimed. This represents perfectly proper qualifying expenditure and in such cases every step should be taken to see that this is identified and capital allowances at the appropriate rate claimed thereon.

While every case must be considered separately, some items likely to fall within this definition are:

- central heating installations;
- double glazing;
- fitted furniture, etc.

A schedule on headed paper should be obtained from the architect or surveyor, upon which is listed the cost of all items falling under this heading and this, with the addition of VAT, will form the basis upon which the claim will be made.

For accounts purposes, this expenditure can be retained within the overall surgery premises account; there is no necessity to make transfers to other asset accounts.

7.5   Unlocking the partnership capital

Many doctors who are partners in medical practices have invested significantly in their practice, in the equity of the surgery premises, in fixed assets and working capital, by some means and upon whatever formula (see **5.8**). These contributions may be in the form of actual cash introduced, but are to some degree likely to have risen through successive restrictions of drawings; or in some cases through an upward revaluation of surgery premises which have been in ownership for some years.

In some cases partners will be responsible for partnership loans on that capital, but they may well also have private loans upon which they obtain no tax relief.

In either of those cases, and provided that sufficient capital is held within the partnership, then those partners may be able to make use of the provisions of s362 ICTA 1988, which provides that interest on a loan taken out to acquire a share in, or contributing money to, a partnership is eligible for tax relief. Furthermore, such relief is allowable not on the preceding (or, in the future, current) year basis, as would be the case with a partnership loan, the interest of which is charged in the income and expenditure account, but on an actual year basis as an annual charge, provided of course that the interest is actually paid during the year (s353 ICTA 1988).

In medical practices, there are two main situations in which this can be used to benefit partners who find themselves in this position.

7.5.1 Division of partnership mortgage

Many partnerships which have acquired surgeries, either through development or purchase, have chosen to do so on the basis of a partnership mortgage. Indeed, this is virtually universal in the case of a new surgery development, where in practice it is extremely difficult to borrow money on an alternative basis.

It is therefore suggested that in such a circumstance and on completion of the development, the partners transfer this mortgage into separate loans in the names of the individual partners, on which the surgery is still held as security, but on which the partners themselves are responsible for the interest payments. Provided that this is done in the correct sequence, the advantages to the client from this course of action will be to convert the allowable interest effectively from the preceding (or current) year to the actual year basis; in the year immediately following the change, or possibly for a longer period depending on the accounting year end in use, there will be a 'double' tax benefit so that relief will be obtainable simultaneously on these two separate bases.

Reorganisations of partnership capital on this basis were common up to the 1993/94 year and were instrumental, with sound planning and advice, in saving significant amounts of tax, possibly over a two-year period. From

31 March 1994, however, new rules were introduced, designed to control changes of this nature in view of the change to current year assessment. These rules provided that in respect of loans taking place after 31 March 1994, for the change to be effective for tax purposes, the Revenue had to be satisfied that the change was for bona fide commercial reasons. In the case of surgery loans in medical practices, it would appear that those commercial reasons would appear not to extend a great deal beyond:

(a) initial transfers where the development was newly completed and by prior arrangement (see above);

(b) where there was a physical change in the partners owning the surgery; and

(c) where the partnership mortgage had been called in by the lender and it was only possible to borrow on the basis of individual loans.

The penalties which may be imposed where procedures of this nature are put in place and then rejected by the Inland Revenue, during the transitional year leading up to the current year basis of assessment, suggest that changes of this nature should only be contemplated when it can be clearly shown that a sound commercial reason exists.

It is emphasised that where it can be established that any or all of these conditions apply, then the reorganisation must be done in the correct sequence:

(i) the loan to the partnership lender must first be repaid. This will create a substantial overdraft on the partnership bank account, which hopefully will have been agreed in advance with the bank, who will presumably charge interest on an overnight situation;

(ii) the following day, again by prior arrangement, loans from the individual partners are advanced and paid into the partnership account to repay the original advance. It is emphasised that the reason for the amendment in treatment of tax relief is that this new loan is taken out for a different purpose; to introduce capital into the partnership, rather than, as previously, for the purpose of developing the surgery. It should be borne in mind that a partner can only borrow on this basis up to the limit of his invested capital in the partnership, which for this purpose will include his share of the book value of the surgery premises, possibly enhanced by revaluation.

7.5.2   Tax-efficient borrowing

We can take a little further the principle of maximising borrowing against shares of partnership capital to apply to individual partners who may wish to take advantage of the principle that tax relief is available on an actual year basis on loans raised to contribute capital into partnerships, at the same time reorganising a personal borrowing situation which may well not be tax-efficient.

Example

Let us consider the separate situation of Dr B who has a total capital investment in the partnership of £30,000. At the same time he has personal borrowings totalling £60,000 made up of a house mortgage of £50,000 and private non-qualifying loans of £10,000.

This is not a particularly tax-efficient situation. He will obtain no tax relief whatsoever on the top £20,000 of interest on his house mortgage and nothing at all on his private loan interest. Even the tax relief on his house mortgage is restricted to 15%.

It is possible therefore for Dr B to rearrange his borrowing so that he will obtain tax relief on the major part of this borrowing. His total tax relief currently on his personal borrowing is, assuming an interest rate of 10%, restricted to £750.

Dr B now proposes to restructure his borrowings by which he will, in correct sequence:

(a)   draw a cheque on the partnership account for £30,000;
(b)   by at least the following day, repay his private and non-qualifying loan of £10,000 and reduce his house mortgage by £20,000; and
(c)   raise an alternative loan with his bank, or other borrowers, for £30,000 which he then repays into his partnership account in order to defray the sum previously paid to him.

As a result of this, his capital will be restored to its correct level, although he will now have a loan standing in his name, taken out for a new purpose and on which the interest will be fully tax allowable as an annual charge.

Figure 7.3 shows the new level of tax relief on this, at £2,190. This assumes an increase in the interest rate to 12%.

As a result of this, Figure 7.3 shows the improvement in his net outgoings as a result of these transactions. It will be seen that the effect of this, even after a modest increase in the interest rate, is to reduce his annual outgoings by about £1,000.

Figure 7.3 *Refinancing the capital*

Partner 'A'	£	
Property capital	20,000	
Fixed assets/working capital	10,000	
	30,000	

Personal borrowing	£	
House mortgage	50,000	
Private loans (non-qualifying)	10,000	
	60,000	

Present tax relief

House mortgage	£
£30,000 @ 10% =	
£30,000 × 25% =	750
Private loans	Nil
	750

New tax relief
(following refinancing)

House mortgage	
(as above)	750
Partnership refinancing	
£30,000 @ 12% =	
£3,600 × 40% =	1,440
	2,190

Net cost

	(1) £	(2) £
House mortgage		
£50,000 @ 10%	5,000	–
£30,000 @ 10%	–	3,000
Private loan		
£10,000 @ 12%	1,200	–
Refinancing loan		
£30,000 @ 12%	–	3,600
	6,200	6,600
Tax relief		
Net cost	750	2,190
	5,450	4,410

Dr B has therefore, by this means improved his net disposable income by over £1,000 per annum.

Provided this is done with proper advice, and the new loan arrangement is set up well in advance, it is highly tax-efficient and there is no reason why it should not be done by one or more partners in a partnership, whose individual tax situations may well be very different.

Points to watch when making arrangements of this nature are:

(a) The question of a penalty on redemption of the original mortgage should be considered. Some lending institutions have attempted to impose conditions of this nature which effectively have increased the expense of the transaction so as to make it non-viable. It may be possible, however, for some negotiation to alleviate this.

(b) Banks and other bodies may wish to make an arrangement fee or legal charges, although again, it may be possible to negotiate this downwards. The GP Finance Corporation, for instance, normally charges a fee of £100 for each loan involved. This applies both to the situation outlined above and to the transfer of partnership mortgages.

(c) The bank or other lender will quite reasonably expect to obtain some security on the new separate loans to individual partners. It may well be necessary, therefore, for some form of cross-guarantees to be given so that if, say, a partner dies in service or retires, the bank has the security of knowing that the loans will continue to be covered.

(d) Consideration should be given to amending the partnership deed to take any new arrangements into account.

(e) The operation outlined above is only relevant up to the limit of the capital invested in the practice by the partner concerned. Therefore, if in Figure 7.3 partner A had only, say, £5,000 invested in the practice, it would not have been possible for him to carry out a refinancing package as illustrated above.

Practitioners should be careful of running up against the 'commercial reason' test (see above). Whilst no guarantees can be given, some operations of this type have been agreed with the Revenue since the imposition of the new rules in 1994.

7.6 Claims for practice expenses

The methods and procedures by which personal practice expenses are claimed by doctors in practice can be one of the most contentious areas to be encountered. It is by no means unusual for disagreements over what constitutes a reasonable claim to produce a minor crisis between the GP and his adviser. In formulating claims of this nature it is essential that the 'wholly and exclusively' rule is understood; that the potential dangers of excessive or unrealistic claims are clearly explained to the client and that before a claim is submitted, this is agreed by the client and every step taken to ensure that the expenses which are the subject of the claim can be clearly justified.

7.6.1 The Inland Revenue attitude

There is clear evidence of a more stringent approach by Revenue offices in their attitude to expenses claims of this nature in more recent years. This is in contrast to a more generous treatment which appears to have been available in the past.

To a large degree, enquiries of this nature appear to be aimed towards:

- motor expenses;
- house expenses;
- wives' salaries/pensions;
- personal telephone costs.

These tend to be expenses which, while they are allowable in principle, are usually subject to discussion on the element of private use.

Where local Inspectors can establish a pattern of overclaiming covering several years, they are within their rights in increasing tax assessments retrospectively, possibly as far back as six years, in order to collect lost tax, interest and penalties. It is essential that clients are made aware that the submission of unrealistic claims could spark off an in-depth investigation, which should be avoided at all costs. In particular, the adviser should do his utmost to ensure that:

(a) all claims submitted on behalf of clients are clearly justified;
(b) the expenditure has actually been paid out for practice purposes;
(c) receipts are provided in support of all claims;
(d) where restrictions for private use are in force, claims are both justified and regularly reviewed; and
(e) estimated expenditure is excluded as far as possible.

Where these are unavoidable, the fact that they are estimates should be clearly shown on the claim submitted to the Inland Revenue.

No claim should be submitted to the Revenue for agreement unless approved and signed by the client. A specimen confirmation letter is set out in Appendix 16.

7.6.2 Preparing the claim

In most cases, the partners' personal expenses claims will be prepared by the partnership accountant. This will not, however, necessarily be the case; at times partners will prefer to use other accountants of their choice (see **4.12**) and every step must be taken to ensure that such claims, when completed and agreed, are delivered to the partnership accountant so that he might include them in his computations of taxable partnership profits (see Figures 7.1 and 7.2).

Such claims, being personal to each partner and maybe considerably different even within the same partnership, should be excluded from the main partnership accounts and prepared as a separate statement for each partner, made up to the same accounting date as is used for the partnership accounts. They will then be shown as deductions on the partnership income tax computation (Figure 7.1).

In the event of the partnership being selected for review under the 'sampling process' by which GPs' pay is calculated (see **2.2** and Appendix 3) any expenses claimed personally will be included within the sample of expenses. There is therefore no loss to the GP or his profession by treating them in this way.

7.6.3   Partnership or personal expenses?

What are personal and partnership expenses, respectively, is a question of fact and may well vary in policy terms as between each partnership. Whatever items are authorised to be paid out of partnership funds or personally by the partners should be clearly set down in the partnership deed (see Appendix 4) and claims prepared accordingly. At its simplest, expenditure paid by the partnership should be claimed through the partnership accounts; that paid personally by the individual partners should be included in their own claim for personal practice expenses.

Appendix 15 shows a typical completed claim for personal practice expenses.

Claims for motor car expenses and in respect of spouses' salaries are dealt with in separate sections (**7.7** and **7.8**) but we should look at other general items which might be included in this claim and which may cause problems to the practitioner and his client.

7.6.4   Practice use of the home

Claims are frequently made for proportionate costs where GPs use their own houses partly for practice purposes. Where justified, it is possible to submit and agree claims for a fractional use of such a house, based upon a system of points being awarded for each room within the house, from which a fraction emerges. An example of the calculation of such a proportionate practice use of the house and of a typical claim for house expenses are shown as Figure 7.4.

Figure 7.4 *Practice proportion of private house expenses (where house used partly for surgery purposes)*

Dr B Fuller 'Adnams', 19 Burton Road, Charrington on Bass

	Practice	*Private*	*Total*
Downstairs			
Garage	12	8	20
Kitchen	1	14	15
Lounge (waiting)	2	18	20
Dining room	–	15	15
Study (consulting)	7	3	10
Entrance hall	1	4	5
Cloakroom	1	4	5
Storage room	1	4	5
Upstairs			
Main bedroom	–	20	20
3 bedrooms (15 each)	–	45	45
Bathroom	–	10	10
WC	–	5	5
	25	150	175

Proportion of claim: one-seventh

Assumes element of genuine practice use.

Practice proportion of private house expenses – example

House expenses	£
Rent	–
Council tax (not community charge)	592
Lighting and heating	729
Repairs and renewals[a]	604
Window cleaning	85
Insurance	225
Domestic assistance (£12 per week)	624
Garden expenses (1/4 whole £800 – subject to negotiation)	200
	3,059
Claim: one-seventh	437

[a] includes:
  £200 interior decorating
  £150 electrical repairs
  £225 part (half) cost of replacement windows

It is suggested that claims of this nature are submitted in respect of GPs who operate from a surgery other than their private house when most or all of these conditions apply:

(a) there is clear evidence of use of the house for consulting or treatment of patients on a regular basis;
(b) a professional plate is displayed outside the house. Although not mandatory, this can make the acceptance of a borderline claim more likely;
(c) an appropriate entry at that address in the local telephone directory;
(d) the house is either within or adjacent to the practice area;
(e) the practice car (owned personally by the partner) is garaged there.

At times GPs, normally sole practitioners, may have their surgery within their house and in those cases will be likely to receive a notional rent allowance (see **3.2**) based on this accommodation. In those cases a far higher element of charge would potentially be available and this could well be based on the proportion of the practice element of the house which is awarded by the District Valuer.

For many years, GPs preparing claims of this nature included domestic rates as an item of such expenditure. Now that council tax is levied on the ownership or occupation of buildings, it seems reasonable to include such an expense in claims of this nature.

In justifying claims of this type to the Inland Revenue, apart from the criteria outlined above, it is suggested that the following may be of assistance:

(a) It may be that the GP's partnership deed has a clause that he must reside in a house within the practice area.
(b) The GP's contract for services with the HA lays down that he will provide 24-hour cover. If, as is likely to be the case, he is a partner in a practice operating from a central surgery, then that surgery will not be open round the clock; there are times when effectively the practice will have to be run from the doctors' private houses and this can be a lever in justifying such a claim, providing all the other circumstances are right.

7.6.5 Study allowance

Where the house is not regularly used for consultation but the doctor, nevertheless, spends time working from home, it is much less contentious to claim a 'study allowance' based on a lump sum estimate of the additional cost to the doctor of using his house for that purpose.

144

Although it may be invidious to quote figures in this context, claims have been accepted by the Inland Revenue on the basis of £1 per hour worked. On that basis, therefore, a GP using his house for that purpose for 10 hours per week, over 46 weeks a year, would have a claim of £460.

7.6.6   Capital gains tax

One reason which at times deters GPs from making a claim for house expenses is that they have been advised that, in the event of the house being sold at a gain, they will be liable for capital gains tax on a proportion of the gain realised. This is, in fact, unlikely provided that no part of the house is used exclusively for practice purposes. In such a case, the CGT private residence exemption (s222 TCGA 1992) will apply. Where there is no exclusive use of any part of the house for business purposes, then private residence exemption would apply to that house, so long as it qualifies in other respects.

Even if such a claim were invalid, the possibility of claims for rollover relief and retirement relief makes it highly unlikely that a GP submitting a claim for house expenses would become liable to a CGT charge.

7.6.7   Locum fees, etc.

Many GPs make payments to locums for temporarily looking after their own patients. Where these are paid personally and charged to the individual partners, these are legitimate expenses and should be included in such a claim. It may be necessary to consider this in conjunction with locum fees paid out of the partnership accounts but charged to the individual doctor during periods of sickness, maternity leave, etc. (see **6.4.1**), possibly through his own current account with the practice (see **5.11**).

7.6.8   Accountancy fees

In some cases partners will pay personal fees to their accountants for dealing with their own personal taxation affairs. Such a fee can be included in a personal practice expenses claim but any fees relating to personal tax returns must be excluded. The fee for dealing with an expenses claim can, however, be included.

7.6.9   Security expenses

In many cases doctors keep valuable drugs and equipment in their houses and these may attract certain elements of the criminal fraternity if they are aware of it. Burglar alarms and annual maintenance charges can be paid for and these, together with the provision of security locks should all be claimed for tax purposes, although there may be a risk of a 'dual purpose' challenge. It may be both necessary and diplomatic to accept a small private use restriction. Alternatively, a modest claim for the upkeep of a guard dog might be made.

7.6.10 Private telephone bills

In some partnerships it is the policy of the practice for all private telephone accounts to be paid from partnership funds. In other cases, these will be met personally by the partners and included in their PPEC. In some cases, the Inspector will insist on the rental charge of such a line being excluded from the claim.

Whichever course is adopted, it will be necessary to try and identify some element of private use for home telephones and an adjustment made either through the partnership tax computation or in the PPEC itself.

7.6.11 Computers and videos

Many GPs invest in such equipment. If this is held at the GP's private house a proportionate claim should be made, although it is fair to say that Inspectors of Taxes are perfectly aware of the recreational element in such items. The GP should be in a position to provide examples of business use, where necessary.

Where such equipment is kept within the surgery, there will normally be no restriction for private use.

7.6.12 Permanent health/locum insurance

Most GPs pay premiums on insurance policies designed to cover the payments to locums during periods of sickness. These policies are invariably marketed as 'locum insurance', whether or not that is, strictly speaking, the case.

It has also been assumed that premiums on such policies were not allowable for tax purposes in any event, but any benefit paid under the policy would be free of tax up to a period of one year. This position was confirmed and clarified by the Inland Revenue as recently as 1995, reference being made to Extra-Statutory Concession A83.

The position has now changed radically as a result of the issue of an Inland Revenue press release on 30 April 1996. This confirms that, after taking legal advice, the Revenue have conceded that premiums on genuine locum insurance policies are indeed allowable for tax purposes. Where such policies are allowed, then it follows that any benefit received falls into charge to tax.

It should be emphasised that this rule refers to genuine locum insurance policies only, i.e., those where a direct refund is made, during or following a period of sickness, of costs directly incurred in payments to locum doctors. It does not cover a standard PHI policy, where a lump sum payment is made, and which the recipient can use at his discretion.

The Revenue also stated that retrospective claims under the 'error and mistake' provisions can be made up to a maximum of six years. Therefore, if claims of this nature are made before 5 April 1997, then these can relate back to the 1990/91 tax year.

See also Appendix 19 for the full text of the press release.

7.6.13   Courses and conferences

GPs like to attend seminars, courses and the like. Some of these are necessary to qualify for the PGEA and in such cases, provided the course has received PGEA approval, the claim for the course fee and expenses would normally be allowed.

In some cases, such events may coincide with an overseas holiday and it may be necessary, on enquiry, to produce a synopsis or programme to establish that there was a serious content. Claims for spouses or other members of the family should normally be excluded (see also **7.12**).

7.6.14   Conclusion

It is by no means surprising to find that some GPs have pressed their accountants to make small dubious fringe claims, possibly quite unsubstantiated, while inadequate recordkeeping ensures that, in many cases, no such claim is made. Clients should understand that a claim can only be made for a particular item as and when advised, provided that reasonable evidence is produced. In many cases this is down to the efficiency of the individual doctor, who is unable, as with his partnership affairs, to delegate most of his work to a practice manager.

7.7   Motoring expenses

While one hears apocryphal stories of GPs who travel around their practice area in all manner of outlandish modes of transport, in this section we shall assume that virtually all GPs decry the use of horses and bicycles and use motor cars as their principal means of private transport.

In preparing a claim for motoring expenses, the difficulty is not so much in calculating the total costs for the year of the claim, which is a relatively simple accounting exercise, provided all the information is made available, but rather in deciding the element of private use which is on the one hand acceptable to the client, and on the other unlikely to provoke undue enquiry from the Inspector of Taxes.

Broadly speaking, the Inland Revenue is invariably prepared to accept a claim for up to two cars, normally upon the basis of a major claim for the main practice car and a relatively low level claim for a second or back-up car. It makes eminent sense, provided this can be organised, that the most expensive car will be the main car for this purpose.

The claim itself should include all amounts expended on running the car during the year: licence and insurance, repairs, petrol and oil, cleaning, etc. It is infinitely preferable if such a claim can be prepared from original records and that evidence is available of every single item of expense.

The question is frequently asked whether GPs can lease cars for use in their practice. There is indeed no reason why not, if this is the GP's preference, the only major advantage appearing to be that this may obviate the need for a substantial capital payment for deposit if the car is to be bought on credit.

Experience does show, however, that the VAT cost is likely to be higher than that of an outright purchase as the GP is unlikely to be able to reclaim the cost of VAT on the leasing premiums.

There are many types of leasing contacts and it is essential that each scheme is evaluated separately and considered on its merits. The inability to reclaim VAT, however, normally militates against this type of contract.

7.7.1 'Private use' factor

It is the calculation of the restriction for private use which causes the most difficulty in preparing claims of this nature. In this, of course, GPs are in no different a position to many other self-employed taxpayers. There may well be occasions when some cars genuinely have 100 per cent practice use; this is likely to be where the doctor lives adjacent to the surgery and does not use his car on journeys from home to the surgery.

It is generally understood that journeys between home and surgery are not allowable for tax purposes. In practice, this would be relevant when a GP was preparing a mileage log as a base for calculating the fraction of private use. However, it seems clear that where the GP is on call and he must of necessity during those hours effectively practice from home, then such a journey, say on a call-out to a patient during the night, would be genuine business use. It has been held (*Sergeant* v *Barnes* [1978] 52 TC

335) that, in a case where a dentist stopped to collect dentures on his journey between home and surgery, then the whole of that journey was disallowed.

The current tax regime is such that a practitioner would be well advised to encourage his clients to keep a mileage log, probably for a specimen period of two months which, when summarised and each journey analysed between practice and private use, would produce a relevant fraction. Experience tends to show that if such detailed information is made available upon enquiry, the Inland Revenue will be less likely to disagree with such a claim. A summarised version of a mileage log is shown in Figure 7.5.

Figure 7.5 *Mileage log for GPs' cars*

Dr David Boddington and his wife, Diana, each run a car, both of which are used to some degree in his medical practice. David has been advised by his accountants to keep a detailed mileage log for each car for a specimen period of two months in order that his proportion of private use can be accurately calculated. Both David and Diana produce weekly mileage figures which, when collated, show the following results:

| | David (Rover) Miles | | | Diana (Fiesta) Miles | | |
	Total	Practice	Private	Total	Practice	Private
April	1,623	1,327	296	450	95	355
May	2,645	2,301	344	478	91	387
	4,268	3,628	640	928	186	742
Percentages		85.0	15.0		20.0	80.0

From this log it would seem that David could justify a practice claim for 85% of the Rover (15% restriction) and for 20% of the Fiesta (80% restriction).

7.7.2 Capital allowances

It is not proposed to go into any detail upon the question of claiming capital allowances, which are subject to normal taxation rules and in which GPs are treated no differently than any other taxpayer. The private use restriction for cars will normally follow that agreed for running expenses.

7.8 Spouses and families

An accepted means of tax saving is available to the married GP who, properly advised, can make a significant reduction in his taxation liability by proper and careful planning.

In this paragraph it is assumed that the GP client is a married male doctor who wishes to make certain claims in respect of his wife. The question of married female doctors is considered separately.

7.8.1 Wives' salaries

The facility for paying a salary to a doctor's wife for assistance in his practice is a perfectly legitimate means for recompensing her for the services she provides to his practice. There is, however, some evidence that these claims are currently being looked at more closely by the Inland Revenue and a number have been queried.

It is firstly important to recognise the duties for which she is being paid, which could well be some or all of the following:

(a) telephone answering;
(b) secretarial services;
(c) chauffeuring duties;
(d) advice to patients if the wife is medically or nursing qualified;
(e) general counselling;
(f) appointment scheduling and reception;
(g) chaperone duties.

The salary which it is recommended to pay the wife is that which will maintain the annual level at below the Class 1 National Insurance threshold (£61 per week for 1996/97) or £3,171 per annum.

It has been shown that current Whitley Council rates will give the level of income required. On current rates, using the practice manager scale (Grade 4) the top incremental grade is £6.60 per hour, which at a weekly duty of 10 hours, say, 47 weeks per year, works out at £3,102, marginally below the level required.

It is frequently proposed that if the wife has other income, which will use up her personal allowance for tax purposes, the salary should not be paid. It is suggested that this is by no means the case; the payment of a salary to a wife in those circumstances cannot have any detrimental effect on the finances of the family unit, unless she is paying tax at a higher rate than her husband, which, given the circumstances, is unlikely. It is therefore standard practice that a salary should be paid to a wife in such circumstances. This may well give rise to other benefits which flow from that salary and will, at the least, set a precedent which could be useful when the payment of such a salary is more tax-efficient.

In negotiating with the Revenue, it is as well to be aware of the areas of attack which have been used in several cases:

(a) Are bona fide duties being performed?
(b) Is the payment commensurate with the duties performed?
(c) Is cover already provided by a deputising service?

The comparison has been raised with an unmarried GP who has carried out similar duties without paying such a salary.

The more regular use of outside agencies to cover out-of-home responsibility, together with the development of co-operative arrangements (see **2.18**), mean that the practitioner should anticipate opposition by the Revenue to such claims for spouses' salaries and be able to justify their payment.

7.8.2 Method of payment

It is strongly recommended that such a salary is paid by some form of physical transfer of funds between the two parties. This would normally represent a payment by a GP, either in cash or preferably to his wife at the end of each month, for one-twelfth of the agreed salary.

7.8.3 GPs in partnership

It is recommended that where such salaries are paid, this is done out of the personal funds of the individual partners and not out of partnership funds. Such a salary (together with any pension contributions) should be paid accordingly and claimed through the practice expenses claims of the individual partners. There are a number of reasons for this:

(a) The partnership may not be fully made up of married men or GPs who are eligible to make such a payment. If, in those cases, the salaries are paid out of partnership funds and effectively divided between the partners in their profit-sharing ratios, then an element of injustice can result.
(b) Some of the partners may wish to make pension payments (see **7.8.5**) on behalf of their wives. While this is highly beneficial, the premiums on those policies are required to be paid by the individual by whom the salary is paid. In a typical partnership the partners' wives will be of very different ages and premiums will vary as a result of this. It would be unfair, therefore, if those premiums were merely charged in the partnership accounts and divided in similar ratios.

7.8.4 The female GP

In many cases, however, the doctor will be a female partner who in theory has the same opportunity to pay a salary to her husband, provided of course – and this is less likely to be the case – that he is performing similar duties as one would expect to be performed by the wife of a male GP. In practice, however, there may be several reasons to the contrary:

(a)   The husband may well be a high-earning professional so that payment of a salary may merely increase his tax liability and he may have a higher marginal rate of tax than his wife.

(b)   Depending on the nature of his occupation, he may be required to be away from home for lengthy periods, as well as working irregular hours. This could make it difficult to justify to the Inland Revenue a salary on the grounds that he is available to perform the necessary duties. This may well, of course, not be the case in respect of a retired or non-working husband.

A frequent cause of dissent among female GPs is that they are unable to claim tax relief on payments to childminders. It may, however, be possible, if an individual is employed with dual duties, to make a claim – possibly under a claim for house expenses, or for a telephone answering service – that a claim on these grounds can be justified.

7.8.5   Pension schemes

The payment and full justification of a salary to a spouse means that a contribution can also be made to a pension scheme on behalf of that spouse. These policies are normally written as executive pension schemes with the doctor paying the premiums and claiming these through his own PPEC. The contributions will, subject to Inland Revenue approval, rank for full income tax relief at the doctor's own rate of tax.

Upon retirement and commencing to receive a pension, this will be treated as earned income in the hands of the recipient. Depending on the spouse's other level of income, this could well result in exemption of all or part of this pension for tax purposes.

The Inland Revenue, on receipt of such claims, have been known to evaluate the claim not merely on the basis of the salary or pension individually, but of the entire package. Where it has been shown that the combined sum was felt to be excessive, a reduction in the claim has been requested. It is suggested that a practitioner faced with this situation should contest this to the ultimate degree so far as practical. Provided payment of a salary can be justified, and the duties are of a conventional nature, the allowability for tax on the pension scheme naturally follows this and it is unreasonable to try and evaluate these as a combined figure.

7.8.6   Medical insurance premiums

Relief on payments to private health schemes for an employer's spouse can also be claimed. It is recommended that a separate policy be taken out for a spouse in such an event, although where a combined policy is in existence, it will be possible to claim an appropriate fraction. Payment of such premiums will only rank as a benefit in the hands of an employee earning £8,500 or over (s154(6) ICTA 1988).

7.9   Schedule E remuneration in partnerships

One problem which many GP partnerships encounter at some time is dealing with a situation where the partners have appointments either with a public body, or more likely, local hospitals which are subject to PAYE deductions at source.

This is a situation which in some cases has proved virtually intractable. In the worst possible scenario, those doctors who hold the appointment in question are charged not only with the Schedule E tax deducted but also their full share of the partnership Schedule D remuneration, which may or may not include that same income. It goes without saying that this is a situation which should not be allowed to occur, yet it is not noticeably made easier by the attitude of some Revenue districts, which insist on sticking to the strict letter of the law and treating the partners in whose names the appointments are held as the holders of those offices (which in strict law they are), and that they are taxed fully on the salaries thus arising.

In many of these situations, the salaries arising from these appointments are, both in equity and in accordance with the terms of the partnership deed, not the property of those partners at all, but must be paid to the partnership pool of income for division in agreed ratios.

This is not a problem which applies to sole practitioners, who, if they held such appointments, would merely retain the income in their own names, and the calculation of tax will take place in the normal manner through the assessment system.

It is only in partnerships that this problem arises, with the purpose of the exercise being to ensure that the partners all pay their fair and equitable share of the income from the partnership, according to accepted rules, however this arises. Indeed, the question of the amount of tax payable on this income is not at issue, but rather the manner in which this can be fairly distributed between the partners.

It is suggested that where this problem arises, the practitioner should seek to treat it as outlined below, in descending order of preference:

(a)   The PAYE tax district dealing with this appointment should be invited to issue an NT coding, possibly after discussion with the Schedule D district. Historically, some districts have proved more co-operative than others in doing so and it will invariably be found that where this agreement is obtained in respect of one appointment, this will continue without undue enquiry in the future.

Where this applies, the income will be paid without any tax deductions, but would still remain subject to superannuation (see **9.2**) and National Insurance (see **7.10**) deductions. For tax purposes, however, the income will be shown in the partnership accounts and will merely form a part of the aggregate profits upon which the Schedule D tax assessment is based. It is an expedient which is attractive to some tax districts, bringing with it a resulting saving in work, without any effect on the ultimate tax payable.

(b) Where this proposal is not acceptable to the Inspector, it is suggested that the following negotiating points may bring some influence to bear and indeed, may encourage him to alter his position:
  (i) It should be pointed out that no expenses will be claimed specifically against income from these appointments.
  (ii) It should be pointed out that the amount of the appointments, if indeed it is the case, are minimal compared to the totality of partnership profits.
  (iii) His attention may be drawn to the effect of ESC A37, by means of which directors of companies who also happen to be solicitors or accountants can, by concession, include director's fees from those appointments in their own Schedule D assessments. While not exactly a parallel case, it has been found that some Tax Inspectors are prepared to accept that the situations are not dissimilar and will allow it on that basis.
  The case which the Inland Revenue use in this connection is *Mitchell and Eden* v *Ross* (1962), which involved a hospital consultant who attempted to obtain Schedule D expenses against Schedule E income. The case has nothing at all to do with GPs or their partnerships but this is quoted by the Revenue as authority to assess GPs in this manner. It is suggested that in negotiations it is pointed out that the two situations are entirely different.

(c) It will, however, be found that in by no means all cases will these approaches be successful. Therefore, the next avenue of approach is that, if the Inspector insists on assessing through normal PAYE procedures, the Schedule D Inspector should be asked to assess the income to Schedule D in the normal way, but to make a deduction in the eventual partnership assessment in respect of the Schedule E tax paid. This will to some degree resolve the objection of Revenue offices who feel that by including it within the Schedule D assessment they are delaying the time at which the tax is paid. Whether this attitude will change following the introduction of the actual year basis of assessment remains to be seen. However, many Inspectors do find this second option to be acceptable as a reasonable compromise.

(d) If all else fails, it then becomes necessary to adjust the partnership income tax computation to take this Schedule E income into account. This is a system which has several imperfections; it is necessary to wait until the end of the fiscal year before the adjustment can be made and problems arise on partnership changes where doctors holding such appointments have left the partnership by the time the profits fall due for assessment.

However, where necessary, the partnership tax assessment must be adjusted to take this into account and this is done by revising the allocation for each fiscal year to take into account the gross income from each such appointment and deducting it from the shares of the partners in whose names the appointment is held.

The tax paid on such appointments must be charged to those partners through their current accounts.

Following on from the assessable profits and allocation outlined in Figure 7.2, let us assume that two of those partners hold outside appointments. Gross income from those appointments, both for the basis period and for the consequent year of assessment (1996/97) is shown in Figure 7.6.

Figure 7.6

	Actual to June 1994 £	Tax year 1995/96 (est.) £
Dr Boddington	4,100	4,500
Dr Courage	3,400	3,750
	7,500	8,250

With this information, it is then possible to prepare re-allocation of the 1996/97 assessment giving effect to these appointments. How this is done is set out in Figure 7.7.

It will be noted from Figure 7.6 that:

(a) There has been deducted in the assessment the Schedule E income received during the basis period (£7,500) and which has already been included in the partnership income and profits.

(b) In adjusting the assessment we have taken into account the estimated income from these appointments for 1996/97. It must be noted that at the time this computation is prepared these figures are estimates only and the assessment will have to be further advised once actual figures, shown on the partners' P60s, are available.

(c) The required effect is obtained by adding to the adjusted profits (£190,401) the estimated Schedule E income for 1996/97 (£8,250) and then deducting this from the respective shares of Dr Boddington and Dr Courage. It will be seen then that the ultimate shares of those partners, as compared with their colleagues, are reduced by those amounts, so giving an element of justice, bearing in mind that those partners have already effectively paid tax on those appointments by charging this through their current accounts.

(d) It will be noted that the quantum of the assessment (£163,954), is identical to what it would have been had such adjustments not taken place.

Indeed, if compared with the figures shown on Figure 7.2, it is reduced from that total figure only by the amount of £7,500 which it is now apparent is assessed under Schedule E and can no longer remain in the quantum of the assessment in order to avoid this being taxed twice.

It may well be thought that this is a somewhat tortuous and time-consuming procedure. This indeed is the case, but where all other avenues have been closed, this is the only one remaining open if some equity is to be maintained as between the various partners.

The reader may reasonably enquire what will be the position as regards the adjustments with the advent of the current year basis of assessment. At the time of writing it is understood that the Revenue have proposed that GPs holding such appointments, from 6 April 1997 are dealt with under the provisions of extra-statutory concession A37, which already entitles partners in legal and accountancy firms who have similar outside appointments, to include these in their accounts for assessment under Schedule D provided that the Schedule E income does not exceed a small proportion of their gross earnings. This apparent change in policy does not as yet have any written authority.

7.10 National Insurance

It is assumed that the reader has a working knowledge of the National Insurance system and it is not proposed here to go into the various classes of insurance and how these are paid.

Figure 7.7 *Drs Ansell, Boddington, Courage, Flowers & Tetley: income tax computation and allocation of adjusted profits for the year of assessment 1995/96*

	Total £	£	Dr Ansell £	£	Dr Boddington £	£	Dr Courage £	£	Dr Flowers £	£	Dr Tetley £	£
Partnership profit for the year		197,462										
Add: Depreciation	4,965											
Entertaining	347											
Eligible for improvement grant	9,000											
Dr Ansell's seniority/PGEA	6,765	21,077										
		218,539										
Less: Bank/Building Society interest	1,926											
Assessed Schedule E	7,500											
Assessed separately (see below)	15,712											
Improvement grant	3,000	28,138										
		190,401										
As above:	190,401											
Assessable Schedule E 1995/96 (est)	8,250											
		198,651										
Divisible: 28%, 28%, 28%, 16%		198,651				55,623		55,622		55,622		31,784	
Assessed separately												
Seniority awards	9,412		4,665		2,166		2,166		415			
Post graduate education allowance	6,300		2,100		2,100		2,100		–			
	15,712											
Less: adjustment for Dr Ansell's seniority/PGEA	(6,765)		(6,765)		–		–		–			
	8,947				4,266		4,266		415			
	207,598				59,889		59,888		56,037			
	8,250				4,500		3,750					
Less: Assessable Schedule E: 1995/96 (est)	199,348				55,389		56,138					
Less: personal practical expenses												
Per previous computation, as adjusted (Figure 7.2)	19,260				6,690		5,910		5,160		1,500	
	180,088				48,699		50,228		50,877		30,284	
Capital allowances:												
Per previous computation, as adjusted (Figure 7.2)	16,134				5,249		4,794		4,337		1,754	
	163,954				43,450		45,434		46,540		28,530	

157

In the case of GPs, however, problems can arise from the situation outlined in **7.9**, where some of the partners have earnings from outside appointments. The income from such posts will unquestionably be chargeable to Class 1 National Insurance, regardless of the success or otherwise of any negotiations as outlined above for adjustment of the respective tax liabilities.

Such Class 1 NIC deductions should be charged to the current account of the partners in whose names the appointments are held.

Where the appointments are insubstantial it may be preferable to allow this to stand and reclaim the employee's contributions after the end of the tax year. Where, however, they are more substantial, applications should be made for deferment of Class 4 and, in some cases, Class 2 contributions. The GP should, however, understand that this is a deferment and not a cancellation; there will come a time when this liability has to be balanced up and this could well result in his being called upon to pay arrears of contributions to the DSS.

7.11 VAT and the GP

7.11.1 VAT exemptions

Until fairly recently, GPs have been secure in the knowledge that they were largely unaffected by VAT, having no requirement to register for VAT purposes but being unable to recover VAT charged on normal practice expenditure. GPs were therefore able to ignore the effect of VAT, being neither required to make a charge to their patients nor able to recover the input tax. This exemption is extended to individuals such as ophthalmic opticians, nurses, midwives, etc.

The exemption is restricted entirely to the supply of medical services by persons who are registered or enrolled in any of the recognised medical registers as listed in VAT Act 1995, Sch 9, Group 7.

Exemption does not extend to individuals who are registered only with one of the various alternative medicine faculties, such as osteopaths, chiropodists and the like.

Where such exemption applies, the ultimate effect on the practice is that, to the same extent as VAT is not added to fees, the additional cost on routine practice expenditure cannot be recovered either, so that this represents a real additional cost to the practice. However, bearing in mind the manner in which GPs' remuneration levels are calculated (see **2.2.2**), by reference to an average refund of expenses, this additional cost is refunded to GPs through their annual pay award.

7.11.2   New surgeries and self-supply

The provision for a self-supply charge, originally introduced in the 1989 Finance Act, was repealed with effect from 1 March 1995.

Where surgery developments commenced after that date, there is no requirement for practices to register under this scheme. Where developments were in progress at that date, practices may still register, recovering the VAT on the builders' charges, professional fees and the like.

7.11.3   Partial exemption and the *de-minimis* rule

From 1 April 1992 those businesses which were partially exempt from VAT and which could demonstrate a regular source of vatable income were entitled to reclaim income tax provided certain criteria were met. Largely due to its use by dentists in selling certain appliances, the scheme became generally known as the 'toothbrush scheme'.

Changes introduced in November 1994 resulted in such schemes being effectively blocked. Any practice which registered under the scheme should reconsider its position with its professional adviser.

7.11.4   Dispensing practices

Some practices obtain dispensing status (see **2.8**), by which they are entitled to dispense medicines to patients living in certain areas. From 1 April 1995 drugs dispensed by GPs in such a position are zero-rated. The practice may register for VAT and reclaim the VAT separately on the purchase of drugs, together with a proportion of overheads which relate to the NHS dispensing activities. Where this applies, practices should understand that they will not be refunded the VAT, with the cost of drugs refunded through the Prescription Pricing Authority, as would be the case with a non-VAT registered practice.

Practitioners should be aware that the transitional arrangements for VAT, whereby NHS dispensing suppliers could be treated as being outside the scope of VAT ceased with effect from 1 October 1995.

Only tax incurred on drugs purchased for dispensing and on hand at the date of registration and which are used to make zero-rated supplies can be treated as input tax and claimed on the first VAT return.

VAT on services supplied, relating to the zero-rated drugs and received in the six months prior to registration may be claimed similarly.

7.12 Avoiding Inland Revenue enquiries

One of the most traumatic experiences for any businessman is being exposed to an in-depth Inland Revenue investigation. GPs are by no means immune from this, although their scope for possible tax evasion is very much less than with many other conventional trades and professions. The practitioner dealing with GP clients will be advised to do his utmost to ensure the avoidance of such a situation, for which he will almost certainly get a share of the blame – rightly or wrongly – finding that his client is not prepared to pay the costs of such an investigation and that he may well, at the end of the day, lose the client.

7.12.1 Expenses claims

In the majority of cases where investigations have resulted for GPs, it has been shown that the trigger point has been the unjustified claiming of practice expenses (see **7.6**). It should never be forgotten that to all intents and purposes these claims are part of the normal income and expenditure account and are deductions in arriving at the Case II profit of the partnership as a whole. The Case II profit is not merely the profit shown in the accounts before deducting individual partners' expenses. If one expense claimed (or part of a claim) is held to be incorrect, the Inspector can, with justification, question the reliability both of the partnership accounts and the claims of the other partners.

This is particularly evident where more than one accountant is acting. While the partnership accountant may well be aware of the realities of the practice, another accountant may not and a claim irresponsibly prepared and submitted could well lead to problems for other partners who are not clients of that practitioner. The points for which the Inspector generally seems to be looking in examining claims of this nature are the justification for:

(a)   private use element of motoring expenses;
(b)   claims for proportion of house expenses;
(c)   spouses' salaries and pension contributions;
(d)   home telephone use;
(e)   expenses for attending courses and conferences.

Make sure that records of payments to casual staff are maintained, showing the nature of the payment, the name of the recipient and ensuring that all PAYE obligations are fulfilled.

7.12.2 Non-disclosure of income

It is in this area where GPs are less likely to fall foul of the Revenue rules than other traders. The standard NHS fees and allowances are a matter of public record and are unlikely to be understated. Certain other subsidiary sources, such as hospital appointments and payments from other public bodies, are also unlikely to be omitted.

Scope for non-disclosure is found in the field of cash receipts and for cheques made payable to individual partners. This is one reason why it is so advantageous for all earnings of the partners to be pooled within the partnership accounts.

A case in point here is in the field of cremation fees, where the Revenue have taken to checking amounts paid by crematoria, undertakers, etc., tracing these back to individual doctors. Again, there is a ready source of information in respect of fees paid by insurance companies, private medical insurance and the like.

Nevertheless, it is a fact that for many years there has been a somewhat irrational view that cash receipts of this nature, in the form of certificate payments by patients and the like, are in some way, non-taxable 'perks' of the practice and that there is no need to return them. The practitioner dealing with these accounts must therefore do his utmost to disabuse his clients of that notion and ensure that all fees of this nature are paid into the practice accounts. If maintained in a separate tin the proceeds should be paid to the bank account at regular intervals.

It should be impressed upon the client that, while he may choose not to disclose those receipts, this situation is unlikely to last permanently and in the event of detection by the Inland Revenue, the likely cost to him would be far more than any tax he had 'saved' by this process.

7.12.3 The client

It should be impressed upon clients that in the last analysis they are responsible for returns and accounts submitted on their behalf, which they should be invited to sign as correct.

Even if there is a client who it is felt is vulnerable to investigation on the lines of some or all of the matters discussed above, it is by no means too late to remedy the situation. Meet the client and ensure that future returns, especially PPECs, are put together in such a way as will leave no scope for challenge. In particular, ensure that the client assumes responsibility for claims submitted on his behalf, preferably by signing a confirmation letter, as shown in Appendix 16. This means that the client assumes responsibility for the accuracy of restrictions for private use and any estimates included in the claim.

Perhaps the worst potential scenario of all would be that the Inland

Revenue conclude a successful investigation, only for the practitioner to be sued by his client on the basis that the client did not authorise production and submission of the figures which had given cause for enquiries to be started.

7.13   The trainee car allowance (see 2.9)

Those GPs who become trainers are responsible for the vocational training of a trainee doctor in the practice. We have seen that the trainee will be paid a salary, which is taxable and subject to Class 1 NIC in the normal way as for any other employee. This salary and employer's NIC will be refunded to the practice through the direct refund system so that there will, in theory, be no additional cost to the practice. In addition to this salary, however, there will be paid to the practice a car allowance, which is the trainer's (or in more practical terms, the partnership's) to do with as they wish.

In a minority of cases one may find that the trainee, during his period with the practice, uses a car owned by the partnership and in those cases the car allowance will merely be included as an item of income in the partnership accounts and effectively set against the cost of running the car. However, this is not the position in most practices, where the trainee will use his own car for practice journeys. It is the manner in which this car allowance is taxed which is the subject of some controversy and misunderstanding, both by trainers themselves and their professional advisers.

There is no doubt that this car allowance is, if paid to the trainee, a taxable emolument of his office (s121 ICTA 1988). Yet again, one of the assumptions which circulated for many years was that this car allowance was a 'tax-free perk' which could merely be added on to the trainee's monthly salary cheque without PAYE being deducted. When this had been picked up by the Revenue on several occasions and substantial arrears charged to employing doctors, in many cases the message was received but it is clear that there are others where this is still occurring and GPs are potentially at great risk as a result of this.

However, this is not to say that the trainee must necessarily pay tax in full on the whole of the car allowance. The amount of this allowance changes from year to year and the latest information at the time of writing is that this is at the rate of £3,719 per annum. It is suggested that those advising medical practices make it a regular point of enquiry to ensure that this car allowance is being properly taxed and, in the absence of contrary instructions, included on the trainee's tax deduction card with the remainder of his salary.

Subject to this, the following course of action is suggested, in order to try and ensure the most beneficial result possible, without loss of tax to the trainee:

(a)   That a dispensation should be applied for from the PAYE tax office concerned. Some districts are prepared to grant this on the grounds that it saves a great deal of work in the tax office and eventually a claim for expenses could well cover the whole of the allowance. Where such a dispensation is granted it should not be for each individual trainee appointment but should cover a succession of these.

It is suggested that the practitioner obtains a copy of this dispensation to be retained on his client's permanent file (see **4.7**).

(b)   If such a dispensation cannot be negotiated, trainers must deduct tax from both the salary and car allowance using the code number advised to them. The trainee may then approach his tax office with a view to having an estimated amount of the likely car expenses included as an additional allowance in his coding. If granted, this will to all intents and purposes restore the position. It must be emphasised that the negotiation of such a code number is the responsibility of the trainee and not of the employer.

(c)   If all else fails, the trainer has no alternative but to make such deductions of tax and Class 1 NIC when paid. The trainee must then, at the end of each tax year, make a claim to the tax office for properly incurred motor and travelling expenses. Form P87 is convenient for this purpose.

This situation as regards the liability of the trainee car allowance to Class 1 National Insurance is even more convoluted and by no means certain. The authoritative position seems to be that Class 1 NIC is chargeable, but only on the profit element (i.e., the gross allowance less any tax-deductible expenses). It goes without saying that this cannot be calculated until some time after the allowance is actually paid to the trainee and practices are advised to seek advice from their own DSS office as local agreements have quite clearly been made.

It must again be emphasised that the responsibility for deducting tax and National Insurance from this car allowance lies entirely with the employer (trainer). If the Revenue find that he has not operated tax according to the rules in force he could in the last analysis find himself being obliged to pay over to the Revenue large sums of unpaid tax, covering several years. This is a prospect best avoided if at all possible.

7.14 Gifts and donations

From time to time practices will receive various gifts and donations from a number of separate people and for various reasons. There continue to be conflicting opinions as to exactly how these should be treated for tax purposes. It is suggested that generally the following rules should apply:

(a) If the gift is in the form of a legacy, and it emanates from the estate of a deceased person which has been properly dealt with for probate purposes and upon which inheritance tax has been paid, then this is not taxable in the hands of the recipient, whether paid into partnership funds or retained by a partner. The partners should check to ensure which policy applies. Ideally, this should be set out in the partnership deed (see **5.6**).
Ideally any such legacy should be in the name of an individual partner, rather than a practice.

(b) Some practices on a regular basis receive donations from pharmaceutical companies, frequently as a recognition for providing some form of training or for giving them access to GPs for the purpose of promoting their wares.
These donations are received in recognition of the profession of the GP; they should be included as such in a separate item in the accounts and without question are chargeable to tax with the remainder of practice income.

(c) Donations for capital equipment. From time to time individuals form patient or support groups in order to help a surgery with the acquisition of needed equipment. Again, it is felt that where this is paid to the practice and utilised for a revenue purpose and the consequent revenue expenditure is to be claimed for tax purposes, then any gift which is intended to be set against this is chargeable to tax. Where, however, this is intended to cover capital gifts, if the money is paid to the practice, then it should be set against any capital allowances which are to be claimed on the asset purchased. The allowance will therefore be reduced by a proportionate amount.

(d) Donations of equipment. From time to time, donations of equipment are received and which are paid out of a fund which is never in the control of the practice. This is in some ways an ideal arrangement; the doctors are not beneficial owners of the money and cannot therefore be taxed on it. If the donors wish to give equipment to the practice, then this should be done on the basis that the equipment will not be the property of the practice/partners, but will be 'community property', or held in trust in such a way that the doctors are not the true owners. It is preferable if, on purchase, an invoice does not show the name of the practice or the doctors in any way. It is important in these cases that such assets are excluded from the balance sheet of the practice and that they are acknowledged in a place of record as being 'community property', which will not be taken into account when the assets are valued, for instance, on a change in partnership.

7.15   Bank interest and charges

The question of the allowability of loan interest in connection with surgery development projects is considered in Chapter 5.

However, at times practices will run regular overdrafts at their bank upon which interest will be paid. One would normally expect this to be allowable without dispute and in many cases this will be so. Where, however, the Inspector sees that the partners' current accounts are overdrawn and an overdraft at the bank results from borrowing over and above the level of partnership profits, then he may seek to disallow some or all of this interest charge.

7.15.1   Overdrawn current accounts

Where possible, the partnership accounts should be organised so as to eliminate debit balances on partnership current accounts. This may, on occasion, be achieved by the inclusion of correct and full debtors (see **6.3.12**), accruals and provisions in the accounts. Similarly, practices should be encouraged to run their bank accounts on a credit basis so as not to incur heavy interest charges of this nature. Despite best endeavours this is not always possible (see Figure 5.9).

Where, despite this, the practice is unable to run without overdrawn current (or in even more unfortunate cases, capital) accounts, the Revenue will frequently attempt to disallow at least a proportion of the bank interest arising on bank overdrafts and loans.

Some advisors have sought to correct this situation by introducing upward valuations of assets, particularly surgery premises, into the accounts. However, the Revenue have stated (Revenue Interpretation No. R12) that they will not be prepared to accept that a revaluation of a partnership's assets in such circumstances can bring the partners' accounts back into credit, at least for this purpose.

Of some help to practitioners finding themselves in this position is the fact that the Inland Revenue appear to have accepted that depreciation should not be taken into account in determining the level of such an overdrawn balance. In these circumstances, it would appear that accumulated depreciation (normally shown in a fixed asset note) could be added back in order to determine whether the account in question was overdrawn. The reader is referred to *Tolley's Practical Tax* (18 August 1993, page 1135).

In similar cases, where reserves for future income tax have been charged against the capital/current account of the partners, then this again can be added back in a similar manner.

Where GPs incur overdrafts on their personal bank accounts, the interest is not allowable for tax purposes in any event. There may be a limited facility here for effectively transferring such borrowing to the partnership account, particularly where partners have large sums invested in the practice capital (see **7.5**)

7.16   Capital expenditure

Practices from time to time acquire capital assets. It is common for a grant to be received, usually from the FHSA, with regard to such expenditure and this particularly applies to computer grants and expenditure financed out of the fundholding management allowance. In one case only (improvement grants: see **3.10**) such expenditure is not allowable for tax purposes in any event. Where other grants are received, of whatever nature, and those grants do not fully cover the cost of such an asset to the practice, then there is no reason why capital allowances at the rate currently in force should not be claimed on the residual cost.

7.17   Domestic mortgage interest relief

As we have seen (see **7.6.4**) many GPs use their private houses wholly or partly for practice purposes. This may extend, at one end of the scale, from a GP with a genuine and regular surgery at the house, to, at the bottom end of the scale, a property which is used merely for reading, studying and the like. We have seen how expenses claims can be calculated in those cases.

However, in many such cases, GPs have sought to claim relief for additional interest on their mortgages. Currently, a domestic mortgage attracts tax relief only at 15 per cent on interest on the first £30,000.

A concession introduced in 1995, however, accepts that an additional amount can be claimed in respect of a proportionate part of the interest which applies to business use of the property. It is considered that such a claim is likely to succeed only where a GP can produce evidence of a regular practice use of the house, preferably by patients, rather than merely as a place for administration and study.

Let us consider a GP with a mortgage of £80,000, upon which he is paying interest of 8 per cent or £6,400 in all. He will receive tax relief only on interest on the first £30,000, or £2,400. Even then, relief will be limited to 15 per cent or £360.

If, however, he is in a position to claim for genuine additional business use of the house and that proportion is agreed at, say, one-fifth, then he could justify a further claim of £1,280 (20 per cent of £6,400).

By virtue of the fact that he can include such an item in his annual claim for personal practice expenses, he will therefore receive relief at his top rate, presumably 40 per cent, so bringing about a reduction in his liability of £512.

It is emphasised that such a claim should only be countenanced where it is abundantly clear that there is an element of genuine practice use.

Chapter 8 – GP fundholding

Some general practices will be accepted as GP fundholders. By this means, they are allotted a sum of money from which they may purchase a defined share of healthcare services for their patients. This chapter looks at the regulations concerning fundholding practices, with particular emphasis on the manner in which the practising accountant will be able to advise his clients, to ensure that certain transactions are passed through the partnership accounts, and other relevant matters.

Fundholding has undergone many changes since its original proposal in 1989. Some of the original regulations concerning GP fundholding have fallen by the wayside and are now of no more than historical interest. They will not be covered in this chapter.

8.1   Origin

The then somewhat revolutionary concept of GPs holding their own budgets, controlling large amounts of public money for which they were to be directly responsible, was originally proposed in the white paper 'Working for Patients' in 1989. Following the later issue of a prospectus, a number of practices entered the scheme from 1 April 1991 as 'first-wave' practices. Since then the scheme has grown steadily each year until, with the entry of 'sixth-wave' practices on 1 April 1996, it is estimated that some 53 per cent of the UK population is now catered for by fundholding practices.

The legislation governing fundholding was set out in the National Health Service and Community Care Act 1990. This was further defined in the National Health Service (Fundholding Practices) Regulations 1993. A regular pattern of NHS guidelines is issued and this chapter includes information included in HSG (9614) dated 23 February 1996.

8.2   Eligibility rules

Where a practice wishes to join the GP fundholding scheme, it is required to meet several criteria:

(a)   a list size of at least 5,000 patients registered with the practice;
(b)   participation by all members of the practice;

168

(c)   the practice is capable of managing the budget and is able to display the necessary facilities which will enable it to do so. This includes a facility for running an approved computer program;

(d)   all members of the practice agree to comply with the conditions for continuing recognition;

(e)   all members of a fundholding facility where more than one practice shares the allotted sum agree to be bound by an act of a member of the practice with regard to that sum.

Having been accepted into the fundholding scheme, a practice must be able to meet the following criteria for continued recognition:

(a)   they must continue to meet the conditions for original entry as set out above;

(b)   the fund can only be applied for the purposes set out in the regulations;

(c)   the practice is responsible for ensuring the continued employment of suitably qualified and trained staff, as well as the competence of the provider of any services purchased by the practice;

(d)   a separate bank account must have been opened;

(e)   monthly accounts must have been submitted to the HA in accordance with details set out in the GP Fundholder's Manual of Accounts;

(f)   annual accounts must be submitted to the appropriate HA within six weeks of the end of the financial year;

(g)   the practice may not accept any payment or benefit in kind from patients for whom GMS are provided, in respect of any treatment either provided by a member of the practice or purchased by the practice.

The Regional Health Authority (RHA) has ultimate responsibility for the approval or removal of a practice from the fundholding scheme. The HA, however, will exercise immediate control of fundholding within their area.

Practices in course of admission to the scheme will do so from 1 April in the year of commencement. The previous year is known as the preparatory year. Thus, for sixth-wave practices entering the scheme on 1 April 1996, 1996/97 will be the first full fundholding year and 1995/96 the preparatory year.

8.3   Setting the budget and scope of the fund

The overall budget for any single year is initially calculated by the HA, following negotiations with the practice. The RHA is responsible for ultimate approval before final agreement is reached.

The budget is set both with reference to historical data and capitation details. The fund is comprised of four main elements:

- hospital and community health services (including community nursing costs);
- cost of drugs prescribed and dispensed;
- practice staff costs;
- practice fund management allowance (see **8.7**).

Once the level of the overall fund is set it is treated as a single fund. The practice may elect to incur expenditure on those elements in different proportions to those in which the original budget is set, so long as expenditure is in accordance with regulations. This facility to offset a deficit in one budget element against a surplus in another is known as 'virement'.

The practice may generate savings if the budget is underspent (see **8.10**).

The practice is not normally allowed to increase the element of staff salaries included in the overall budget, either by virement from another element of the budget, or by other means.

8.4   Community fundholding

Community fundholding was a concept introduced in 1995 and is a type of 'halfway house' between non-fundholding and full standard fundholding status.

By this means, practices which enter the scheme enjoy rather less autonomy than those which have become standard fundholders. In return for this they receive a reduced level of payment of PFMA but are entitled to a transitional payment upon eventual conversion to standard fundholding status (see Figure 8.2).

8.5   The role of the accountant

The accounts of the fund itself are separate and distinct from the normal practice accounts. In theory, a practice which is able to employ suitably trained and qualified staff, where salaries are paid out of the PFMA, should be capable of preparing the accounts of the fund, using the computer system in place, submitting reports to the HA as required and submitting accounts for audit.

Whilst in many cases, practices have now been able to do this, in other cases a certain element of support is required and the practice accountant should always be in a position to offer advisory services of this type to his client.

The practitioner must ensure that all transactions concerning the PFMA are passed through the annual practice accounts as payments and refunds (see **8.8**). If this is not done then there is a great danger that this will ultimately distort the overall level of indirect refunds (see **2.2**). Apart from this, practices are likely to require initial assistance in preparing management and business plans; setting and agreeing budgets; preparing forecasts of PFMA expenditure and, in general, offering support as and when required.

8.6 Fundholding accounts

As we have seen, the fundholding accounting system, detailed regulations of which are included in successive issues of the Fundholders' Manual of Accounts, is a 'stand-alone' system, entirely outside the main practice accounts.

All fundholding accounts are made up to 31 March annually. They are based on normal double entry principles and show, among other things, cumulative figures for a year set against the available budget. An example of a computerised fundholding income and expenditure account (FIEA) is shown in Figure 8.1.

The accounts will be maintained on a computer system designed for the purpose. Fundholders are not allowed to use systems which have not been approved by the Department of Health.

An integral element of the system is the inclusion of accruals in respect of expenditure incurred but not paid at each year end. It is essential that these accruals are properly and fully included in the accounts to ensure accurate comparisons with the original budget.

The practice will be required to submit monthly reports, extracted from the computer accounting system, to the HA at the end of every month together with, in some cases, more frequent reports. An annual account should be prepared within six weeks of the end of each accounting year and submitted for audit.

The original intended timing for audits was that these would be carried out at triennial intervals by the National Audit Office. It now appears that all fundholding practices will have their accounts audited within the first two years, with successive audits being required where it is felt the practice has fallen in some way below required standards. Otherwise, annual audits will be carried out by HA internal auditors.

Figure 8.1 *Fund income and expenditure account*

		Month of June 1996					Year to date estimated annual outturn				
		Actual DR £	Budget CR £	Variances Better/(worse) £	Act%Bgt	Last year £	Actual DR £	Budget CR £	Variances Better/(worse) £	Act%Bgt	Last year £
Purchase of hospital services											
Excess costs > £6,000		73,821	54,000	(19,821)	137	56,870	156,362	162,611	6,250	96	140,598
		(3,398)				0	(3,398)	0			0
Approved fund adjustment			0					0			
Transfer from FSA	1	70,423	54,000	(16,423)	130		152,964	162,611	9,647	94	
Subtotal							698,361	651,611	(46,750)	107	
Estimated annual outturn						56,870					140,598
Drugs and prescribing		44,206	46,000	1,794	96	39,000	129,952	138,338	8,386	94	113,837
Approved fund adjustment			0					0			
Transfer from FSA		44,206	46,000	1,794	96		129,952	138,338	8,386	94	
Subtotal							538,952	559,338	20,386	96	
Estimated annual outturn						39,000					113,837
Staff costs		7,228	9,000	1,772	80	6,667	21,365	24,994	3,629	85	19,663
Approved fund adjustment			0					0			
Transfer from FSA	2	7,228	9,000	1,772	80		21,365	24,994	3,629	85	
Subtotal							91,365	99,994	8,629	91	
Estimated annual outturn						6,667					19,663
Community nursing		11,174	10,000	(1,174)	112	28,471	31,174	30,044	(1,130)	104	28,471
Approved fund adjustment			0					0			
Transfer from FSA	12	11,174	10,000	(1,174)	112		31,174	30,044	(1,130)	104	
Subtotal							121,174	121,044	130	100	
Estimated annual outturn						28,471					28,471
Other approved fund adjustment			0					0			
Other transfer from FSA			0					0			
Sub-total above		133,031	119,000	(14,031)	112	131,008	335,455	355,987	20,532	94	302,569

Figure 8.1 *Continued*

| | Month of June 1996 | | | | | Year to date estimated annual outturn | | | | |
	Actual DR £	Budget CR £	Variances Better/(worse) £	Act%Bgt	Last year £	Actual DR £	Budget CR £	Variances Better/(worse) £	Act%Bgt	Last year £
Supp fund allocation (re overspend)							0			
Sub-total above						335,455	355,987	20,532	94	302,569
Estimated annual outturn						1,449,853	1,431,987	(17,866)	101	
Savings transferred to FSA										
Balance (variance carried foward to FBS)						335,455	355,987	20,532	94	302,569
Reconciliation Initial budget		119,000					355,987			
Fund adjustments		0					0			
Savings transfers		0					0			
Totals		119,000					355,987			

Report complete: Produced at 11.13 on 26/07/96 for June 1996 month of account (final)

173

8.7 The practice fund management allowance (PFMA)

Fundholding practices are allocated an agreed sum of money out of which they can pay expenses of managing, financing and controlling the fund. It is the payment and reimbursement of the PFMA which will most closely affect the practitioner dealing with the accounts of the general practice and it is important that the regulations governing the fund and practical application of these are understood.

The PFMA is effectively a reimbursement of expenditure incurred in the course of managing a fundholding budget. It is subject to a maximum level beyond which additional expenditure will be borne by the practice. The NHS (Fundholding Practices) Amendment Regulations 1995 brought the management allowance within the scope of the fundholding budget for the first time. This does not affect the practical aspects of reclaiming expenses and accounting for this resource.

Until 31 March 1995 the management allowance was a set annual amount which was effectively repaid to the practice by claim and reimbursement. For 1994/95, this maximum was £35,000.

From 1 April 1995, the structure of the allowance was changed so as to take into account various factors affecting the level of costs likely to be incurred, as well as the community fundholding option (see **8.4**) introduced from that date.

From 1 April 1996, however, the management allowance element of the fund will be paid to practices in advance on a quarterly basis, in line with the practice's agreed annual requirement. Any amounts incorrectly reimbursed through this system will be recoverable from the practice.

The amount which fundholding practices are permitted to spend on costs associated with managing the fund will continue to be restricted to the level of the management allowance element provided for that purpose. No virement (see **8.3**) will be possible *into* the management allowance element.

However, practices which plan not to (or do not) spend the full management allowance will be able to vire the planned (or actual) underspend into other elements of the fund, to be used for the benefit of patients.

Figure 8.2 sets out the scales to be used in calculating the annual management allowance, for 1995/96 and 1996/97.

Figure 8.2 *Practice fund management allowance: 1995/96 and 1996/97*

		1996/97 (2) £	1995/96 £
Standard fundholding practices			
In preparatory year:			
Fixed allowance: per fund		21,840	21,255
Site allowance (for major branch surgery)		668	650
Group allowance (for each additional practice)		2,877	2,800
In full fundholding year:			
Fixed allowance: per fund		28,008	27,258
List size allowance per patient:	1–6,999	1.93	1.88
	7,000–10,999	1.65	1.61
	11,000–14,999	1.56	1.52
	15,000–20,999	1.20	1.17
	21,000 and over	1.05	1.02
Site allowance (for major branch surgery)		668	656
Group allowance (for each additional practice)		1,439	1,400
Locum allowances (part of fixed management allowances)			
Preparatory and full fundholding years:			
Equivalent of one full day per week		7,449	7,250

(1) This table is for standard fundholding practices only; a separate scale applies for community fundholding practices.

(2) Alternatively, 1996/97 PFMA can be calculated by using 1995/96 rates and adding 2.75%.

Each practice will prepare a preliminary calculation based upon its known factors, i.e., number of patients, separate practices, branch surgeries, etc. An illustration of how the management allowance is likely to be calculated for 1996/97 is set out in Figure 8.3.

Where a community fundholding practice (see **8.4**) wishes to become a standard fundholder, it is eligible to claim a transitional allowance of £13,484 in respect of the cost incurred during the preparatory year for standard fundholding. This is in addition to the full year's allowances applicable for community fundholding in the same year.

The fund can be used generally for all expenses incurred in administering the fund. Practices are also entitled to a locum allowance, however this is reimbursed within the overall management allowance and is not additional to the maxima agreed.

Areas where expenditure against the PFMA would be appropriate are:

Figure 8.3 *Calculation of practice fund management allowance: 1996/97*

A practice with a list size of 15,800 patients and one major branch surgery would be eligible to claim expenditure up to a maximum of £55,985 calculated as follows:

	£	£
Fixed allowance		28,008
List size allowance		
6,999 @ £1.93	13,508	
4,000 @ £1.65	6,600	
4,000 @ £1.56	6,240	
801 @ £1.20	961	
	———	27,309
Site allowance		668
		———
		55,985

- the employment costs of staff to manage the fund (including those employed for data collection);
- the cost of training members of the practice or staff in connection with the management of the allotted sum;
- the running costs of fundholding computer systems (e.g., software and hardware maintenance charges);
- postage, telephone or other suitable office costs;
- minor modifications to premises to house additional staff employed in connection with the fund, for example, for internal partitioning to accommodate a fund manager;
- rent payable on accommodation used to accommodate staff employed in connection with the management of the allotted sum;
- the purchase of relevant specialist advice (e.g., accountancy);
- an amount to reimburse the practice locum costs or to enable GPs to be involved in the work related to managing a fund as an alternative option to employing a locum. The limit on such costs for standard GP fundholding practices is the annual equivalent of one full day of locum costs per week per fund, and for community fundholding practices is one half day of locum costs per week per fund;
- the capital cost of equipment necessary for the management of the fund (such as photocopiers or faxes). These should not in any year exceed 25 per cent of the annual management allowance element for that fund, except in the preparatory year when a limit of 50 per cent of the relevant preparatory level of the management allowance element will apply;
- capital costs of the purchase (or lease) of accredited computer systems (agreed by the Health Authority) necessary for managing the fund.

Items which are excluded from the PFMA are:

- the purchase of equipment for the treatment of patients;
- major capital expenditure such as extensions to surgery premises;
- expenditure on administration or management of the practice relevant to the delivery of general medical services.

8.8   Connections with practice accounts

The fundholding system, as we have seen, is entirely separate from the general practice accounts and these are prepared separately from one another. However, fundholding does affect the general practice accounts in certain areas and it is necessary to look at these items and consider how they might be properly treated.

(a)   The PFMA, both for preparatory and fundholding years, must be shown as a separate item of income so far as it is used to reimburse revenue items. This is so that the expenditure is grossed up for Review Body purposes (see also **6.3.1**).

(b)   Reimbursements of the cost of capital assets, both out of the management allowance and from other sources, should be shown as reductions in the fixed asset note to the accounts (Appendix 1, page 11), thus reducing the cost of the assets to the amount contributed by the practice. In most cases, this will be nil.

(c)   The fundholding bank account should be clearly annotated as such by the bank and the funds held therein are not in the beneficial ownership of the partners. The balance held on this bank account is not the property of the partners and should not appear on the balance sheet of the general practice.

(d)   Interest and charges on this account would best be debited directly from the practice current account by the bank, but alternatively reimbursed to the fundholding bank account out of practice funds. They can then be included in any claim for the PFMA (see **8.7**).

(e)   Interest credited on any monies in this or other interest-bearing accounts does not accrue to the practice and will be credited to the HA in the fundholding accounts. It should not, therefore, be included as an item of income in the annual practice accounts or included in the partners' income tax returns.

(f)   Reimbursements out of the staff fund to the general practice must be included in ancillary staff refunds and care must be taken to see that all monies due to the practice at the year end have been included.

(g)   If either too much or too little has been transferred from the fundholding bank account to the general practice current account, the balance will appear on the fundholding balance sheet under the heading of 'general practice account'. An equal and opposite entry should in this case be included on the general practice balance sheet, or within an omnibus figure of debtors or creditors, as appropriate. The required information will be found in Schedule 7 in the fundholding accounts. In many cases, this will in practice show a nil balance.

8.9   Computer reimbursement scheme

Since 1991, all practices have been able to claim an element of reimbursement in respect of new computer systems, acquired either by lease or outright purchase.

This reimbursement scheme, since its inception, has been favourable to GP fundholding practices, which have been able to claim a higher level of reimbursement than those in non-fundholding practices.

SFA 58 makes provision for GP fundholders to receive (normally):

- 75 per cent of the cost of computer hardware (including leasing costs);
- 100 per cent of the cost of computer software.

Normally, maintenance costs of running computer systems are met out of the PFMA.

From 1 April 1996, reimbursement for the purchase or lease of computer systems, currently authorised through SFA 58, will be replaced by an additional element within the PFMA. This element will be allocated to the PFMA element of the fund upon agreement of any such purchase or lease by the HA.

GP fundholders will be able to use this allowance for the acquisition or lease of fundholding computer systems with prior agreement of the HA, the amount being agreed in each case as part of the practice plan.

8.10   Fund savings

Since the inception of the scheme, the manner in which fund savings are to be used, the types of expenditure which will qualify and the manner in which these are to be passed through practice accounts, have been major items of concern to the practitioner with GP fundholding clients.

If there is an underspend on the fund in any single year, i.e., the total actual expenditure is less than the amount of the original budget then, following completion of the accounts and issue of an audit certificate, any such saving is available for the practice to spend on improving the standard of care for patients. All expenditure out of fund savings must be approved in advance by the HA. It is not permitted either to spend savings before they are approved by the auditors or to reimburse expenditure retrospectively out of fund savings.

Within the fundholding accounting system there is a running fund savings account (FSA) from which the cumulative savings at any time can be readily ascertained.

The fund savings can be carried forward for four years only, after which they are forfeited and will revert back to the HA.

8.10.1 Ownership of assets

Any assets acquired out of such fund savings are the property of the partners to dispose of as they wish. Whilst it is to be expected that in a majority of cases, such assets (which may be medical equipment, machinery, transport facilities, etc.) will remain in the use of the practice until for some reason they are no longer available, problems can arise where a partner leaves the practice and wishes to realise his own share of such assets.

This can lead to disputes within the partnership, which are best avoided if at all possible.

In many cases this can be done by inclusion of a clause in a partnership deed (or a separate agreement signed by all the partners) to the effect that assets purchased out of fund savings will represent 'community property', to be used in perpetuity in the surgery and the ownership will not vest in any or all of the partners.

8.10.2 Surgery buildings

In some cases, HAs have allowed practices to spend fund savings on improving their surgery premises. Inequity can arise, for instance, where the surgery is not owned equally by all the partners in the practice or, in some cases not at all (see **5.7**). Where a non-surgery owning partner leaves the practice, he may well feel that he is unjustly treated by virtue of the fact that he is unable to take with him his share of the fund savings which have effectively been invested in the surgery premises, of which he is not a joint owner and could not normally expect to receive a share of valuation on retirement. In some cases this has been resolved by an ex-gratia payment to a partner leaving in such circumstances.

8.10.3 Doctors leaving the practice

In other cases a GP may leave the practice which already has unallocated fund savings, possibly totalling substantial amounts of money.

He is unable to take those savings with him in the form of cash as these are to be used for the benefit of improvement of patient services. Savings do not belong to GPs personally, unless and until they are released for investment in practice assets. However, where a partner leaves in order to join another fundholding practice, he will be able to transfer his share of any such unallocated savings to his new practice.

Where a partnership splits, in the absence of any agreement between the partners, any accumulated savings will be allocated to the partners in proportion to their list size. Again, the savings can only be used for the benefit of patients.

8.11   Taxation implications

The amount of the fund has no effect on the taxable income of the practice, being offset by the effect of eligible expenditure. The fund itself and disbursements made from it should not be included in the practice accounts. On the other hand, the management allowance, as we have seen, is in theory taxable on the practice, although in practice this will be fully offset by expenditure which is ultimately reimbursed.

Where a practice incurs administration costs, etc. over and above the management allowance limit, then there is no reason why such total expenditure should not be included in the practice accounts and tax relief obtained upon it.

Where the practice acquires equipment which is fully reimbursed out of the management allowance or otherwise, then this must be shown in the accounts (see **8.8**). Capital allowances may be claimed on this but only to the extent that this represents the net cost to the practice. In cases where the costs of acquiring assets are fully reimbursed, there will obviously be no claim for capital allowances.

Similarly, where assets are acquired and fully paid for out of fund savings (see **8.10**) then these assets become the property of the partners in every way and are theirs to dispose of as they think fit. Whilst they must be treated as outlined above, any capital allowances due will be restricted to the net cost, if any, to the practice.

Where any such asset is disposed of and a chargeable gain results, then the base cost for capital gains tax purposes will be nil.

Any bank charges incurred on the fundholding bank account are not expenses of the general practice and must fall for reimbursement with the remainder of qualifying expenditure under the management allowance.

Similarly, any interest credited to fundholding bank accounts is not the property of the practice and must be returned or credited to the HA. This should not be shown in the practice accounts or tax returns of the individual partners.

Chapter 9 – Superannuation, pensions and retirement

The practitioner who acts for medical clients will, inevitably, at some time find himself asked to advise his client on certain aspects of providing for retirement, whether it be the manner in which eventual pension benefit might be enhanced, the way in which he might organise his retirement, or on many other matters.

All of us have to retire at some time. For large sections of the population, with anticipation of eventual retirement on a final salary basis, the problems are by no means as complex as for the GP, who will find his eventual retirement income dependent on a number of factors, such as his length of service, the level of earnings from his practice and, perhaps above all, the quality of advice he has received regarding how his eventual pension and retirement are to be organised.

This chapter looks at how the NHS pension scheme works; how an eventual pension can be enhanced and other matters of which almost certainly the practitioner will wish to be aware.

This chapter also applies, with certain adaptations, to general dental practitioners.

The NHS pension scheme (NHSPS) is likely to bring significant benefits to the GP who is prepared to take advantage of the opportunities available, hopefully with knowledgeable and relevant advice.

General medical and dental practitioners are unique in that they are the only individuals in the country who have both the opportunity of subscribing to an occupational pension scheme and, at the same time, an entitlement to subscribe to a private pension scheme, accepting tax relief on whichever set of contributions is most advantageous to them. The NHS scheme is complex to a degree and is constantly changing. Certain radical changes within the last year have totally altered the dates at which a GP might retire, the procedure in respect of abatement and partial retirement.

9.1 The NHS scheme

This section looks at a number of aspects of a GP in the NHSPS of which the practitioner should be aware. It must be emphasised that in a publication of this size only a summary of the scheme can be given. Readers who wish to obtain more complete details should apply to the NHS Pensions Agency, Hesketh House, 200/202 Broadway, Fleetwood, Lancs FY7 8LG. Doctors who are members of the British Medical Association can obtain a series of comprehensive guidance notes from BMA House or from their local Regional Office.

9.2 The two schemes

The somewhat ambivalent position of the NHSPS, being the only occupational pension scheme available to the self-employed, with contributions partly funded by a 'principal' (i.e., the Department of Health) dates from the formation of the National Health Service in 1948, and from negotiations at the time which saw GPs emerge as 'independent contractors' (see **1.3**) rather than the original intention of a full salaried service. Whilst the scheme exists using principles laid out at the time, it has seen numerous changes over the years.

The NHSPS is divided into two distinct schemes:

(a) *The 'officer' scheme*, which covers employees of the NHS, i.e., hospital consultants, senior and junior house doctors. This is a final salary scheme, in which the eventual pension and lump sum entitlement is based upon the highest year's earnings prior to retirement. The scheme is outside the scope of this book and will not be considered further, except in passing.

(b) *The 'practitioner' scheme*, which applies to GMPs, GDPs and certain ophthalmic doctors. The basic feature of this scheme is that the eventual pension and lump sum entitlement are calculated on a formula using the accumulated earnings of the practitioner concerned during his period as an NHS principal.

The NHS pension scheme, with all its variations and complexities, holds tremendous opportunities for the GP. It is essential that it is understood in all its elements by those who are charged with advising GPs on such matters. In this, as the reader will by now have realised, it is not materially different from most other aspects of GP finance.

9.3 Membership of the scheme

Membership of the NHS pension scheme for practitioners, apart from dentists for whom slightly different considerations apply, is available to:

- principal practitioners;
- associate practitioners;
- assistant practitioners (in certain circumstances);
- ophthalmic medical practitioners.

Locum GPs and retainer scheme doctors (see **2.17**) are not entitled to join the NHS scheme, except for locums who are appointed by a Health Authority.

GP trainees and those engaged upon a salaried basis may join the scheme but their pensions are calculated using the 'officer' method of calculation.

9.4   Opting out of the scheme

Since 1988, when new social security legislation required that it become a voluntary scheme, membership of the NHSPS has not been compulsory. Doctors can, if they so wish, decline to join the scheme at the outset or, having joined, opt out at some future time, probably in favour of contributions to a personal pension scheme.

The GP in normal circumstances would be extremely unwise to exercise this option. Such a course of action is likely to result in the loss of a number of valuable ancillary benefits (see **9.8**) which are available under the scheme, apart from the standard pension and lump sum entitlement.

9.5   Contributions levels

All GPs who are members of the scheme will pay 6 per cent of their superannuable income as the 'employee's' contribution to the scheme. These contributions will effectively be paid by deduction from quarterly payments. A further amount is theoretically contributed by the Department of Health as the 'employer', although this has no material effect on the eventual benefit.

Superannuable income can be defined as all earnings by the GP from NHS fees and allowances. From most headings of income there will be deducted a notional allowance for expenses. This deduction varies from year to year and for the 1996/97 year will be 33.6 per cent. Some headings of income, however, such as seniority awards (**2.3.2**) and the trainer's supervision grant (**2.9.4**) are fully superannuable, without deduction. Some other items of income are non-superannuable, normally in respect of reimbursements of expenditure and similar items.

A full schedule of the various sources of income showing into which category they fall is set out in Figure 9.1.

Figure 9.1 *The NHS superannuation scheme – superannuable income*

Fully superannuable (100%)
- Seniority allowance
- Training grant
- Course-organiser fees
- Target payments
- Designated area allowance
- Inducement payments
- Hospital appointments (clinical assistantships, hospital practitioners, clinics, locums staff funds)

Partly superannuable (66.4%)
- Basic practice allowance
- Assistant allowance
- Capitation fees
- Deprivation payments
- Maternity medical service fees
- Contraceptive service fees
- Temporary resident, immediately necessary treatment, emergency treatment, dental haemorrhage arrest and anaesthetic fees.
- Night visit fees
- Capitation addition for out-of-hours cover
- Initial practice payments
- Dispensing fees, on-cost, oxygen therapy service rents and fees
- Post graduate education allowance.
- Students' allowance
- Registration fees
- Health promotion banding payments
- Child health surveillance fees
- Minor surgery sessional fees

Non-superannuable
- Non-NHS fees
  - private patients
  - insurance medicals
  - sundry fees: cremations, private certificates, etc.
- Notional and cost rent allowances
- Sickness and maternity payments
- Prolonged and study leave locum payments
- Locum payments for single-handed rural GPs attending courses
- Reimbursements; rent and rates; practice staff; computing costs; trainees' salaries
- Associate allowance
- Doctors retainer scheme allowance
- Net ingredient cost, container allowance and VAT paid in respect of supply of drugs and appliances
- Trainee car allowance and other trainees' expenses
- Fundholding payments and management allowance

9.5.1   GP partnerships

As we have seen (Chapter 5), many GPs practise as members of partnerships. In those cases, the total superannuation contribution will be calculated by the HA which will then divide it for each quarter according to profit-sharing ratios. Where there is a change in ratios, either through a partner retiring or some similar reason, the HA will divide the income on a time apportionment basis and apply the correct allocation to each separate period. If no notification is given of a new partnership, the contributions will be divided equally. It is essential that partnerships give the HA a notification of every change in profit-sharing ratios, including physical changes in the partnership, whenever relevant, so that these can be reflected in the individual superannuation contributions. Failure to do so could result in partners suffering in future when their eventual pension entitlement is calculated.

The practitioner will, at times, come across situations where this allocation has been made using incorrect ratios, usually because the partnership has not notified the HA of a recent change.

It is always desirable to check that these contributions are being made in correct ratios. Errors can and do arise at fairly regular intervals. Where it is found that such errors have been made and an application is made, the HA will normally be prepared to make a retrospective adjustment, but only to the preceding 1 April and no earlier.

The HA quarterly statement is the definitive document for obtaining information about superannuation deductions. Not only must this information be used when drawing up the annual accounts, but if drawings calculations are to be made on a reasonably accurate basis, then account must also be taken of any such deductions. Failure to do so will be a contributory factor in the partners' current account balances requiring adjustment at the end of each financial year.

Figure 9.2 shows a typical calculation of superannuation contributions in a single year, although in practice this would be deducted in variable quarterly amounts, depending on the amount earned in each quarter, by the HA.

9.6   Tax relief on contributions

GPs are not salaried employees of the State and hence there is no statutory entitlement for tax relief on their NHS pension contributions to be granted. However, it would clearly be unjust not to do so and GPs are therefore able to obtain concessionary tax relief through Extra-statutory

Figure 9.2

Dr A has gross income for 1996/97 from NHS fees and allowances of
£45,000, with a Stage III seniority award of £5,015. He is a GP trainer and
receives the training grant of £4,570.

His superannuation contribution is calculated thus:

	£	£
Fees and allowances	45,000	
Less: Notional expenses (33.6%)	10,120	
		34,880
Seniority	5,015	
Training grant	4,925	
		9,940
		44,820
Superannuation contribution @ 6%		2,689

Concession (ESC) A9. This is set out in full in Appendix 17. While it has
been mentioned elsewhere in this book, this factor is of such importance
that it will bear repetition.

To ensure that this is granted in a proper manner it is essential that when
the annual accounts are drawn up, contributions are shown separately in
the current accounts of each partner, rather than being shown as a
deduction in the income and expenditure account in calculating partnership profits. This will ensure that each partner is charged with the correct
amount of his contributions, so that if one partner was purchasing added
years of benefit (see **9.9.1**) that partner will pay his correct share of the
contributions.

This will ensure that tax relief is granted on those contributions on an
actual year basis, rather than on the preceding (or, from 1997/98, current)
year basis, as would apply if these were passed through the partnership
accounts. There is an obvious time benefit in tax relief being granted in
this manner.

Tax relief on these contributions should be claimed on the GP's personal
tax return and not by inclusion in the practice accounts, nor in a separate
claim for personal practice expenses. It should properly be shown as a
deduction through the partnership (or individual) income tax assessment.

With the advent of self-assessment, it will be necessary to obtain details of such superannuation contributions for the last fiscal year and these will rank as deductions in determining the amount of tax payable for that year.

9.7   The dynamising factor

In most occupational pension schemes, including the NHS 'officer' Scheme, the calculation of eventual pension is made using a formula based upon salary earned in the final year or years of service.

This system cannot apply to GPs, who do not earn a salary in the accepted sense of the term. In addition, a GP's earnings tend to peak earlier in his career and frequently fall to the end of his working life. This is by no means unlikely if the GP decides to take a 'part-time' commitment of some type.

If no adjustment were to be made, a pension based on figures earned, say, 30 years earlier, would produce benefits very much lower than for a doctor in employment.

To counteract this, there was devised some years ago a system known as 'dynamising' (or 'uprating') which is intended to ensure that a GP's career earnings are properly protected against inflation during his career and have not lost real value by pensionable age. By this means, the super-annuable remuneration of each individual year is 'uprated' in order to convert the amount of income in the year it was earned to its equivalent value at the date of retirement. A full list of dynamising factors is set out in Figure 9.3.

Example

Dr Burton retired on 31 March 1996. As a part of calculating his uprated career earnings, and to take the year 1960, when he earned NHS superannuable income of £4,926, if this is uprated by the given factor of 11.434, this gives 'dynamised' earnings for that year of £56,324. This procedure must be applied to each of the years of his career.

Uprating is done each year, from 1 April. Where a doctor works for part of the month, one-twelfth of the annual rating factor is applied for the whole of that month. This is why it is sound practice to time a GP's retirement on the first two or three days of each month.

188

Figure 9.3 *Dynamising factors for GPs' pension calculations*

Years ended 31 March

Year	Factor	Year	Factor
1949	25.894	1973	7.743
1950	25.894	1974	7.507
1951	23.594	1975	6.867
1952	23.594	1976	4.942
1953	23.594	1977	4.816
1954	23.954	1978	4.635
1955	23.954	1979	3.554
1956	23.954	1980	3.022
1957	23.835	1981	2.546
1958	21.637	1982	2.402
1959	21.337	1983	2.273
1960	20.399	1984	2.128
1961	19.505	1985	1.997
1962	19.505	1986	1.860
1963	19.505	1987	1.750
1964	17.109	1988	1.608
1965	17.109	1989	1.499
1966	15.555	1990	1.388
1967	14.556	1991	1.284
1968	11.666	1992	1.151
1969	11.434	1993	1.079
1970	10.791	1994	1.063
1971	8.993	1995	1.030
1972	8.325	1996	1.000

9.8   Benefits of the scheme

There are numerous benefits which arise from membership of the NHSPS, to a far greater degree than merely the basic pension and lump sum entitlement:

(a)   a pension of 1.4 per cent of the total uprated career earnings of the GP concerned;

(b)   the pension is indexed-linked by a factor announced each year, linked to the Retail Price Index;

(c)   a lump sum retiring allowance, free of tax, which is normally 4.2 per cent of the uprated career earnings. Different arrangements may apply where a GP was a married man in practice before 1972;

(d)   widows', and in some cases widowers', pensions;

(e)   children's benefit for the younger GP whose career is terminated by death;

(f)   a death gratuity;

(g)   ill-health retirement benefit, if a GP is obliged to cease work through illness after two years or more of service.

The NHSPS offers to members an attractive and secure package, particularly for those members with younger dependants. These benefits can, however, be relatively modest during the earlier years of service and the younger GP may be well advised to 'top up' this benefit with some form of family income benefit insurance to ensure that there is a guaranteed and continuing level of income for his surviving family.

9.9   Purchase of additional benefits

One feature of the NHSPS, which is by no means unique but works in a rather different way to many other comparable schemes, is that members have an opportunity of buying further years of service where, provided the circumstances are right, their eventual total service appears unlikely to provide them with a full pension.

One problem facing the GP wishing to enhance his eventual pension is the multitude of schemes available. We shall look later at such schemes as are available through the private sector but this section looks at the means of enhancing eventual retirement benefit through schemes available through the NHSPS.

The standard retirement age for GPs is 60. Some GPs choose to work later although normally a principal will be unable to continue working past the age of 70. GPs may now choose (see **9.13**) to retire at an earlier date, provided they are prepared to accept the reduction in pension which will ensue.

9.9.1   Added years

The earliest date at which a GP can retire on a full pension is aged 60. According to Inland Revenue rules, total superannuable service cannot exceed 45 years, of which not more than 40 may accrue by the normal retiring date, i.e., by age 60.

As most practitioners qualify in their mid twenties, it is not possible for more than about 35 years of superannuable service to be completed by age 60. In many cases it will be rather less, and if nothing is done to enhance this entitlement, a GP will be obliged to face the fact that he will be unable to obtain a full pension on retirement. For this reason, there has been introduced a scheme known as 'added years' (roughly equivalent to AVCs for those in occupational pension schemes) which gives a GP an opportunity of buying sufficient years to allow him to build up a full career entitlement.

Purchase of these 'added years' is subject to two limitations:

(a) total service, both worked and purchased must not exceed 40 years at age 60 or 45 years at age 65; and

(b) the maximum contribution to the scheme is 15 per cent of his NHS superannuable income. This figure includes the standard 6 per cent, so that the maximum allowable payment for 'added years' cannot exceed 9 per cent of NHS net remuneration.

For younger practitioners, the cost of buying their own entitlement is likely to be rather less than the 9 per cent maximum, but for those doctors in their later years of service the 9 per cent limit will be substantially less than the cost of purchasing their entitlement. This may well mean that they are unable to purchase all the 'added years' required but they would be better advised to consider some other scheme of enhancing their eventual benefits.

In practice, the optimum age for buying 'added years' appears to be about age 40. Below that level a GP's financial commitment may well mean he is unwilling to contribute up to 9 per cent of his income to buying an additional pension. When he begins to reach his mid forties, the 9 per cent maximum rule commences to operate.

Example

Dr A, a GP aged 38, has entered service as a principal at age 28. If nothing is done, his career service to age 60 will be 32 years.

He decides to buy the additional 8 added years (taking his total years up to 40) and to purchase these on the 'age 60' scale. Using the age next birthday as 39, each added year will therefore cost him 1.03% of his NHS superannuable income. The purchase of 8 added years will cost him 8.24% in all, just within the maximum 9% contribution.

9.9.2   The unreduced lump sum

Married practitioners in the NHS before March 1972 will receive a lump sum retiring allowance for each year of service prior to that date at one-third of the rate applicable to each year subsequent to March 1972. A facility has, however, been made available which enables such GPs to purchase the remainder of their normal lump sum entitlement. The cost is subject to the same restrictions as for buying added years.

The cost of buying into added years and the unreduced lump sum are set out in Figure 9.4. It is generally considered that GPs should opt for the

Figure 9.4 *Additional NHS benefits*

1 Cost of buying added years (fixed percentage to nominated birthday)

Extra % of pay required as additional contributions to buy one year of additional service – when paid from the 'age next birthday' to the 'chosen birthday'

Age next birthday	Chosen birthday 60 %	65 %	Age next birthday	Chosen birthday 60 %	65 %	Age next birthday	Chosen birthday 60 %	65 %
20	0.50	0.36	35	0.85	0.67	50	2.25	1.38
21	0.52	0.38	36	0.89	0.69	51	2.53	1.48
22	0.54	0.40	37	0.93	0.72	52	2.86	1.60
23	0.56	0.42	38	0.98	0.74	53	3.26	1.74
24	0.58	0.44	39	1.03	0.77	54	3.80	1.90
25	0.60	0.46	40	1.09	0.80	55	4.58	2.08
26	0.62	0.48	41	1.15	0.83	56	5.77	2.30
27	0.64	0.50	42	1.22	0.87	57	7.77	2.56
28	0.66	0.52	43	1.30	0.91	58	12.06	2.92
29	0.68	0.54	44	1.39	0.95	59	–	3.40
30	0.70	0.56	45	1.48	1.00	60	–	4.10
31	0.72	0.58	46	1.58	1.06	61	–	5.20
32	0.75	0.60	47	1.70	1.13	62	–	6.97
33	0.78	0.62	48	1.85	1.21	63	–	10.42
34	0.81	0.64	49	2.03	1.29			

2 Cost of purchasing the unreduced lump sum (GPs practising before 1972 as married men)

Extra % of pay required as additional contributions to buy a bigger lump sum for one year – when paid from 'age next birthday' to the 'chosen birthday'

Age next birthday	Chosen birthday 60 %	65 %	Age next birthday	Chosen birthday 60 %	65 %	Age next birthday	Chosen birthday 60 %	65 %
30	0.08	0.07	41	0.13	0.10	53	0.38	0.20
31	0.08	0.07	42	0.14	0.10	54	0.45	0.22
32	0.09	0.07	43	0.15	0.11	55	0.54	0.24
33	0.09	0.07	44	0.16	0.11	56	0.68	0.27
34	0.10	0.08	45	0.17	0.12	57	0.91	0.30
35	0.10	0.08	46	0.19	0.12	58	1.42	0.34
36	0.11	0.08	47	0.20	0.13	59	–	0.40
37	0.11	0.08	48	0.22	0.14	60	–	0.48
38	0.12	0.09	49	0.24	0.15	61	–	0.61
39	0.12	0.09	50	0.27	0.16	62	–	0.82
40	0.13	0.09	51	0.30	0.17	63	–	1.23
			52	0.34	0.19			

age 60, rather than the age 65 scale. This is because if they choose the age 65 scale and opt to retire earlier, there is an actuarial penalty on their retirement and the return on their investment will be a great deal less.

The cost of buying both added years and the unreduced lump sum is fully allowable for income tax purposes, in the same way as standard contributions (see **9.5**).

9.9.3   Additional voluntary contributions (AVCs)

There is available, through the NHS, a scheme of contributions to AVCs through Equitable Life. This is subject to similar contribution limits as 'added years'.

9.10   Death and sickness benefits

As part of the NHSPS, the doctor is effectively insured against loss of earnings through death or sickness. If a GP dies whilst a member of the scheme, a lump sum gratuity is paid to the spouse and children's pensions become payable.

The death gratuity is an insurance cover for which the doctor is covered during his period in the NHSPS. This is a tax-free lump sum equal to twice the average annual dynamised remuneration (see **9.7**). This is paid direct to the GP's spouse or otherwise direct to his estate.

For doctors with five or more years in NHSPS membership, a continuing pension will be paid to a widow or widower. These benefits become due three months after the GP's death. For those three months, a short-term pension equal to the actual rate of the doctor's pensionable remuneration at the date of death is payable. Where there are dependent children, this three-month period is extended to six months.

Where a NHSPS member is obliged to retire on grounds of ill health, an enhanced pensionable lump sum will be payable in most cases. A GP must have at least two years' service before applying for ill-health retirement. Where a doctor retires on health grounds, full credit is given for the 'added years' being purchased, although these will not have been fully paid up.

The conditions of payment for death and sickness are complex and should be read fully. Where necessary, specialist advice should be taken.

9.11   Leaving the scheme: refunds and transfers

Where a GP leaves the pension scheme, for whatever reason, with less than two years' service, a refund of contributions can be claimed unless he returns within 12 months or avoids a disqualifying break. This is not sound practice if it can be avoided because the pension scheme membership benefits are lost and any refund suffers not only income tax but a proportion of National Insurance contributions.

If the service has lasted over two years, then a refund cannot be taken but accrued benefits can be left in the scheme or transferred out. Careful consideration should be given to all these options, taking into account the age of the GP, his career prospects and intentions.

9.12 Hospital service

Most GPs have at some time worked in the hospital service, in most cases immediately after qualifying and before taking up a GP appointment. If this service exceeds a period of 10 years, a separate pension under the 'officer' scheme will be paid. If the service is less then 10 years, it will be pensioned as part of the GP pension. This is done by using a formula by which the GP pension is increased in proportion to the amount of pre-GP service.

Similarly, many GPs continue to do part-time work in the hospital service, such as clinical assistant posts, in conjunction with their GP service.

If this outside work in total, after reducing any part-time work to its full-time equivalent, equals more than one whole time year, then this is pensioned separately on the final salary basis. If the outside work is less than one whole time year in total, the income deriving from it is merely added to the GP's superannuable income and treated as his income for pension purposes.

9.13 Voluntary early retirement

Until 1995, a GP was unable to retire, apart from on the grounds of ill health, before the normal retiring age of 60, at the same time attracting a pension and lump sum benefit. These would have previously been held in abeyance and paid to him at age 60. Under new regulations, however, applying from 5 March 1995, a NHSPS member is entitled to opt for voluntary earlier retirement after his 50th birthday, although his benefits will be actuarially reduced.

Where this option is taken, the pension and lump sum accrued to the date of retirement will be reduced actuarially to take into account payments commencing before the normal retirement age of 60.

Figure 9.5 shows how this might work. It will be seen that a GP proposing

---

Figure 9.5

GP aged 60: Retirement benefits, with total uprated career earnings £1.4m

		£
Pension	(1.4%)	19,600 pa
Lump sum	(4.2%)	58,800

Actuarial reductions on early retirement:

Age	Pension	Lump sum
50	0.599	0.747
55	0.754	0.864
59	0.943	0.971

GP qualified age 25: average practice earnings £43,000 pa

Benefits on early retirement:

Age	Pension £	Lump sum £
50	8,805	39,942
55	13,300	45,722
59	18,859	58,236

---

to retire at the age of 50, after about 25 years' service, will receive a pension significantly lower than had he continued to work until age 60.

This is indeed the major stumbling block in making such a decision. Whilst to a harassed GP it may well be superficially attractive to retire at age 50, at that age his family commitments are unlikely to have disappeared and if he wishes to maintain his present standard of living, almost certainly he will have to obtain some alternative source of income. This may well defeat the object of the exercise and he will probably be financially better off continuing with his work as a GP, with all the problems this might bring.

Appendix 18 shows the factors by which the pension benefit will be reduced by voluntary early retirement.

9.14 Partial retirement

It should be noted that doctors who choose to take voluntary early retirement (see **9.13** above) are unable to rejoin the NHSPS if they return to work after retirement. In addition, until age 60, if they return to work in the NHS their pension will be subject to abatement. Under the abatement rule the total of continuing pension plus post-retirement earnings must not exceed their pre-retirement earnings.

Until March 1995 it was possible for GPs to take '24-hour' retirement, under which they took their pension but were immediately re-engaged. This no longer applies. In an arrangement dating from 6 March 1995 (1 April 1995 in Scotland and Northern Ireland) these new arrangements only apply where a doctor has genuinely retired and there is a break between returning to practice of at least one calendar month. If the break is less than one month, the pension will be suspended completely until the doctor takes final retirement.

9.14.1   Abatement

Abatement applies only in certain circumstances, whereby the NHS pension is reduced, or removed completely, if the NHS pension plus NHS superannuable post-retirement earnings exceeds his pre-retirement earnings. Those GPs who retired before 6 March 1995 will continue to suffer abatement, where appropriate, unless they retire again, at which point they will not be abated unless they have not reached the age of 60.

Those GPs who have retired since 5 March 1995 will only suffer abatement so long as they remain under the age of 60.

9.15   The private options

Up to now we have looked at the NHS pension scheme, which in itself, over a full career, is capable of giving GPs a perfectly adequate pension on retirement. Exactly what proportion of their final earnings this pension represents, is subject to a number of variable factors; chiefly the earnings levels of the practice(s) in which they may have worked over their career, but also their length of service, and the extent to which they have purchased additional benefits.

This is by no means the end of the story. Many GPs faced with the prospect of retiring at some foreseeable future date at what they see to be little more than half of an acceptable income level, with a consequent drop in living standards, seek to augment this eventual pension by making contributions to private pension schemes. They have every advantage and encouragement to do so; whereas for most individuals, employees can only contribute to AVCs up to a certain level and self-employed people again are restricted to the level of their contributions, GPs have the opportunity of contributing to two separate schemes and choosing from which one of these they will take their tax relief.

Authority for this is set out in ESC A9 (Appendix 17).

Generally speaking, if a GP is claiming tax relief on contributions to the NHS scheme he cannot also make private contributions. There are, however, several means by which, whilst remaining in the NHS scheme, he may also make, and obtain tax relief on, personal pension payments.

9.15.1 The 'grossing-up' formula (also known as 'topping-up')

A GP can pay personal pension premiums in respect of any non-superannuable income he receives. This non-superannuable element of his net relevant earnings is calculated by grossing up his actual contributions (excluding any added years or any unreduced lump sum payments) in any one fiscal year by a factor of 100/6. The resulting figure effectively represents his superannuable NHS income during that year. If this is compared with his net relevant earnings, which in effect will be the amount of his Schedule D tax assessment, then he is entitled to obtain tax relief at the scale applicable to his age, on the balance. In practice, many GPs are unlikely to be able to pay premiums of more than a few hundred pounds a year from this source. It will frequently be found that the NHS superannuable income calculated by this formula is higher than the net relevant earnings, so that no contributions at all can be paid.

If relevant, and provided he has non-superannuable income calculated by this means, he can pick up unused tax relief for the previous six years.

Practitioners advising GPs on this subject should be aware that if a doctor has income from any medical source, which he may retain personally outside his partnership income, this must all be taken into account in calculating the relief. The effect of this can, at times, be such as to either reduce or completely cancel any relief which might otherwise have been available.

An example of how this calculation is made is shown in Figure 9.6.

It will be seen that this GP's net relevant earnings (1) for 1994/95 are lower than (3) his NHS superannuable income so that there is no margin upon which he can claim. For 1995/96, however, either through an economy in expenses, or the receipt of more income from non-NHS sources, his net relevant earnings (1) have risen to £28,425 whilst his NHS superannuable income (3) has risen at a much lower rate, to £26,083. This gives him a margin of £2,342 (4) upon which he may pay personal pension premiums of 30 per cent, or £703 (6).

It will be seen that in making this calculation there has been deducted (2) from his total contributions the amount of the added years element in each case.

Figure 9.6 *NHS Superannuation: calculation of non-superannuable income*			
GP aged 52			
		1994/95	*1995/96*
		£	£
Net Schedule 'D' assessment			
(less capital allowances)	(1)	22,845	28,425
NHS superannuation contribution (actual)			
1994/95		2,535	
1995/96			2,765
Less: added years element	(2)	1,150	1,200
		1,385	1,565
'Grossed up' @ 6%:			
1994/95: £1,385 × 100 =	(3)	23,083	
6			
1995/96: £1,565 × 100 =	(4)		26,083
6			
Non-superannuable income:			
1994/95		Nil	
1995/96	(5)		2,342
Available relief:			
£2,342 × 30%	(6)	–	703

In using this formula, it is frequently the case that the margin of non-superannuable earnings is either small or non-existent.

9.15.2 Renunciation of concessionary tax relief

We have seen that the tax relief granted to GPs is by way of concession rather than statute. As a result of this, GPs can if they so wish, renounce the tax relief which they would otherwise be granted on their NHS contributions. If this is done, the GP then becomes entitled to make his maximum available contribution to a personal pension scheme. He can, by this means therefore, effectively pension that income twice.

Such a renunciation can be carried out in the current year, by election for the preceding tax year and also in respect of any year where the assessable profits have not become final and conclusive. The election remains in force until revoked and the GP can opt in and out as he wishes from year to year.

Although this course of action can bring significant benefits to the GP, in order to make it worthwhile and particularly to recover the additional cost of renouncing the tax relief on standard contributions, the cost can be substantial and GPs should understand and accept all the implications before going ahead.

If a GP renounces his concessionary tax relief, this applies also to added years contributions. If these are substantial it may well mean that the project is not viable.

A GP does not necessarily have to make these contributions out of disposable income; they can be paid out of any capital sums available and can be, for instance, an ideal vehicle for investment of parts of the lump sum on retirement (see **9.16**). This is illustrated in Figure 9.7.

Figure 9.7 *NHS Superannuation: renunciation of concessionary tax relief*

Dr BL Theakston, a GP aged 57 is contemplating taking out a personal pension policy for 1995/96. His agreed Schedule D assessment for that year is £42,000. For 1994/95 the actual superannuation contributions were £2,800.

The net cost to him can be illustrated as follows:

	NHS Only £	After renunciation £
Standard contributions 1995/96	2,800	2,800
Private pension premiums: £42,000 @ 35%		14,700
		17,500
Tax relief: £2,300 @ 40%	1,120	
£14,700 @ 40%		5,880
Net cost	1,680	11,620
Average rate of tax relief	40%	33.6%

It will be seen that Dr Theakston, if he takes his option, can contribute an additional £14,700 to private pension contributions and obtain substantially higher tax relief. However, he must accept that there will be a fall in his net disposal income by some £9,940. In return for this, of course, he will obtain a substantial pension entitlement which will be a useful supplement to his income if he contributes over a number of years.

The example assumes that he will obtain tax relief under both schemes at 40 per cent.

9.15.3 Free-standing additional voluntary contributions (FSAVCs)

First introduced in 1987, these are to all intents and purposes the private sector alternative to added years. They can also be paid in addition to added years, provided that, if the GP will have more than 38.1 years of pensionable service, worked or purchased, by age 60, he cannot contribute to FSAVCs.

Subject to this, the maximum aggregate contribution of NHSPS payments, added years and FSAVCs cannot exceed 15 per cent of superannuable income.

A further restriction is that FSAVCs cannot be implemented by GPs who have renounced their NHS tax relief under ESC A9.

In effect, FSAVCs are most useful to GPs who do not wish to commit themselves to paying added years over the rest of their career and do not feel able to afford the substantial cost of the full private pension alternative by renouncing their NHS tax relief.

9.15.4 Pensions for spouses

We have already seen (**7.8**) how the potential benefits of paying a salary to the spouse of a GP and the consequent pension contributions can be advantageous in terms of tax planning, if properly organised.

A useful addition to the GP's pension planning strategy is that of taking out a pension for a spouse. The taxation advantages here, although real, must be by the nature of things relatively small as compared to the total level of a GP's earnings, but such a facility can add to the eventual pension of the couple in retirement, and taking out a wife's pension has a great advantage in that it does not require the survival of the GP for the pension to be paid.

9.16 Investing the lump sum

GPs on retirement will frequently come into possession of a substantial amount of money, by way of the lump sum entitlement. This is not taxable in their hands and (for a GP under 60) is not subsequently affected by the abatement rule.

However, GPs should accept and understand that this is part of their pension entitlement and is awarded to them as a supplement to their

200

pension. It is dangerous, therefore, for them to seek to use it for other purposes, i.e., repayment of outstanding loans or commitments.

A retired GP will frequently find himself in possession of sufficient funds which will enable him to live as he wishes and he has no need for additional taxable income, which will merely be taxed at its top rate. Such income would be surplus to requirements and he would be better advised to invest this by some means which will ensure, so far as is possible, a level of capital growth, so that when needed his invested lump sum will at least have kept pace with inflation. It may well be, for instance, that he can renounce his tax relief in his final two years of practice and invest some of his lump sum in private pension contributions.

9.17 Timing of retirement

A GP will usually choose the date of his retirement to suit his own personal preference. Indeed, many GPs retire as soon as is practical. However, it should be borne in mind that he can obtain a minor advantage by timing his retirement so as not to coincide with the end of the month, but for the first few days in the following month. This gives him a slight advantage in that he obtains the benefit of the dynamising factor (see **9.7**) on his income for the whole of that month.

GPs are now required to retire at 70, which in effect is the maximum age to which they can work.

9.18 Superannuation on outside appointments

We have seen (**7.9**) the taxation problems which can arise when some partners have outside taxed appointments. Similar problems can arise where superannuation contributions are deducted from these salaries, regardless of how they are dealt with for tax purposes.

Hospital pay offices will make payment of salaries direct to the practitioners concerned and any deductions for superannuation will automatically be charged to them. Again, it is important that those deductions are charged to the partners holding the appointment through their current accounts.

Where the partnership so elects, the HA will equalise out the superannuation contributions so that no partner in effect pays more than his parity colleagues. This is done by re-allocating the total partnership shares and then deducting the hospital superannuation already paid by the partners concerned. This will then leave the total charge for superannuation from the HA as previously, but this will be distributed amongst the partners so

Figure 9.8 *Re-allocation of superannuation contributions in partnership where some partners receive income from outside superannuable appointments*

Drs A, B, C and D are equal partners in their practice, each paying superannuation on an income from the HA of £40,000 pa. Drs B and D have outside appoopintments which bring an annual income into the partnership of £5,000 and £8,000 respectively. They decide to equalise their contributions.

	Total £	Dr A £	Dr B £	Dr C £	Dr D £
Superannuable pay	160,000	40,000	40,000	40,000	40,000
Hospital pay	13,000	–	5,000	–	8,000
	173,000	40,000	45,000	40,000	48,000
Re-allocated	173,000	43,250	43,250	43,250	43,250
Less: hospital pay	13,000	–	5,000	–	8,000
	160,000	43,250	38,250	43,250	35,250
Contributions (6%)					
Revised HA	9,600	2,595	2,295	2,595	2,115
Hospital pay	780	–	300	–	480
Total contributions	10,380	2,595	2,595	2,595	2,595

that when both sources are accounted for, their contributions are equal. A calculation showing how this is dealt with is set out in Figure 9.8.

As will be seen, the partner who has a hospital appointment will, after the exercise of this option, be paying one amount of superannuation under the officer scheme and the remainder under the practitioner scheme. It is generally accepted that the eventual benefit in terms of final pension from the practitioner scheme is likely to be greater than that from the officer scheme and for this reason those doctors who hold hospital posts of this nature are advised not to undergo this procedure but to accept the additional cost of those contributions, in return for a higher ultimate pension.

It is inevitable that this procedure will never be entirely fair to all the partners concerned:

(a)   If the election is made and the superannuation equalised, one or more doctors will find that their eventual pension benefit for an equal contribution may well be rather less than their colleagues.

(b) Those doctors without hospital appointments in their names may well feel aggrieved that they are not earning extra pension although they share in the income from which it derives.

(c) On the other hand, if the election is not made, the partner(s) in whose name(s) the appointments are held may object to paying more contributions than their colleagues.

Different considerations may well apply if the income from the hospital work is retained by any partner personally rather than retained in the partnership for division in agreed ratios, although as a matter of partnership policy such arrangements are frequently found to be unacceptable (see **5.1.1**).

This is a decision which should be taken consciously by all partnerships which find themselves in this position, with the requisite advise.

Appendix 1 – Specimen partnership accounts

Authors' note: These accounts are an example of how a particular type of practice accounts could be set out. It is not suggested that these cover all possible variations or that they are the definitive layout.

Drs Sample, Alpha, Beta, Gamma and Delta partnership accounts: year ended 30 June 19..

Contents

Page(s)

    1 *Accountant's report*

    2 *Distribution of profit*

    3 *Income and expenditure account*

    4 *Balance sheet*

5–14 Notes to the accounts

   15 *Current accounts*

   16 *Drawings*

Drs Sample, Alpha, Beta, Gamma and Delta Accountant's report

We have prepared the accounts for the year ended 30 June 19 . ., on pages 2–16, from the records produced to us and from information and explanations given to us.

We have not carried out an audit.

Wonderland   **March Hare & Co**
31 August . . . .   *Chartered Accountants*

Confirmation by the partners

We approve the accounts on pages 2 to 16 and confirm that the accounting records produced, together with information and explanations supplied to March Hare & Co, constitute a true and correct record of all the transactions of this practice for the year ended 30 June 19 . .

_____   _____   _____

_____   _____   _____

_____

Dated: _____

[Page 1]

Drs ....

Distribution of profit

year ended .... 19..

	Page	19.. £	19.. £
Income			
Expenditure		————	————
Investment income		————	————
Net profit	3	════	════

Allocated as follows:

	Prior shares *(Note 2)* £	*Share of* *balance* *(Note 3)* £	*19..* *Total* £	*19..* *Total* £
Dr				
Dr				
Dr				
Dr				
Dr				
	————	————	————	————
	════	════	════	════

[Page 2]

Drs ....
Income and expenditure account
year ended .... 19..

	Notes	19.. £	£	19.. £	£
Income					
National Health Service fees	4				
Reimbursements	10				
Appointments	11				
Other fees					
Other income	12				
Fundholding management allowance	16				
Total income					
Expenditure					
Practice expenses	14				
Premises expenses	14				
Staff expenses	14				
Administration expenses	14				
Financial expenses	14				
Depreciation	19				
Fundholding expenses	16				
Total expenditure					
Investment income					
Bank interest receivable					
Building society interest receivable					
Net profit for the year (page 2)					

[Page 3]

Drs ....

Balance sheet

.... 19..

	Notes	19..		19..	
		£	£	£	£
Partners' funds and reserves					
Property capital accounts	22				
Capital accounts	23				
Current accounts	24				
Taxation provision	*				
			————		————
			════		════
Employment of funds					
Surgery premises	18				
Fixed assets	19				
Current assets					
Stock of drugs					
Debtors					
Due from former partner	20				
Balance at building society					
Cash at bank and in hand					
		————		————	
		————		————	
Current liabilities					
Bank overdraft					
Creditors					
Due to former partner	20				
		————		————	
		————		————	
Net current assets					
Net assets			————		————
Long-term liabilities					
Property mortgage	21				
Net assets			————		————
			════		════

* *Where applicable*

[Page 4]

Drs ....

Notes to the accounts

year ended .... 19..

1 Accounting policies

1.1 The income and expenditure account is prepared on an accruals basis so as to reflect actual income earned and expenditure incurred during the year.

1.2 The stock of drugs is valued at the lower of cost or net realisable value.

1.3 Fixed assets are written off over their estimated useful lives. The following rates of depreciation are applied to the assets in use at the balance sheet date:

Computer equipment — 33⅓% per annum on cost

Office and medical equipment — 20% per annum on cost or book value

Furniture and fittings — 10% per annum on cost

The surgery premises are not depreciated.

1.4 The income and expenditure for the year has been allocated between the periods shown on page 2 on the time apportionment basis.

1.5 The accounts are prepared taking into account principles outlined in the General Medical Services Statement of Fees and Allowances.

2 Prior shares of profit

	Night visit fees £	Seniority £	PGEA £	Surgery income (note 18)	Total £
Dr					
Dr					
Dr					
Dr					
Dr					

[Page 5]

208

Drs ....
Notes to the accounts
year ended .... 19..

3 Distribution of profit

The following profit-sharing ratios have been applied in the allocation of profit between the partners:

	Period to 30 September 19.. %	Period to 31 December 19.. %	Period to 30 June 19.. %
Dr			
Dr			
Dr			
Dr			
Dr			
	100	100	100

Share of balance

	£	£	£	Total £
Dr				
Dr				
Dr				
Dr				
Dr				

4 National Health Service fees

	Note	19.. £	19.. £
Practice allowances, etc.	5		
Capitation fees	6		
Sessional fees	7		
Item of service fees	8		
Other fees	9		

[Page 6]

Drs ....

Notes to the accounts

year ended .... 19..

	19.. £	19.. £

5 Practice allowances, etc.

Practice allowances
Seniority awards (note 15)
Post graduate education allowances (note 15)
Rural practice payments
Trainee supervision grant

6 Capitation fees

Capitation fees
Registration fees
Child health surveillance fees
Deprivation payments
Target payments:
    Cervical cytology
    Childhood immunisations
    Pre-school boosters

7 Sessional payments

Health promotion clinics
Minor surgery
Medical students

8 Item of service fees

Night visits
Temporary residents
Contraceptive services
Emergency treatment and INT
Maternity
Vaccinations and immunisations

[Page 7]

210

Drs ....

Notes to the accounts

year ended .... 19..

	19..	*19..*
	£	*£*

9   Other NHS income

Dispensing fees

10   Reimbursements

Premises
Rent
Rates and water rates
Refuse disposal

Ancillary staff salaries
Salaries
National Insurance
Pension contributions
Training
Trainees' salary
Courses and conferences
Computer maintenance
Drugs
Maternity allowance

11   Appointments

Dr .... :
   Clinical Assistant
XYZ Ltd: Retainer
ABC Nursing Home

12   Other fees

Private patients
Insurance examinations, etc.
Cremations
Sundry

[Page 8]

Drs ....

Notes to the accounts

year ended .... 19..

	19..	19..
	£	£

13 Other income

Rent of rooms
Insurance claims
Etc.

14 Expenditure

Practice expenses
Drugs and instruments
Locum fees
Relief service fees
Hire and maintenance of equipment
NHS levies
Practice replacements
Medical subscriptions
Medical books
Courses and conferences

Premises expenses
Rent
Rates and water rates
Heat and light
Insurance
Maintenance and repair
Cleaning and laundry

Staff expenses
Ancillary staff salaries
Nurse's salary
Training expenses
Recruitment costs
Staff welfare

[Page 9]

212

Drs ....
Notes to the accounts
year ended .... 19..

	19.. *£*	*19..* *£*
Administration expenses		
Postage and stationery		
Telephone		
Accountancy fees		
Computer costs		
Sundries		
Professional fees		
	_____	_____
	══════	══════

Financial expenses		
Bank interest and charges		
Permanent health insurance		
Surgery loan interest		
	_____	_____
	══════	══════

15 Seniority, etc. awards

Seniority: Dr		
Dr		
Dr		
Dr		
	_____	_____

Post graduate education allowance		
Dr		
Dr		
Dr		
Dr		
	_____	_____
	══════	══════

[Page 10]

213

Drs ....
Notes to the accounts
year ended .... 19..

	19.. *£*	*19..* *£*

16   Fundholding management allowance

Allowance received for capital assets
Allowance received for revenue
   expenditure

Capital expenditure
Photocopier
Fax machine

Revenue expenditure
Salaries
Training costs
Administration
Etc.

Net income

17   Net surgery income/(expenses)

Notional rent (note 10)
Less: interest (note 14)

18   Surgery premises

Freehold property:
   The Surgery, Main Street,
   Brancaster

At cost and valuation: 1 July 19..

Drs ....

Notes to the accounts

year ended .... 19..

19   Fixed assets

	Furniture & fittings £	Computer equipment £	Office and medical equipment £	Total £
Cost				
At 1 July 19..				
Additions				
Surplus on revaluation				
Less: FHSA grant				
Management allowance (note 16)				
At 30 June 19..				
Depreciation				
At 1 July 19..				
Charge for year				
At 30 June 19..				
Net book amounts				
At 30 June 19..				
At 30 June 19..				

[Page 12]

215

20 Retired partners' account

Dr ......

£   £

Balance at 1 July 19..

Less: withdrawn during year

_____

_____

Balance at 30 June 19..

═══════

21 Property mortgage

The practice has a mortgage loan with ...., secured on the freehold property and repayable by monthly instalments over ....
years.

The term of the mortgage remaining is .... years, the interest rate is fixed at ....%/variable, and at .... was ....%.

The monthly repayments at present are £.................. and the capital outstanding is as follows:

19..   *19..*
£   £

_____   _____

═══════   ═══════

[Page 13]

Drs ....

Notes to the accounts

year ended .... 19..

22 Property capital accounts

	19..	19..
	£	£
Dr		
Dr		
Dr		
Dr		
Dr		

Represented as follows:
Surgery premises (note 18)
Less: property mortgage (note 21)

23 Capital accounts

Dr		
Dr		
Dr		
Dr		
Dr		

24 Current accounts [page 15]

	19..	19..
	£	£
Dr		
Dr		
Dr		
Dr		
Dr		

[Page 14]

Drs ....

Partners' current accounts
year ended .... 19..

	Total £	Dr £	£	Dr £	£	Dr £	£	Dr £	£	Dr £	£	Dr £	£
Balances at 1 July 19..													
Profit for the year [page 2]													
Leave advances													
Surplus on revaluation													
Less: partnership drawings													
Partner's monthly drawings [page 16]													
Superannuation:													
Standard													
Added years:													
Leave advances repaid													
Income tax paid:													
19../..													
19../..													
19../..													
Income tax provision: 19../..													
Transfers to/from property capital accounts (note 22)													
Transfers to/from capital accounts (note 23)													
Balances at 30 June 19..													

[Page 15]

Drs ....
        Partners' monthly drawings
        year ended .... 19..

	Total	Dr	Dr	Dr	Dr	Dr
	£	£	£	£	£	£

19..: July
      August
      September
      October
      November
      December

19..: January
      February
      March
      April
      May
      June

Appendix 2 – Fees and allowances for GPs: 1995/96 and 1996/97

Major elements of remuneration levels for 1996/97 showing comparison with previous year.

To be paid from 1 April 1996. Any overpayment resulting to 30 November 1996 from consequent overpayments will be recovered in future pay awards.

	1996/97 £	1995/96 £	Increase %
Practice allowances:			
Basic	7,200	6,912	4.2
Seniority: Stage 1	445	430	3.5
Stage 2	2,325	2,240	3.8
Stage 3	5,015	4,825	3.9
PGEA	2,260	2,175	3.9
Designated Area: Type 1	3,490	3,360	3.9
Type 2	5,325	5,125	3.9
Assistant's allowance (ordinary)	6,240	6,005	3.9
Capitation:			
Fees: Age to 64	15.35	14.80	3.7
65–74	20.30	19.55	3.8
75 and over	39.25	37.80	3.8
Out-of-hours care	3.05	2.95	3.4
Child health surveillance fee	11.15	10.75	3.7
Registration fee	6.80	6.55	3.8
Deprivation payments: high level	10.75	10.35	3.9
medium level	8.05	7.75	3.9
low level	6.20	5.95	4.2
Night visits:			
Annual allowance	2,078	2,000	3.9
Target payments:			
Childhood immunisation: higher rate	2,235	2,145	4.2
lower rate	745	715	4.2
Pre-school boosters: higher rate	660	630	4.8
lower rate	220	210	4.8
Cervical cytology: higher rate	2,505	2,415	3.7
lower rate	835	805	3.7

Health promotion:

Band 1	450	435	3.4
Band 2	1,220	1,175	3.8
Band 3	2,165	2,085	3.8

Chronic disease management:

Diabetes	380	365	4.1
Asthma	380	365	4.1

Item of service fees:

Night visits: standard rate	20.00	20.80	4.0
Temporary residents: to 15 days	9.05	8.70	4.0
over 15 days	13.60	13.05	4.2
Maternity (Obst. list: complete service)	178.00	171.00	4.1
Anaesthetic fee	37.70	36.30	3.9
IUD fee	47.70	45.90	3.9
Contraceptives	14.25	13.70	4.0
Emergency treatment	22.60	21.75	3.9
Vaccination: lower rate	5.45	5.20	4.8
higher rate	3.75	3.60	4.2
Dental haemmorage: higher rate	22.60	21.75	3.9
lower rate	15.40	14.80	4.1
Minor surgery	111.90	107.70	3.9
Trainee supervision grant	4,925	4,740	3.9
Locum allowance (weekly)	437.60	415.60	5.3

Appendix 3 – Inland Revenue: enquiry into GPs' expenses

There is published here for the first time, and made available to accountants, the form which is completed by local Inspectors of Taxes as a preliminary to the gathering and collation of information preliminary to the completion of information to be included in each year's annual Review Body award and for the indirect expenses sampling process.

This form is revised slightly each year. That published here is GP/96, which would be submitted to tax offices during 1996, returns being requested in respect of accounts ending within the period 1 January to 5 April 1995.

Publication of this form will indicate to accountants the level of information they are required to show in partnership accounts and the reasons this is required.

© *Crown copyright. Reproduced with the permission of the Controller, Her Majesty's Stationery Office.*

Inland Revenue: enquiry into GPs' expenses

FOR THE ATTENTION OF THE ACCOUNTS INSPECTOR

GP/96

P L E A S E   R E T U R N   B Y   2 AUGUST 1996

TO:

1. **HMIT** ....

   District file no: ....

2. **New District:** ....

   New District file no: ....
   (Only enter if case has been transferred)

3. If no trace of the undermentioned Doctor please tick this

   box [ ] and return this form to the Worthing address

   shown below.

   ON COMPLETION PLEASE RETURN TO:

4. Inland Revenue
   Statistics & Economics Office   (ref GP/96)
   Room 41   East Block
   Barrington Road
   Worthing
   Via IR Sorting Centre

Please make and keep a copy of **PAGES 1 AND 2 [AND IF APPROPRIATE A(96)] WHEN SECTIONS B TO J HAVE BEEN COMPLETED.** This will help in the event of queries or of duplicates being required.

In case of query phone (01903) 509923 or GTN 3541 extension 2923.

STATISTICAL INFORMATION ABOUT DOCTORS

The doctor identified below has been selected in this year's sample enquiry which is designed to gather information for the Department of Health to provide assessments of the level of doctors' income and expenses for the Doctors' and Dentists' Review Body.

I think that you are the Accounts District but, should I be wrong, would you return this form to the Worthing address, on the left, indicating the correct District if known.

Thank you for your assistance.

R G Ward
Director of Statistics

DO NOT POST TO THIS ADDRESS

Enquiry in respect of:

NAME

ADDRESS

General   **NOTES FOR COMPLETION**

1. Enter the District file number at the head of this page and the name of the Inspector to contact in the event of queries next to the District Date Stamp below. Enter the District number at Box 06, near the top right hand corner of page 2, overleaf.

2. a. Please enter at Box 07 the accounting period end date showing, for example, 30 September 1994 as 30 | 09 | 94

   b. A full report is required for all cases where the accounts are on an earnings basis (IM1751) and the accounting period ends between 1 January 1995 and 5 April 1995 inclusive and it relates to a period of exactly 12 months.

   c. If figures have not been agreed please give what you expect will be the final figures and enter "Not Agreed" in the Remarks section, at the bottom of page 3.

   See pages 3 and 4 for further notes relating to the completion of this form—including those about specific items.

Please remember to make and keep a copy of **PAGES 1 AND 2 [AND IF APPROPRIATE A(96)] WHEN SECTIONS B TO J HAVE BEEN COMPLETED.**	Report herewith from Inspector Name .... *(block caps)* Signature .... Telephone no (incl extension) .... GTN No .... *District Date Stamp*

1.

W1489-4-96(1) G

223

AP ENDED IN 1994-95

GP/96

	Tick appropriate box		

A. Accounts for AP ended in 1994-95

i. not yet received ....

ii. no AP ended in this period ....

iii. for period other than exactly 12 months

iv. accounts <u>not</u> on earnings basis

If A.i. is the current position please retain until 2 August in case accounts are received.

If box at A.i., A.ii., A.iii. or A.iv has been ticked, no further information is required.

v. enter AP end date of the accounts made up to date between 6 April 1994 and <u>5 April 1995</u> (inclusive) ....

FOR HO USE ONLY

DH Ref No	01

DISTRICT NUMBER OF RETURNING DISTRICT

(see Note 1) 06

07

Please complete Sections B to J for all cases with a 12 month AP ending between 1 January 1995 and <u>5 April 1995</u>. No further information is required for cases with a 12 month AP ending between 6 April 1994 and 31 December 1994.

B. Total number of partners in partnership <u>at end of AP</u> (excluding salaried partners, assistant and trainee doctors). If sole practice only enter"1" 09

SCH D ONLY (Earnings basis only — see Note 2) Expenses should be shown gross and recoveries should be included in incomings (see Note 10)	Col 1 Sole practice or on own account (see Note 5) £	Partnerships	
		Col 2 Partnership income and expenses — All partners (see Note 6) £	Col 3 This partner (see Note 7) £

C. Gross professional incomings (before deduction of superannuation contributions but <u>excluding</u> amounts chargeable Sch E eg Hospital Fees) taken into account for the AP .... **(see Notes 8, 9 & 10)**

11	26

D. Partnership expenses borne jointly and admitted for the AP

Personal superannuation contributions should be <u>excluded</u> entirely from expenses

Expenses not allowable should be excluded **(see Notes 9 & 10)**

i. Medical supplies (Note 12) 27

ii. Expenses of premises (including interest) (Note 13) 28

iii. Salaries, wages and Nat Ins (Note 14) 29

iv. Car and travelling (Note 15) 30

v. Other (Note 16) 31

Total 32

E. Net partnership profit <u>after</u> admissible expenses but <u>before</u> capital allowances

This should equal box 26 minus box 32

20

F. **This partner's share of profits <u>before</u> deduction of personal expenses or any capital allowances (see Note 7a)** 33

G. This practitioner's expenses borne personally and admitted for the AP

Personal superannuation contribution should be <u>excluded</u> entirely from expenses

Expenses not allowable should be excluded **(see Notes 9, 10 & 11)**

i. Medical supplies (Note 12) .... 12 | 34

ii. Expenses of premises (including interest) (Note 13) .... 13 | 35

iii. Salaries, wages and Nat Ins (Note 14) .... 14 | 36

iv. Car and travelling (Note 15) .... 15 | 37

v. Other (Notes 11 & 16) .... 16 | 38

Total .... 17 | 39

H. Net profit <u>after</u> admissible expenses but <u>before</u> capital allowances

This should equal box 11 minus box 17, or box 33 minus box 39

18		40
		42 For HO use only

I. i. Capital Allowances claimed and made for the IT year* for which the AP forms the basis period (see Note 17).

(*If there are two or more such years, give allowances for the earliest which is a full year)

21	see Note 7c	43

ii. Balancing charge on sales etc during the AP .... 22 | 44

J. **SCH E ONLY**

Gross professional income chargeable Sch E 1994-95 wherever assessable (<u>excluding</u> pensions) 23

Allowable expenses (<u>exclude</u> Superannuation) 24

Net income chargeable Sch E 1994-95 25

2.

224

3.   If "A" is entered in the HO Use Only box on page 1, a supplementary enquiry form A(96) is attached. This should be completed as indicated <u>only if a full report</u> is made for the corresponding year on the main form GP/96.

4.   If the accounts for the AP ended in 1994-95 have not been received—part A.i. overleaf—please RETAIN this form in a prominent place in the accounts pad in order to action it on (or by) 2 August if the accounts should come to hand before that date. DO NOT RETURN the form with only Box Ai. ticked UNTIL 2 August.

5.   Entries in <u>Column 1</u> are required where the doctor:

     a.   has a sole practice, or

     b.   has professional earnings etc unconnected with the partnership. Amounts entered in Column 1 should <u>not</u> be included in Columns 2 or 3.

     If the doctor has changed his status during the year (eg from sole practice to partnership) or has changed partnership, please give the figures to cover his earnings for the whole year. Give details of any change in the Remarks section below.

6.   Entries in <u>Column 2</u> should relate to the total partnership incomings and total allowable expenses borne jointly within the partnership.

7.   Entries in <u>Column 3</u> should be restricted to:

     a.   the doctor's share of the net income of the partnership (total partnership incomings <u>less</u> total allowable expenses borne jointly) — box 33;

     b.   the expenses borne personally by the doctor, outside of the partnership (boxes 34 to 39);

     c.   the doctor's share of partnership capital allowances etc <u>plus</u> any personal capital allowances (boxes 43 and 44);

     d.   the doctor's share of profit for the AP (ie PY basis) which is usually the same as his share of profit assessable for the following IT year (ie CY basis). Where it is not the same (eg if there is a change of partnership and an election made for continuation basis of Assessment—S154 ICTA 1970), please report this partner's share of the <u>profit for the AP</u>.

Specific items

8.   Incomings

     Professional incomings should <u>include</u> fees and other payments from Family Health Services Authorities, (Health Boards in Scotland), local authorities, other government departments and private practice.

     The following should be <u>included</u> as professional medical income if received:

       i.   Income from drug trials.

       ii.   Inducement payments — usually to doctors in sparsely populated areas with small lists.

       iii.   Trainers' grants — paid to doctors who supervise newly qualified GPs.

       iv.   Seniority payments — paid according to length of service with NHS.

     Incomings chargeable Sch D Case I and II should be shown at box 11 and/or 26, while incomings chargeable Sch E should be shown at box 23.

(CONTINUED OVERLEAF)

REMARKS

W1489-4-96(2) G

9. Superannuation

Family Health Services Authorities (Health Boards in Scotland) withhold from the payments made to doctors an amount representing the doctor's contribution to NHS superannuation. Please report as Gross professional incomings (boxes 11 and 26) the amount of the payment <u>before</u> deduction of superannuation contributions.

Personal superannuation contributions should be <u>excluded</u> entirely from expenses, both 'partnership' and 'borne personally'.

PLEASE READ <u>ALL</u> NOTES 10-16 INCLUSIVE BELOW BEFORE DECIDING TO WHICH BOX A SPECIFIC ITEM IN THE ACCOUNTS SHOULD BE CATEGORISED.

10. Expenses

Expenses should be reported <u>only</u> if they are allowable.

Certain expenses incurred by doctors which are wholly or partly reimbursed by the National Health Service include rent, rates, salaries and the cost of drugs dispensed. For this report, expenses should be shown gross and any recoveries should be added to incomings. If it is believed that the expenses shown in the accounts are <u>net</u> and the recoveries are not known, please report this in the Remarks section. Expenses should <u>exclude</u> depreciation, amortisation, personal superannuation contributions and any expenses disallowed for private use etc.

11. Expense sharing agreements

If the doctor is party to an expense sharing agreement and contributes to a common fund which meets some of his practice's expenses, please report his payments to the fund as a personal expense. If the expenses met by the fund are known in total and by type it should be assumed that the doctor's payment may be apportioned by type of expense pro rata to all expenses met from the fund. If the expenses met from the fund are not known, <u>include</u> payments to the fund in "Other" expenses and note the amounts in the Remarks section.

12. Medical supplies

This item should <u>include</u> gross expenditure on drugs, dressings and containers, disposable equipment and reagents and sundry equipment and replacements not capitalised (eg stethoscopes).

Where separate accounts are prepared for the pharmacy <u>and</u> the AP ends in the same quarter as the GP's main practice accounts, the income and expenses of the pharmacy should be <u>included</u> as appropriate. Otherwise <u>exclude</u> income and expenses of the pharmacy and make a note in the Remarks Section.

13. Expenses of premises (<u>including</u> interest)

This item should relate to expenditure on practice premises and <u>include</u> rent, rates, repairs, heating, lighting, insurance, laundry and cleaning materials/services, security system rental and maintenance, exterior/interior maintenance and decoration and interest on mortgages or other loans for the purchase or improvement of premises. Amounts disallowed for private use etc should be <u>excluded</u>.

14. Salaries, wages and Nat Ins

This item should cover the staff costs (gross wages and employer's national insurance and superannuation payments) of assistants, trainees, dispensers, nurses, receptionists and other staff (<u>including</u> salaries relating to wives), staff advertising and agency fees. It should also <u>include</u> all locum and deputising costs.

15. Car and travelling

This should <u>include</u> car tax, insurance, petrol, repairs, maintenance, AA/RAC, parking and garaging, car rental/lease/hire and taxis and other travel expenses (rail, ship, air) but <u>exclude</u> amounts disallowed for private use etc.

16. Other

This should <u>include</u> all other expenses borne jointly or personally and admitted but not elsewhere specified, (eg telephone, postage, stationery, magazines, technical literature, professional subscriptions, accountancy and legal expenses, hire purchase charges). All the following <u>not</u> related to property should be <u>included</u> in this category — bank and interest charges, laundry and cleaning, repairs and renewals and insurance.

It should <u>exclude</u> depreciation and amortisation and amounts disallowed for private use etc.

17. Capital Allowances/Balancing charges

These should <u>include</u> the doctor's share of partnership CAs/BCs <u>plus</u> any personal CAs/BCs but should <u>exclude</u> any amounts disallowed for private use etc.

4.

Appendix 4 – Sample partnership agreement

The specimen agreement presented here is of a type widely in use, although the precedent is by no means universal.

The deed would, in practice, be varied in such a manner and as necessary in order to express fully the intentions and policy of the partners.

THIS DEED OF PARTNERSHIP is made the _____ day of _____ One thousand nine hundred and _____

BETWEEN

WHEREAS:

(1) The parties hereto all of whom are medical practitioners on the list kept by the _____ Family Health Services Authority (FHSA) of practitioners _____ undertaking to provide general medical services have for some time past carried on practice in partnership as general medical practitioners.

(2) _____ was admitted as a partner in the said partnership practice on the _____ day of _____ One thousand nine hundred and _____ but had no share in the capital of the partnership.

NOW THIS DEED WITNESSETH as follows:

1 The partners will as from the _____ day of _____ One thousand nine hundred and _____ (hereinafter called 'the commencement date') carry on the profession of general medical practitioners in partnership under the name of _____

2 Subject to the provisions for determination hereinafter contained the partnership shall continue for the joint lives of the partners

3 (1) The seniority of the partners shall be deemed to be in the order of priority in which their respective names are set out above as parties to this deed

    (2)   If there is any difference of opinion on any matters or thing connected with the policy or conduct of the partnership practice then the decision of the majority in number of the partners on any such matter shall prevail and be binding on all the partners

    (3)   Each partner shall in relation to voting on any such matters or things as aforesaid have one vote only and in the case of an equality of votes for and against any proposition or resolution the matter or thing shall remain in status quo ante

    (4)   Nothing in this clause contained shall in any way preclude affect or detract from the provisions of this deed which are mandatory or confer specific rights on the partners individually

4   The partnership practice shall be carried on from the premises referred to in the first column of Part I of the First Schedule hereto and (subject to the approval of the appropriate Health Authority) from such other place or places (whether in addition to or in substitution for all or any of the aforesaid premises) as the partners may from time to time agree upon

5   The initial capital assets of the partnership shall consist of those assets which are specified in Part I A and B of the First Schedule hereto the values hereof as at the commencement date having been agreed between the partners. Such capital assets shall belong to the partners in the proportions specified in Part II of the said Schedule

6 (1)   The profits and losses of the partnership (other than profits and losses of a capital nature) shall belong to or be borne as the case may be by the partners in the shares specified in the Second Schedule hereto in each of the financial years of the partnership therein mentioned

    (2)   Medical earnings by the partnership and individual partners, from whatever source, will be pooled with partnership profits and divided between the partners in the ratios set out in the second schedule hereto, with the exception of:

        6.2.1   all income from seniority awards and other payments in recognition of length of service in general practice.

        6.2.2   income from the post graduate education allowance.

        6.2.3   any other items of income which the partners might unanimously agree may be retained by the partners, such agreement to be given in writing.

    (3)   Profits and losses of a capital nature shall belong to and be borne by the partners in the ratios in which the respective capital assets specified in Parts I and II of the First Schedule hereto are owned by the partners

7   If any statement of account of the partnership shall show that in the period covered by the account any of the partners drew in excess of his share of the profits for that period such partner shall repay the excess forthwith

8   (1)   Proper books of accounts giving a true and fair view of the partnership business shall be kept properly posted and such books shall be available for inspection by each of the partners and by the partnership accountants at all times

    (2)   An account of income and expenditure shall be taken in every year on the _____ day of _____ (or on such other date or dates as the partners may from time to time mutually agree upon which date is hereinafter referred to as 'the account date') and a balance sheet as at the same date shall also be prepared

    (3)   Every such account and balance sheet shall be prepared by _____ Chartered Accountants of _____ in the City of _____ or such other firm of accountants as the partners may from time to time appoint as accountants. The accounts will be signed by all the partners and shall thereupon become binding on them except that any of the partners shall be entitled to require the rectification of any manifest error discovered in any such account or balance sheet within six months of the date of such signature by the partners

9   (1)   The bankers of the partnership shall be _____ at its branch at _____ in the County of _____ or at such other branch of the said bank or at such other bank as the partners may from time to time agree upon

    (2)   All receipts in respect of the partnership practice shall be entered in the partnership books of account and shall be paid into the partnership bank account which shall be designated

    (3)   All cheques on the partnership bank account shall be drawn in the name of the partnership and may be so drawn and signed by any two of the partners

10   (1)   Each of the partners shall be entitled in each calendar year of the partnership to _____ weeks' holiday to be taken at such times as may conveniently be arranged between the partners

    (2)   The priority of choice as to the dates between which such holidays are to be taken in relation to the first three consecutive weeks of the overall holiday period referred to in sub-clause (1) hereof shall be based on the order or seniority of the partners in the practice

    (3)   When the dates between which each of the partners are to take

the said part of the overall holiday period have been determined under the provisions of sub-clause (2) hereof then the
dates between which each of the partners are to take the
remaining part of their holiday period shall then be decided on
the same principle as referred to in sub-class (2) hereof

(4) Should the partners (other than the absent partner) consider it
necessary to engage a locum tenens during the absence of a
partner on holiday or on study leave they shall be at liberty to
engage a competent registered medical practitioner as such
locum tenens at the expense of the partnership

11 Each of the partners shall provide for himself at his own cost all the
surgical instruments which he may require and such motor cars or
other vehicles as he may need for the efficient working of the practice
and shall bear and pay all expenses connected therewith and shall
pay the wages of all his own servants and all his other personal
expenses AND each of the partners shall provide and maintain at
least one motor car for the purposes of the practice PROVIDED
ALWAYS that in the event of any special instrument or apparatus
being required for any particular operation case or forms of
treatment the same may with the consent of the majority of the
partners be purchased or hired out of the funds of the partnership

12 Subject to the express provisions of clause 10 hereof in relation to the
expenses referred to therein the following other expenses shall be
expenses of the partnership practice and so treated in the accounts of
the partnership

(1) The salaries wages allowances and statutory and pension
contributions (if any) payable in respect of all employees of the
practice

(2) All payments to be made under any mortgage on any of the
freehold properties from time to time forming part of the
partnership

(3) Rates and all other outgoings in respect of the said premises
including (but without prejudice to the generality of the
foregoing provision) telephone charges insurance premiums
lighting and heating charges stationery postage

(4) The rent and all other outgoings as aforesaid in respect of any
other premises acquired by the partners' practice or of which
they are tenants and which are used for the purposes of the
partnership practice

(5) Debts losses or damages incurred in carrying on the said
practice

(6) The cost of all medicines drugs and instruments and other
things necessary for carrying on the said practice

(7) The cost of keeping proper accounts and of the taking of a profit and loss account and balance sheet under the provisions of clause 8 hereof

(8) Any other expenses agreed by the partners to be an expense of the partnership practice

13 Each partner shall at all times:
(1) Show the utmost good faith to the other partners in all matters relating to the partnership
(2) Devote his whole time and attention to the business of the partnership except during any holidays to which he is entitled and except during incapacity due to illness or injury or other cause
(3) Conduct himself in a proper and responsible manner and use his best skill and endeavour to promote the partnership practice
(4) Duly and punctually pay and discharge his or her separate and private debts and liabilities and keep the partnership property and the other partners and such partners' estates and effects indemnified against the same and against all actions proceedings costs claims and demands in respect thereof

14 In the event of a partner absenting himself or herself from the practice (except during holidays taken under and in accordance with the provisions in that behalf hereinbefore contained) or becoming incapacitated from performing his or her fair share of the work of the said practice the other partners shall be at liberty to engage at the expense of the partnership a competent registered medical practitioner as substitute for such absent or incapacitated partner PROVIDED ALWAYS that:
(a) If such absence is due to illness incapacity or pregnancy and shall continue for:
(i) more than 4 consecutive weeks
(ii) for a total of more than 28 days during any period of 12 consecutive months
the expense of engaging such a substitute shall in respect of any period in excess of 4 weeks or 28 days respectively be borne and paid by the absent or incapacitated partner
(b) If such absence is not due to illness incapacity or pregnancy the whole cost of employing such substitute shall be at the sole cost and expense of the absent partner

15 PROVIDED FURTHER that nothing herein contained shall be taken to imply any right on the part of a partner to absent himself or herself to the neglect of his or her duties in respect of the partnership practice and provided also that if any monies are received from the

231

Family Health Services Authority under the Statement of Fees and Allowances payable to General Medical Practitioners in England and Wales in respect of the period during which the expense of engaging a locum tenens is to be borne and paid by the absent partner then the absent partner shall be entitled to retain such monies in part or full reimbursement for providing a locum tenens

16 No partner shall without the consent of the others:

(1) Engage directly or indirectly in any business or any professional practice other than the partnership practice or accept any appointment or office requiring substantial personal attention by him

(2) Engage or (except for gross misconduct) dismiss any employee of the partnership

(3) Except in the ordinary course of the practice and for the benefit of the partnership (but subject nevertheless to the provisions of sub-clause (5)) hereof pledge the credit of the partnership or incur any liability or lend any monies on behalf of the partnership

(4) Lend money or give credit on behalf of the partnership or have any dealings with any person company or firm with whom the other partners shall have previously requested him not to deal and any loss incurred through breach of this provision shall be made good to the partnership by the partner committing the breach

(5) On behalf of the partnership by order or contract for any goods or property exceeding the value of £500 and any goods or property bought ordered or contracted for by any partner in breach of this provision shall be taken and paid for by him and shall be his separate property (unless the other partners shall elect to adopt the transaction on behalf of the partnership) or contract any partnership debt exceeding the said sum

(6) Give any guarantee on behalf of the partnership

(7) Enter into any bond or become bail or surety for any person or knowingly cause or permit or suffer to be done anything whereby the property of the partnership may be taken in execution or otherwise endangered

(8) Assign mortgage or charge his share in the partnership with any other person concerning such share or any part thereof

(9) Compromise or compound or otherwise (except upon payment in full) release or discharge any debt due to the partnership

17 (1) Each of the partners shall keep all records that are usually or ought to be kept by persons engaged in general medical practice including a record of every attendance upon a patient and of

the treatment prescribed or advised and any other action taken and all records necessary for the purpose of the National Health Service or required by any Act or any regulation made by a competent authority

(2) There shall also be kept a record showing the number of patients on the National Health Service lists of the partners and of any assistants from time to time employed by the partnership

(3) All the said records shall be available at all reasonable times for inspection by any partner

18 Each of the partners shall be a member of the Medical Defence Union or such other medical defence organisation as the partners may agree upon

19 If any partner shall give to the other partners or partner at any time not less than six months' notice in writing of his retirement expiring on any account date he shall retire from the partnership on the expiry of the notice. If more than one notice shall be given on the same date that of the more senior partner shall be deemed to have been served first

20 A partner shall be deemed to retire from the partnership

(1) On the expiry of not less than two months' notice in writing requiring him to retire given to him by the other partners at a time when by reason of illness injury or other cause he is unable to perform his duties as a partner and has been unable so to do throughout the period of nine months immediately preceding the service of such notice or for more than a total period of nine months in the aggregate during the period of twelve months immediately preceding the service of such notice:
  (i) unless before the expiry of such notice
  (ii) he resumes his partnership duties to the reasonable satisfaction of the partners who gave the notice

(2) Or the service upon him of a notice in writing requiring him to retire given by the other partners or partner at any time after he has become a patient within the meaning of the Mental Health Act 1988

(3) On the account day next following his sixty-fifth birthday or on such later account date as the partners may agree in writing

21 If any partner:
(1) shall commit any breach of the provisions of this deed or shall commit other persistent breaches thereof after warning by the other partners; or
(2) shall commit an act of bankruptcy or shall suffer his share in the

partnership to be charged as a separate debt under the Partnership Act 1890 or without the consent of the other partners shall assign charge or incumber such share or any part thereof; or

(3) shall fail to pay any monies due from him to the partnership within 28 days of being requested in writing to do so by the other partners; or

(4) shall absent himself (otherwise than under the provisions of Clauses 10 and 14 hereof) from the partnership practice without the consent of the other partners for more than three months in any period of twelve months; or

(5) shall be guilty of habitual insobriety or of flagrantly immoral behaviour likely to prejudice the partnership practice or of any grave breach or persistent breaches of the ethics or etiquette of the medical profession or of any other behaviour or conduct likely to have a serious adverse effect on the partnership practice; or

(6) shall have his registration in the medical register suspended; or

(7) shall have his name removed from the list of medical practitioners hereinbefore referred to

then the other partners shall be entitled by notice in writing given to such partner to expel him from the partnership

If the name of any of the partners is erased from any register maintained under the Medical Acts 1956 to 1978 he shall automatically be expelled from the partnership upon the date when his name is so erased PROVIDED that if such erasure is made pursuant to the provisions of Section 3(5) of the Medical Act 1969 his expulsion shall not be automatic but the other partners shall be entitled to give notice to expel such partner from the partnership if he or she shall fail to apply for the restoration of his or her name to the register forthwith upon becoming aware of such erasure or shall fail to secure an order for the restoration of his or her name to the register within such period after such erasure as such other partners or partner shall consider reasonable

22 (1) The provisions contained in the Third Schedule hereto (hereinafter called 'the Third Schedule') shall apply on the death of a partner or on his deemed retirement under the provisions of clause 19 hereof or on his expulsion from the partnership under the provisions of clauses 20 or 21 hereof and the partnership shall continue hereunder between the other partners

(2) Subject nevertheless to the provisions of clause 22 hereof the

provisions contained in the Third Schedule shall also apply if and whenever any of the partners retires under the provisions of clause 18 hereof

23 (1) If and whenever a partner retires under the provisions of clause 18 hereof the other partners shall be entitled by notice in writing given to such partner or his receiver or trustee in bankruptcy as the case may be to elect that the following provisions of this clause shall apply instead of the provisions contained in the Second Schedule PROVIDED that such notice shall be given in writing at least three months before the retirement under the said provisions is due to take effect

    (2) If any right of election provided for in this clause is exercised the partnership shall be dissolved on the date specified in the notice given under the provisions hereof and on such dissolution the affairs of the partnership shall be wound up in accordance with the provisions of the Partnership Act 1890

24 In consideration of the covenants by the other partners herein contained each of the partners hereby irrevocably appoints the other partners his attorneys for the purpose of signing executing and doing all notices documents deeds acts and things which in accordance with the provisions set out in the Third Schedule or any request made pursuant to those provisions are at any time required to be signed executed or done by him

25 In this deed and the Third Schedule hereto unless the context otherwise requires:

    (a) 'Account date' means the date on which accounts and balance sheet is to be taken in accordance with Clause 8.2 of this deed

    (b) Every reference to any Act or section of an Act or any statutory instrument or regulation is to be construed as a reference to that Act or section or statutory instrument or regulation as amended or re-enacted from time to time

    (c) 'Outgoing partner' refers to any of the partners who has ceased to be a partner by reason of his death or in consequence of his retirement or deemed retirement or expulsion and where the circumstances so require the expression shall be deemed to include a reference to his personal representatives trustee in bankruptcy or receiver

    (d) 'Succession date' means in relation to the outgoing partner the date of his death retirement deemed retirement or expulsion as the case may be

    (e) 'Continuing partners' refers to the persons or person in partnership with an outgoing partner immediately prior to the succession date applicable to that outgoing partner PROVIDED that if at a time when not less than three of the partners remain partners all but one of them shall become outgoing partners on the same date the expression shall be taken also to refer to the remaining partner

(f)   Every covenant or agreement given or made by any party hereto shall be deemed to have been given or made by him with the other parties jointly and with each of them separately

(g)   Words importing any gender include the other gender

26   If any partner shall so require in relation to any transaction effected or proposed to be effected pursuant to the provisions of this deed all the partners shall join in an application to the Medical Practices Committee for a certificate that such transaction is not a transaction involving the giving of valuable consideration in respect of the goodwill of a medical practice or part thereof and all the expenses of every such application shall be a partnership expense

27   Any notice hereunder shall be sufficiently given to or served on the person to whom it is addressed if it is sent in a prepaid letter by registered post or the recorded delivery service addressed to that person at his last known address and shall be deemed to have been received by that person on the date on which it would have been delivered in the ordinary course of post

28   If any new partner shall with the consent of the partners be admitted to the partnership he shall as a condition of such admission execute a deed of accession containing a covenant to perform and observe the provisions of this deed subject to any such modifications thereof as are agreed and set out in the deed of accession

29   If during the continuance of the partnership or at any time afterwards any dispute difference or question shall arise between the partners or their respective representatives touching the partnership or the accounts or transactions thereof or the determination or winding-up thereof or the construction meaning or effect of this Deed or anything herein contained or as to the rights and liabilities of partners under this Deed or otherwise then (save in circumstances in which express provision is made in this Deed for determining any particular disputes differences or questions in another way) such dispute difference or question shall be referred in accordance with the provisions of the Arbitration Acts 1950 to 79 to a single arbitrator to be agreed upon by the parties hereto or if they shall be unable to reach agreement on such appointment within four weeks after the dispute difference or question shall have arisen to be appointed on

the application of any party hereto by the President for the time being of The Royal College of General Practitioners PROVIDED that if the said President shall refuse to make such an appointment or shall fail to do so within a period of six weeks after application has been made to him so to do then any party hereto may apply to the Court to appoint an arbitrator

30   The Outgoing partner if he shall be living shall not without the prior express written consent of the continuing partners during the period of three years following the succession date and within a radius of five miles from any premises at which the partnership practice is carried on at such date attend as a general practitioner any person who was a patient of the partnership

IN WITNESS whereof the parties hereto have hereunto set their hands and seals the day and year first above written

SIGNED SEALED AND DELIVERED   )
by the said   )
in the presence of:)

SIGNED SEALED AND DELIVERED   )
by the said   )
in the presence of:)

SIGNED SEALED AND DELIVERED   )
by the said   )
in the presence of:)

THE FIRST SCHEDULE

above referred to

PART I

Description of Capital Assets
1. Freehold property at
2. Furniture, fittings and effects (including surgical instruments)
3. Drugs

PART II

ASSETS REFERRED TO IN PART I OF THIS SCHDULE

Name of Partner	Existing Share of Partner in these assets

THE SECOND SCHEDULE

above referred to

DIVISIONS OF PROFITS AND LOSSES
(other than of a capital nature)

Partnership Financial year ending	Dr	Dr	Dr

THE THIRD SCHEDULE

above referred to

1   The share of the outgoing partner in the capital and assets (including goodwill) of the partnership shall vest in the continuing partners and if more than one in the shares in which they were entitled to share in the capital of the partnership immediately prior to the succession date.

2   The continuing partners shall pay and discharge all debts and liabilities of the partnership at the succession date except any debt or liability in respect of income tax attributable to the outgoing partner's share of the profits of the partnership or any capital taxes attributable to the outgoing partner's share in the capital assets of the partnership firm and except any debt or liability in respect of any claim arising from any wrongful act or omission of the partners or any of them to the extent that such claim is not covered by insurance and shall keep the outgoing partner and his estate and effects indemnified against such debts and liabilities except as aforesaid and against all actions proceedings costs claims and demands in respect thereof.

3 (1) Any unpaid interest which has accrued on the outgoing partner's capital to the succession date shall be paid to him immediately.

     (2) Any undrawn balance of the outgoing partner's share of the net profits of the partnership for the financial year of the partnership in which the succession date occurs shall be paid to him as soon as the amount thereof has been ascertained PROVIDED that:

         (a) unless the succession date coincides with an account date such share shall be deemed to be a proportionate part calculated on a time basis (in accordance with the relevant provisions of the Apportionment Act 1870) of the share of the net profits of the partnership in the relevant year of the partnership to which the outgoing partner would have been entitled if he had continued to be a partner for the whole of that year.

         (b) the continuing partners may retain from such undrawn balance such sum as the partnership accountants shall estimate to be the amount of any income tax assessable on the partnership which is attributable to outgoing partner's share of profits and of any capital taxes which would be recoverable from the partnership firm but are attributable to the share of the outgoing partner in the capital assets of the partnership but the continuing partners shall account to the outgoing partner promptly for any amount remaining owing after payment of the income tax and capital taxes so attributable.

4 The outgoing partner shall not be entitled to any payment in respect of his share of the goodwill of the partnership but shall be entitled to receive in respect of his share of the remaining assets a purchase price equal to the value thereof after deducting therefrom his share of the debts and liabilities of the partnership at the succession date but subject to the right of retention referred to in paragraph 3(b) hereof.

5 For the purposes of paragraph 4 hereof the value of the partnership assets (other than goodwill) shall be agreed between the outgoing partner and the continuing partners and in default of such agreement shall be assessed by a valuer to be nominated by them or in default of such nomination to be appointed by the President for the time being of the Royal Institution of Chartered Surveyors. In agreeing or assessing the value of any freehold leasehold or crownhold property belonging to the partnership the valuation shall be made on the basis of sale price of any such property on the open market with vacant possession and taking into account any value attributable to the fact that such property is especially adapted or suitable for use for the purposes of a medical practice. The expenses of any professional valuation shall be borne by the outgoing partner and the continuing partners in the proportions in which they were entitled to share in the profits of the partnership immediately prior to the succession date

6 The purchase price together with interest calculated from the succession date to payment thereof on the amount or balance thereof for the time being outstanding at the rate of 3% above the base rate from time to time of _____ Bank plc shall be paid to the outgoing partner by the continuing partners within four months after the succession date. The liability of the continuing partners (if more than one) to pay such purchase price together with interest as aforesaid and their liability under the indemnities contained in paragraphs 2 and 8 of this Schedule shall be joint and several but as between themselves they shall bear the amount of such purchase price and interest and any liability arising under such indemnities in the same

241

proportions as those in which immediately prior to the succession date they were entitled to share in the profits of the partnership

7   If the outgoing partner shall cease to be a partner otherwise than by reason of death due notice of the fact that he has ceased to be a partner shall be given in the *London Gazette* and so far as may be reasonably practicable by circular letter to all persons firms and bodies with whom the partnership has had dealings

8   At the request of the continuing partners the outgoing partner shall join with the continuing partners and with any person or persons who may enter into partnership with the continuing partners on the succession date in making any election available under sub-section (2) of section 113 of the Income and Corporation Taxes Act 1988. The continuing partners shall keep the outgoing partner and his estate and effects indemnified against the amount of all income tax suffered by the outgoing partner which the outgoing partner would not have suffered if he had not joined in making the election

9   The outgoing partner shall deliver to the continuing partners all books of account records letters and other documents in his possession relating to the partnership but during the period of 18 months following the succession date the outgoing partner or his duly authorised agent shall be permitted to inspect by appointment the books of account records letters and other documents of the partnership practice so far as they relate to any period preceding the succession date

10 The outgoing partner shall sign execute and do all such documents deeds acts and things as the continuing partners may reasonably request for the purpose of enabling the continuing partners to recover and get in outstanding assets of the partnership or for the purpose of conveying assigning or transferring to the continuing partners any of the partnership property which immediately prior to the succession date is vested in the outgoing partner as one of the partners or in trust for the partnership

Appendix 5 – Internal control questionnaire for medical practices

1 General accounting organisation

1.1 Are the accounting records maintained up to date and balanced monthly?

1.2 Do the partners appear to take a direct and active interest in the financial affairs of the practice?

1.3 Are there any systems of periodic financial reports or budgetary control?

1.4 Are the personal funds and financial transactions of the partners completely segregated from those of the partnership?

2 Receipts

2.1 Is the mail opened by the partners?

2.2 Are sundry cash receipts separately recorded?

2.3 Is all money received banked intact?

3 Payments

3.1 Are all payments made by cheque?

3.2 Can cheques be signed only by the partners?

3.3 Are cheques signed only when complete (i.e., not in blank)?

3.4 Is supporting documentation approved and cancelled by the partners when payment is made?

3.5 Is supporting documentation properly filed, consecutively numbered and cross-referenced to the cash book?

3.6 Are spoiled cheques retained?

3.7 Are payments not made by cheque (e.g., standing orders) authorised only by the partners?

3.8 Do the partners review the bank balances and reconciliations?

3.9 Is petty cash maintained on an imprest system?

4 Fees and debtors (for private patients)

4.1 Are fee notes pre-numbered and all accounted for?

4.2 Is a list of unpaid fees regularly reviewed by the partners?

4.3 Are reminders sent to patients in respect of overdue fees?

5 Drawings

5.1 Are partners' drawings paid regularly (e.g., monthly)?

5.2 Do the calculations for regular drawings take account of tax reserves, disparities in allowances, etc.?

5.3 Are the amounts of regular drawings periodically reviewed during the year in the light of practice income and any changes in profit-sharing ratios?

5.4 Are Class 2 National Insurance contributions paid regularly by the partnership and debited to the partners' current accounts?

6 Wages and salaries

6.1 Are employees taken on or dismissed only by the partners?

6.2 Are references obtained in respect of new employees?

6.3 Do the partners approve the payroll and supervise the payment of wages and salaries?

6.4 Are PAYE and National Insurance deductions paid over monthly to the Collector of Taxes?

7 Fixed assets

7.1 Are detailed records maintained of the assets owned by the practice?

7.2 Are the partners aware of which assets are owned by the practice and which are owned by the individual partners?

7.3 Are disposals and scrapping of assets authorised only by the partners?

8 Stock (for dispensing practices)

8.1 Are continuous stock records maintained?

8.2 Is stock physically counted periodically and reconciled to the stock records and dangerous drugs book?

8.3 Is the stock physically counted and valued at the account date?

8.4 Are obsolete or unwanted stocks properly disposed of?

Appendix 6 – Specimen master index: working papers file

MASTER INDEX	

Client	

A	Planning
B	Accounts
C	Balance sheet items
D	Capital
E	Fixed assets
F	Loan finance
G	Income and expenditure
H	Taxation
I	Correspondence
J	Profit allocation
K	Stock on hand
L	Investments
M	Debtors
N	Creditors
O	GP fundholding
P	Personal expenses claims
Q	Trial balance
R	Accounts to trial balance: receipts
S	Accounts to trial balance: payments
T	Petty cash
U	Statistics
V	Cash at bank/in hand
W	Journals
X	Extract from previous years
Y	Carry forward to succeeding year
Z	Client papers (to return)

Appendix 7 – Accounts preparation checklist

This list is presented in order to formulate a programme for preparation of accounts of a typical NHS general practice.

It does not presume to be exhaustive and practitioners will wish to amend the list in order to comply with their own internal policies and requirements.

It is recommended that a checklist of this type be included in each working papers file (Section A: Appendix 6), being completed as each separate operation is completed. This ensures that at any time it is evident exactly to what stage the work has progressed.

This schedule is to be included in the Working Papers file on completion of the work: To be completed/initialed as the work progresses to conclusion.

A – Preliminary and briefing		Date	Initials	Checked
A–1	Year-end letter sent			
A–2	Visit arranged			
A–3	Confirmation letter sent			
A–4	Last year's c/fwd points checked			
A–5	Briefing meeting held			
A–6	Examine Partnership Deed			
A–7	Establish Opening TB/balances			
B – Petty cash				
B–1	Receipts analysed			
B–2	Payments analysed			
B–3	Summary prepared/reconciled			
B–4	Cash from bank reconciled with bank payments			
B–5	Entered on computer program trial balance			

C – Bank account 1
(for main practice account)

C–1	Summary prepared and agreed			
C–2	Bank balance reconciled			
C–3	Bank entries checked			
C–4	Final statement copied			

D – Bank account 2
(for subsidiary bank/building society accounts)

D–1	Summaries prepared and agreed			
D–2	Bank balances reconciled			
D–3	Bank entries checked			
D–4	Final statements(s) copied			

E – Loan account(s)
(use for all loan accounts during year)

E–1	Summary prepared			
E–2	Balance reconciled			
E–3	Final statement(s) copied			
E–4	Repayments reconciled to bank payments			

F – Payments analysis and summary

F–1	Summary of analysis cash book totals			
F–2	Vouched against receipted accounts/invoices			
F–3	Analyse separate columns (as required)			
F–4	Analyse sundries column			
F–5	Analyse and summarise partners' drawings			
F–6	Prepare detailed analysis (as necessary: from cheques paid)			
F–7	Prepare final payments summary			
F–8	Reconcile total of F–7 to payments figure on bank summary (C–1)			

G – Receipts analysis and summary

G–1	Summary of analysis cash book totals			
G–2	Prepare analysis of NHS income			
G–3	Prepare analysis of NHS fees and allowances			
G–4	Prepare analysis of NHS reimbursements			
G–5	Prepare analysis of NHS drug refunds, dispensing fees			
G–6	Prepare analysis of deductions from NHS fees, etc.			
G–7	Prepare analysis of income from outside appointments			
G–8	Prepare analysis/reconciliation of hospital remuneration (Sch E income)			
G–9	Prepare analysis of sundry receipts			
G–10	Prepare final receipts summary			
G–11	Reconcile total of G–10 to receipts figure on bank summary (C–1)			

H – Dispensing
(for use by dispensing practices)

H–1	Analysis of fees/refunds (see under **9.7**)			
H–2	Analysis of superannuation deductions			
H–3	Stock figure available (see also L)			
H–4	Establish payments to drug suppliers			
H–5	Identify income from private prescriptions			
H–6	Prepare dispensing trading account (see Figure 2.3)			

J – Debtors

J–1	Prepare lead schedule of total debtors (include comparative figures)			
J–2	Summary of NHS debtors (fees & allowances)			
J–3	Summary of NHS debtors (reimbursements)			
J–4	Summary of debtors from other sources			
J–5	Schedule of pre-payments			

K – Creditors

K–1	Prepare lead schedule of creditors & accruals (include comparative figures)			
K–2	Schedule of creditors for accountancy fees			
K–3	Schedule of accruals			

L – Stock on hand

L–1	Check stock calculations per client			
L–2	Stock certificate prepared & signed by client			

M – Fixed assets

M–1	Prepare lead schedule			
M–2	Schedule of acquisitions during year (with copy invoices)			
M–3	Schedule of disposal			
M–4	Calculate depreciation			
M–5	Schedules of surgery transactions (including ownership changes)			

N – Taxation

N–1	Analyse Income Tax Reserve Account			
N–2	Calculate reserves for current year			
N–3	Calculate future tax reserve transfers			

O – Trial balance
(or computer program)

O–1	Enter opening balances (A–7)			
O–2	Post petty cash summary (B–5)			
O–3	Enter bank payments summary (F–7)			
O–4	Enter bank receipts summary (G–10)			
O–5	Reconcile/balance bank entries (C–1)			

O–6	Adjust for loan accounts (E–1)			
O–7	Enter debtors (J–1)			
O–8	Enter creditors (K–1)			
O–9	Enter stock on hand (L–1)			
O–10	Adjust for depreciation (M–4)			
O–11	Prepare trial balance			
O–12	Draft final accounts			

P – Completion

P–1	Complete Letter of Representation (signed by client)			
P–2	Accounts review procedure completed			
P–3	Clear all review points			
P–4	Accounts to client for approval			
P–5	Accounts signed by clients			
P–7	Accounts to HMIT for agreement			

Appendix 8 – Reconciliation of list sizes

Drs ....   Date 31 March 1996

Prepared by:

Four quarters to 31 March 1996:
    To 64   @   13.85
    65–74   @   18.20
    75+   @   35.15

                                          _____

                                          ═══════════

one quarter thereof   ...   .

                                                    _____

                                                    ═══════════

Cross-reference to total of capitation   £
fees

Note:
This schedule can be used to reconcile and verify amounts received by
way of capitation fees, which are likely to be the largest single item in a
GP's remuneration package.

Amounts of list sizes can be extracted from quarterly NHS statements of
fees and allowances.

Appendix 9 – Specimen letter of engagement

It is suggested that this letter be sent to all clients so as to lay down clearly the work the practitioner will perform, the manner by which his fees will be charged and paid, the services he has available and the information he will expect from the client.

Ideally such a letter should be signed by the client (or in a partnership by all the partners), one copy of which should be retained by the client and the other returned to the accountant for his retention and future reference.

The letter is designed for GP partnerships, although it can be suitably adapted for sole practitioners where required.

Dear Dr
We should like to thank you for appointing us to act for you in the provision of accountancy, taxation and allied services.

In order to make clear the relationship between us, we have set down below our understanding of the extent and nature of the work we shall perform on your behalf, together with certain administrative matters which are drawn to your attention and of which the partners should be aware.

We should be grateful if, provided the partners are in agreement with this letter, that this be signed by them where indicated on the last page and returned to us.

Accountancy services
We shall prepare the statement of partnership accounts to the partnership accounting date which has been agreed from time to time. Although at the time of preparing this letter your accounts are prepared annually to .... 19...., we reserve the right to propose alterations to this date as and when it seems to us that it will be beneficial to you.

The first annual accounts we shall prepare for you will be in respect of the year/period ended .....

We shall not carry out an audit of your accounts although where the partners wish us to perform certain functions of an audit nature we shall be pleased to do so, subject to an appropriate fee being agreed in advance.

In carrying out our work we shall examine the records and make any enquiries which are necessary for us to complete our work. Our annual report to the partners will state that we have prepared the accounts from the accounting records produced to us, together with any explanations and information given to us.

The work we perform should not be relied upon to disclose any irregularities, although where these become apparent from tests we undertake, we shall report to you accordingly.

Where there is any change in the partnership during the year, either as regards the doctors making up a partnership, or involving variations in profit-sharing ratios, we shall, unless instructed to the contrary, prepare your accounts to the agreed accounting date, dividing the profits for the year on the basis of time apportionment, thus assuming that all profits have been earned equally throughout the year.

Our standard procedure for dealing with necessary work on your partnership accounts will be to visit the surgery at a time mutually acceptable. We shall then proceed with the preparation of your annual accounts, the timing of which will to a large degree depend on the quality of records produced to us, and the efficiency with which we receive responses to any enquiries we might raise.

Following preparation of the accounts, these will be sent to the partners for agreement and signature. Where required, we shall be pleased to attend a meeting of the partners to discuss any points they may wish to raise, arising from these accounts.

Taxation services
Our basic duties will be to agree the partnership income tax computations based upon accounts prepared by ourselves. We shall check assessment notices, submitting appeals as necessary and making recommendations of income tax due from time to time.

Attached herewith is form 64–8, which will enable HM Inspector of Taxes to supply us with copy assessment notices and to deal through us with all necessary correspondence. We shall be grateful if this can be signed where indicated and returned.

We shall discuss and agree with you schemes for reserving income tax, so as to provide funds to be set aside in order to meet your tax liabilities as these fall due.

We shall deal separately with those partners who instruct us to deal with their personal affairs. These instructions will normally involve the issue of a separate, and personal, letter of engagement. Where we do not receive instructions to act for individual partners we shall, if necessary, correspond with their own accountants and it may be necessary for an additional fee to be charged in respect of any work thus involved.

Consulting services
We are in a position to offer specialist consultancy services under separate headings. Work on these will be carried out by experts in these fields and a separate fee negotiated before work is commenced:

(a) GP fundholding;
(b) business planning;
(c) practice administration;
(d) organisation of profit-sharing ratios;
(e) maximisation of income levels;
(f) retirement and pensions planning;
(g) personal financial planning;
(h) surgery developments;
(i) raising of loan finance;
(j) taxation planning;
(k) partnership capital planning.

So that we might prepare accounts to reflect more accurately the profits generated through the year, we shall be grateful if you will arrange for the stock of dispensing drugs to be valued at each accounting date. We shall invite the partners to sign a certificate setting out this valuation.

Where no valid partnership deed is available, where a previous deed has become invalid or an existing deed requires an element of variation, we shall submit for approval to the partners each year a letter of representation, which we shall invite them to sign and return to us before the work on your accounts is completed.

Necessary correspondence of a partnership nature will be carried on with one partner nominated by you for that purpose. Attached herewith is a letter to that effect, which we shall be grateful if you would sign and return to us.

255

Fees

Our fees each year will be based upon a quotation, which will be prepared and submitted prior to the work being commenced each year. This will be subject to annual negotiation. Such fees will normally include work upon the partnership, accountancy and taxation services, as well as for personal taxation services for the individual partners.

Where acceptable, and in order to assist the cash flow of the practice, we shall invite you to settle quoted fees by means of monthly standing orders. Where it is necessary to render an invoice for any specific assignment, this will normally be issued on completion of that work.

We should like to emphasise that the level of accountancy fees charged, to a large degree, depends on the standard of records produced to us. We shall be pleased to make recommendations as and when necessary in order to improve these accounts.

It will be necessary for VAT at the rate currently in force to be added to all invoices and any fees quoted are exclusive of VAT.

Yours faithfully

On behalf of the partnership we acknowledge receipt of this letter and signify our agreement to its terms.

....

....

....

(In practice, the engagement letter would also be required to include paragraphs concerning the obligations of both the firm and the clients arising from the Financial Services Act.)

Appendix 10 – Specimen letter of representation

The Medical Centre
Watney Street
Charrington-on-Bass

Messrs March Hare & Co.
Chartered Accountants
41 Hatters Road
Wonderland

Dear Sirs

Drs Truman, Bass & Partners
Accounts for the year ended 30 June 1996.

In the absence of a valid partnership deed in force for the above year of account, we hereby authorise and instruct you to take the following items into consideration in preparing our accounts for that year.*/This should be taken as supplementary to our existing partnership deed dated 27 May 1986.*

1. Profit-sharing ratios applicable to general practice profits during the year of account and for the succeeding income tax year are as follows:

Period:	From 1 July 1995 %	From 1 July 1996 %	From 1 July 1997 %	From 1 July 1998 %
Dr Truman	21	20.5	17.94	17.52
Dr Bass	21	20.5	17.94	17.52
Dr Whitbread	21	20.5	17.94	17.52
Dr Young	21	20.5	17.94	17.51
Dr Webster	16	18.0	17.94	17.51
Dr Tetley			10.30	12.42

2. Proceeds from seniority awards, and post graduate education allowances are to be retained in the names of the individual partners in

whose names they are paid*/accumulated with partnership profits for division in agreed profit-sharing ratios as set out in (1) above.*

3. The surgery premises are owned equally by the following partners. Proceeds from notional/cost-rent allowances are to be divided similarly.

Dr Truman	25%
Dr Bass	25%
Dr Whitbread	25%
Dr Young	25%

4. All income of a medical nature, from whatever source, is to be accumulated with practice profits for division, with the exception of the following:

    4.1 Night visit fees, in the proportions advised to you.
    4.2 Proceeds from the appointment of Dr Bass at the Samuel Smith Cottage Hospital.

5. The following amounts are to be treated as paid out of partnership income and charged as such in the partnership accounts:

    5.1 Salaries, pension contributions and National Insurance contributions in respect of partnership employees.
    5.2 All costs of maintaining the surgery.
    5.3 Fees to locums and deputising services.
    5.4 Purchase of drugs and instruments for use in the surgery.
    5.5 Interest and charges on the partnership bank account(s).
    5.6 Any other expenses of an administrative nature agreed to be paid out by the partners.
    *5.7 Salaries, pension contributions and medical sickness premiums in respect of the partners' spouses.
    *5.8 Partners' personal telephone charges.
    *5.9 Medical subscriptions.
    *5.10 Motor expenses of the individual partners.

6. The following expenditure is to be borne personally by the individual partner concerned and, if relevant, claimed for income tax purposes through his own claim for personal practice expenses:

    6.1 Medical subscriptions.
    6.2 Personal fees to locum and relief services.
    *6.3 Salaries, pension contributions and medical sickness premiums for the partners' spouses.
    6.4 Motor expenses incurred by each partner.

   6.5   Expenses of running the partners' private houses.

 *6.6   Partners' private telephone charges.

 *6.7   Attendances at courses, conferences, etc. (PGEA qualifying).

 *6.8   Private subscriptions to books and medical journals.

7.   The partners will contribute to the capital (including working capital) of the practice in the same proportions as those in which they share practice profits.

8.   The required fixed capital (excluding surgery capital) contribution by each parity partner has been set at £8,000.

9.   The practice has received a dispensation from the Inland Revenue under which the Trainee Car Allowance may be paid without deduction of PAYE tax.

Yours faithfully

   ....

   Dr B Truman   Dr J R Bass

   ....

   Dr M Whitbread   Dr D J Young

               ....

               Dr R J Webster

* Alternatives

Appendix 11 – Specimen 'year-end' preparatory letter

It is recommended that a letter based upon the example given, but varied to suit the requirements of a particular client, is sent out some two or three weeks before the accounting date.

This gives the practice due advance warning of the information which will be required to complete their accounts, at the same time enabling the accountant to plan ahead, allocating staff time to the work and ensuring that facilities are made available.

Dr J D Jameson
Drs Jameson, Grant & Partners
Distillery Health Centre
Easy-on-the-Water

Dear Dr Jameson

The accounting year of your partnership ends on 30 September 1996. During the next few weeks we shall be making arrangements to visit your practice to commence our work on preparation of your partnership accounts to that date.

Might I ask you to contact me as early as possible with a view to arranging such a visit.

When the date of the visit has been arranged, I shall send a more detailed letter to you outlining a number of matters to be dealt with during the visit, but in the meantime you could assist me considerably as follows:

1.   Please let me have your Petty Cash Book, duly written up to date.

2.   Could you obtain statements from your bank, not only of your current account but also of any deposit accounts in existence, made up, ideally, to a few days after the year end.

3. Similarly, please have written up to date any pass books in respect of accounts at building societies.

4. Your cash book should be ruled off at the accounting date. Any payments to partners by way of drawings paid at or about the year end should be treated as having been paid on the last day of the accounting year.

5. There will be a significant saving of time on our part if your cash book is balanced at the year end and the balance reconciled with your bank statements. To assist you in this I am attaching:

   *(i) a copy of the bank reconciliation statement at 30 September 1995.
   *(ii) a blank copy of the above to be completed as at 30 September 1996.
   *(iii) a copy of the bank account summary for the year to 30 September 1995.
   *(iv) a blank copy of the above to be completed for the year to 30 September 1996.

   If these could be completed and handed to us on arrival we should be most grateful.

6. It would be of great assistance if you could also balance, reconcile and analyse other bank accounts held by the practice in a similar format to the main current account. It is not normally necessary to use a full cash book as with the main current account unless there are a large number of transactions involved.

7. Would you please prepare a list of sundry creditors, i.e., amounts known to be due from you to suppliers, for example drug purchases, other accounts such as stationery, lighting and heating, telephone, etc. and amounts due to the Inland Revenue in respect of staff PAYE and NIC.

8. Similarly, could you make a list of all debtors, i.e., amounts due to the practice on the same date; fees due from patients but not paid; amounts due from your FHSA for any reason, and any other items. Where necessary, estimates may be made.

9. It is essential, if our accounts are to represent a true picture of the profit for the year, that a value be taken of the stock of drugs on hand at that date (excluding free samples), if it is material. Would you therefore kindly arrange to have the drug stock checked, counted

and valued. The value should be taken as at cost or market value, whichever is the lower, inclusive of VAT. If necessary an estimate can be made, although we would prefer to use actual figures.

The omission of drug stocks from accounts may be used by the Inland Revenue as evidence of the understatement of profits for tax purposes, with possibly adverse results if an accurate figure of stock valuation is not included in the accounts.

We shall ultimately invite the partners to sign a certificate confirming such a valuation.

As mentioned above, we shall attempt to arrange a visit to your practice as soon as possible. With this in mind, perhaps your practice manager would be kind enough to telephone me at the above address, with a list of suitable and convenient dates.

Yours sincerely

* not illustrated

Appendix 12 – Specimen appointment of nominated partner letter

Drs Truman, Bass & Partners
The Medical Centre
Watney Street
Charrington-on-Bass

Messrs Saunders, Nadir & Co
Chartered Accountants
24 Maxwell Square
Granchester

Dear Sirs,

We being the partners in the above medical practice, hereby authorise you to correspond with Dr G B Bass upon all matters on partnership finance, accountancy and taxation.

If you receive correspondence from any other partner in this respect, you are to reply to the letter accordingly and to send a copy of this to the nominated partner. We agree to accept the cost of any further work engendered by such additional correspondence.

....
Dr S W Truman

....
Dr G B Bass

....
Dr D J Whitbread

....
Dr L W Young

....
Dr J S Webster

Appendix 13 – Current (from April 1995) cost rent limits (building costs)

Building cost limits per practice unit:	Rate A £	Rate B £
One GP	46,965	40,820
Two GPs	85,942	74,706
Three GPs	129,222	112,453
Four GPs	157,049	136,594
Five GPs	185,492	161,261
Six GPs	209,281	181,981
Seven GPs	235,617	204,892
Eight GPs	261,602	227,452
Nine GPs	287,939	250,365
Ten GPs	314,361	273,365
Optional extra rooms:		
offices per sq m	429	372
common room per sq m	429	372
dispensary per sq m	429	372
GP reg./consulting room	429	372
plus externals	15%	15%
plus professional fees	11.5%	10.5/12%
with VAT on fees	17.5%	17.5%
plus planning consent fees	100%	100%
plus approved site cost	100%	100%

All costs exclude VAT, which will be added by the HA at the rate currently in force.

Rate A: For new developments and approved works, plus VAT.

Rate B: For modifications of existing buildings.

Published rates are subject to annual amendments.

Appendix 14 – 1995/96 cost rent limit variations: building cost location factors

HA	Factor
Avon	0.96
Barking and Havering	1.11
Barnet	1.11
Barnsley	0.97
Bedfordshire	1.01
Berkshire	1.01
Birmingham	0.95
Bolton	0.99
Bradford	0.95
Brent and Harrow	1.17
Bromley	1.11
Buckinghamshire	1.02
Bury	0.99
Calderdale	0.95
Cambridgeshire	0.98
Camden and Islington	1.17
Cheshire	0.97

City and E London	1.17
Cleveland	0.95
Cornwall and Isles of Scilly	0.92
Coventry	0.95
Croydon	1.11
Cumbria	1.02
Derbyshire	0.92
Devon	0.93
Doncaster	0.97
Dorset	0.99
Dudley	0.99
Durham	0.95
Ealing, Hammersmith and Hounslow	1.13
East Sussex	1.06
Enfield and Haringey	1.11
Essex	1.01
Gateshead	0.97
Gloucestershire	0.94
Greenwich and Bexley	1.17
Hampshire	0.99
Hereford and Worcester	0.95
Hertfordshire	1.08

Hillingdon	1.11
Humberside	0.99
Isle of Wight	0.94
Kensington, Chelsea and Westminster	1.17
Kent	1.05
Kingston and Richmond	1.11
Kirklees	0.95
Lambeth, Southwark and Lewisham	1.17
Lancashire	1.00
Leeds	0.95
Leicestershire	0.92
Lincolnshire	0.91
Liverpool	0.99
Manchester	0.99
Merton, Sutton and Wandsworth	1.11
Newcastle	0.97
Norfolk	0.94
Northamptonshire	0.97
North Tyneside	0.97
Northumberland	0.99
North Yorkshire	1.00
Nottinghamshire	0.92

Oldham	0.99
Oxfordshire	0.98
Redbridge and Waltham Forest	1.11
Rochdale	0.99
Rotherham	0.99
St Helens and Knowsley	0.99
Salford	0.99
Sandwell	0.95
Sefton	0.99
Sheffield	0.97
Shropshire	0.92
Solihull	0.95
Somerset	0.93
South Tyneside	0.97
Staffordshire	0.92
Stockport	0.99
Suffolk	0.97
Sunderland	0.97
Surrey	1.10
Tameside	0.99
Trafford	0.99
Wakefield	0.95

Walsall	0.95
Warwickshire	0.98
West Sussex	1.03
Wigan	0.99
Wiltshire	0.96
Wirral	0.99
Wolverhampton	0.95
Wales	
Clwyd	0.89
Dyfed	0.96
Mid Glamorgan	0.97
South Glamorgan	0.97
West Glamorgan	0.93
Gwent	0.96
Gwynedd	0.96
Powys	0.91

Appendix 15 – Claim for personal practice expenses

DR D J BODDINGTON
PERSONAL PRACTICE EXPENSES CLAIM
YEAR ENDED 30 JUNE 1994

	£	£	£
Use of home for practice/study purposes			460
Motor expenses	*Rover*	*Fiesta*	
Licence and insurance	465	288	
Petrol and oil	1,762	645	
Repairs and servicing	787	429	
HP interest	462		
RAC subscription	100		
Parking expenses	50	20	
Cleaning costs	70	30	
	3,696	1,412	
Less: Private use (15%)	554		
(80%)		1,129	
	3,142	283	3,425

Claim

General practice expenses:

	£	£
Wife's salary	2,900	
Wife's pension contributions	1,675	
Medical subscriptions	1,328	
Telephone (80%)	462	
Accountancy fees (60%)	475	
Postage & stationery (60% (est))	125	
Security expenses	250	
Courses & conferences	480	
		7,695
		£11,580

Capital allowances – 1995/96

Asset: **Cars:**	WDV brought forward	WDA (25%)	WDV carried forward	Proportion claimed	Allowance claimed
Rover (J123 ABC)	9,825	2,456	7,369	85%	2,088
Fiesta (F456 XYZ)	1,468	367	1,100	20%	73
Computer	848	212	636	50%	106
Video recorder	468	117	351	30%	35
					£2,302

Appendix 16 – Personal practice expenses: confirmation letter

'Badgers'
Breakspeare Road
Friary-on-Meux

Messrs March, Hare & Co.
Chartered Accountants
41 Hatters Road
Wonderland

Dear Sirs

Personal practice expenses: year ended 30 June 1994

I hereby confirm that:

1. The claim in general shows a fair representation of expenses paid personally by me, wholly or partly in respect of my medical practice.

2. Apart from as shown in (5) below, a full record has been kept of all expenses actually incurred.

3. The salary paid to my husband/wife is a genuine level of payment for services supplied to my medical practice and has been paid by means of a physical transfer of funds.

4. The following restrictions for private use are in order:

	%
Motor cars: Rover	15
Fiesta	80
Private telephone use	20
Personal accountancy fees	40
Personal computer	50
Video recorder	70

5. The following estimates of expenditure are a fair reflection of claims for the year:

	£
Study allowance	460
Postage & stationery	125

I approve the claim and accept that this is in order for submission to HM Inspector of Taxes for agreement.

Yours faithfully

Dr D J Boddington

Appendix 17 – Inland Revenue Extra-Statutory Concession: doctors' and dentists' superannuation contributions (ESC A9)

Under FA 1970, s 22 (for 1973/74 onwards; ICTA 1970, s 209 for years to 1972/73) contributions required to be made in pursuance of a public general Act of Parliament by the holder of an office or employment towards the provisions of superannuation benefits may be deducted in assessing his emoluments. These sections are in practice treated as extending to assessments under Schedule D on the profits of a medical or dental practitioner who is required to make superannuation contributions in pursuance of the National Health Service Acts. Where, however, the practitioner also pays premiums or contributions towards a retirement annuity within ICTA 1970, s 226 a restriction is imposed either on the amount of the deduction for his statutory contribution or on the amount of retirement annuity relief allowable.

For 1980/81 onwards concessionary relief is allowable on either of the following bases.

Either practitioners may have relief on the amount of their NHS contributions together with relief on the amount of any retirement annuity premium in relation to their non-NHS earnings. For this purpose

(i) non-NHS earnings are taken as the amount of net relevant earnings (as defined in Sec 227(3)) less the sum produced by multiplying the amount of the NHS contributions by $16\frac{1}{3}$.

(ii) retirement annuity relief will be allowable within the normal limit of $17\frac{1}{3}$ (or the higher percentages for older contributors) of the non-NHS earnings plus any unused relief for earlier years. For this purpose unused relief should be calculated on the appropriate concessional basis for years in which relief has been allowed on NHS contributions.

Or, practitioners may have relief on the same basis as set out in (2) above relating to the years 1972/73 to 1979/80.*

274

Finally, practitioners may, instead, have relief on a statutory basis. In this case, they would take retirement annuity relief, up to the limits appropriate for a particular year, on their full net relevant earnings (i.e. including NHS earnings). But in that event no concessionary relief would be available in respect of NHS contributions.

Source   IR1(1970) as amended and updated by each of the Supplements 1971 to 1973; 1977 and 1978 Supplements to IR1 (1976) and amended to present wording by 1981 Supplement to IR1 (1980)

Notes   In view of the number of changes that have been made to this concession (see sources above), careful consideration should be given to the exact form of the concession for earlier years.

Appendix 18 – NHS pension scheme: early retirement factors by age attained

Age	Complete months											
	0	1	2	3	4	5	6	7	8	9	10	11
Pensions												
50	0.599	0.601	0.604	0.606	0.608	0.610	0.612	0.614	0.616	0.618	0.620	0.622
51	0.624	0.627	0.629	0.631	0.634	0.636	0.638	0.640	0.643	0.645	0.647	0.650
52	0.652	0.654	0.657	0.660	0.662	0.665	0.667	0.670	0.672	0.675	0.677	0.680
53	0.682	0.685	0.688	0.691	0.694	0.696	0.699	0.702	0.705	0.708	0.711	0.713
54	0.716	0.719	0.723	0.726	0.729	0.732	0.735	0.738	0.742	0.745	0.748	0.751
55	0.754	0.758	0.761	0.765	0.768	0.772	0.775	0.779	0.782	0.785	0.789	0.792
56	0.796	0.800	0.803	0.807	0.811	0.815	0.818	0.822	0.826	0.830	0.833	0.837
57	0.841	0.845	0.849	0.853	0.857	0.861	0.865	0.869	0.873	0.878	0.882	0.886
58	0.890	0.894	0.899	0.903	0.907	0.912	0.916	0.921	0.925	0.929	0.934	0.938
59	0.943	0.947	0.952	0.957	0.962	0.966	0.971	0.976	0.981	0.986	0.990	0.995
Lump sums												
50	0.747	0.749	0.751	0.753	0.755	0.756	0.758	0.760	0.762	0.764	0.766	0.767
51	0.769	0.771	0.773	0.775	0.777	0.779	0.780	0.782	0.784	0.786	0.788	0.790
52	0.792	0.794	0.796	0.798	0.800	0.801	0.803	0.805	0.807	0.809	0.811	0.813
53	0.815	0.817	0.819	0.821	0.823	0.825	0.827	0.829	0.831	0.833	0.835	0.837
54	0.839	0.841	0.843	0.845	0.847	0.849	0.851	0.854	0.856	0.858	0.860	0.862
55	0.864	0.866	0.868	0.870	0.872	0.874	0.877	0.879	0.881	0.883	0.885	0.887
56	0.889	0.892	0.894	0.896	0.898	0.900	0.902	0.905	0.907	0.909	0.911	0.913
57	0.916	0.918	0.920	0.922	0.925	0.927	0.929	0.932	0.934	0.936	0.938	0.941
58	0.943	0.945	0.948	0.950	0.952	0.955	0.957	0.959	0.962	0.964	0.966	0.969
59	0.971	0.973	0.976	0.978	0.981	0.983	0.985	0.988	0.990	0.993	0.995	0.998

Example: A doctor retiring at the age of 58 years and 2 months would receive 89.9% of the pension that had accrued at that age and 94.8% of the accrued lump sum.

[Source: Government Actuary's Department 15.6.94]

Appendix 19 – Inland Revenue press release 30 April 1996

Tax treatment of premiums and benefits under locum and fixed practice expenses insurance policies

The Inland Revenue today announced revised arrangements covering the way in which premiums paid for insurance policies to cover the cost of engaging a locum tenens, and benefits paid out under such policies, will be treated for tax purposes in the future.

This change of practice has been the subject of detailed consultation with the main parties likely to be affected, and the particulars set out below reflect their views.

Details

1. Some professional people who practise alone or in partnership, in particular medical professionals, take out insurance policies to indemnify themselves against the cost of engaging a locum tenens, or against other practice expenses, in the event of the policyholder's illness or other incapacity. In the past the Inland Revenue's view has been that premiums and benefits under these policies should be excluded from the calculation of taxable professional profits in the same way as other permanent health insurance premiums and benefits are excluded.

Change of view

2. The Inland Revenue have now received legal advice that this view is incorrect. Premiums on policies of indemnification of this nature are deductible in computing profits under Case II of Schedule D. Equally, benefits payable under the policies should be regarded as Case II receipts on the basis that they diminish the allowable expenses of the profession.

3. This treatment of both the premiums and the benefits holds good whether a person is obliged to insure (because of partnership obligations or National Health Service regulations) or does so as a matter of commercial prudence.

4. Where, however, the particular policy also includes insurance against

other, non-business, risks such as the cost of medical treatment for accident or sickness of the insured, the premiums will be incurred partly for a personal purpose. Only the proportion of the premium relating to practice expenses cover, calculated on a reasonable and consistent basis, will then be deductible.

How the change of view will be put into effect

5. In calculating profits for periods of account that begin on or after 1 October 1996, the premiums on locum/fixed practice expenses policies will be deductible and the benefits treated as taxable business receipts.

6. Where the profits for a period of account beginning before 1 October 1996 have **not** been agreed with the Inspector and assessments have **not** otherwise become final, premiums should be deducted and benefits treated as taxable business receipts. Alternatively, where premiums and benefits have been excluded from the computation of taxable profits for earlier settled periods this practice may be continued for unsettled periods of account beginning before 1 October 1996 subject to paragraph 7 below.

7. Where figures for periods of account beginning before 1 October 1996 have become final and premiums and benefits have been excluded from the computation of taxable profits for those periods, claims to repayment under the error or mistake provision (Section 33 Taxes Management Act 1970) may be made subject to the general rules for error or mistake relief, in particular the six year time limit. Under such a claim tax relief may be obtained for previously unallowed premiums but the total unallowed relief will be reduced by any untaxed benefits relating to the earliest period of account to which claims relate and all subsequent settled periods.

8. If an error or mistake claim is made premiums must also then be deducted and benefits treated as taxable business receipts for the unsettled periods mentioned in paragraph 6 above.

© *Crown copyright. Reproduced with the permission of the Controller, Her Majesty's Stationery Office.*

Appendix 20 – Recommended reading

A book of this type, while it can look at the issues involved and highlight several areas which are of special interest and involvement to those involved in GPs' accounts and taxation, cannot by definition look at every single issue which might emerge.

Developments in medical finance tend to take place regularly and the practitioner who wishes to advise his clients fully must take every effort to keep as up to date as reasonably possible. Those readers wishing to avail themselves of additional knowledge will be well advised to make a point of reading one or more of the specialist medical journals which circulate in this field. Where applicable, subscription rates are quoted but these can also change quite regularly.

PERIODICALS
Medeconomics (Haymarket Medical Press, subscription office: PO Box 219, Woking, Surrey GU21 1ZW; monthly): includes statistical information, current fee rates, salary scales, etc. together with articles of topical interest.

Financial Pulse (Morgan Grampian House, 30 Calderwood Street, Woolwich, SE18 6QH; fortnightly): contains similar information but also examines current issues with useful comment on accountancy and taxation matters.

Doctor Magazine (Doctor Mailing Department, P0 Box 60, Loughborough, Leics; weekly): not exclusively financial but includes articles of financial interest.

Fundholding Magazine (Haymarket Medical Press see *Medeconomics* above; fortnightly): exclusively concerned with fundholding practices, contains lists of courses, useful addresses and contacts as well as articles of topical interest.

BOOKS
From Accountancy Books:
Business Briefing 'Doctors': in looseleaf format, not concerned with taxation matters but topicality is assured by regular updates.

280

Tax Briefing 'Doctors': exclusively concerned with taxation matters, in looseleaf format and regular updates issued.

Other publishers:
Radcliffe Medical Press (15 Kings Meadow, Ferry Hinksey Road, Oxford OX2 ODP): this publisher issues a regular series of books aimed at the general practitioner, practice managers and staff.

Making Sense of Practice Finance: aimed specifically at GPs and practice managers; is particularly useful on certain aspects of basic book-keeping; balancing cash books, etc.

Practice Finance: Your Questions Answered: deals with many similar problems on a question and answer format.

Making Sense of the Cost-Rent Scheme: looks in far more detail at the requirements of surgery development, particularly as regards architectural and clinical requirements.

Making Sense of The Red Book: explains in detail the various fees and allowances which GPs are able to claim.

Index

Abatement, 9.14–9.14.1
  rule, 2.12
Accountancy software, 6.2
Accountants acting for doctors,
    4.1–4.13
  accounts preparation checklist,
    Appendix 7
  avoiding problems, 4.13
  charging of fees, 4.8–4.8.1
  clearance from outgoing
    accountants, 4.9
  fundholding accounts, 8.5
  internal organisation, 4.2
  new clients, 4.9
  partnership and personal accounts,
    4.12
  permanent files, 4.7
  planning the work, 4.4
  reviewing of files, 4.6
  working papers, 4.3, Appendix 6
Accountants' certificate, 6.6
Accountants' fees, 4.8–4.8.1
  personal practice expenses claims,
    7.6.8
Accounting year ends, 6.2
  fundholding accounts, 8.6
Accounts
  fundholding *see* **Fundholding**
    accounts
  practice *see* **Practice accounts**
Accounts preparation checklist,
    Appendix 7
  see also **Practice accounts**
Administration of the practice, 1.4.1
  internal control questionnaire,
    Appendix 5
Age of retirement, 9.9, 9.17
AISMA, 1.1, 4.1
Allowances, 2.3–2.3.3, 2.3.8,
    Appendix 2
  accounting treatment, 6.3.12
  basic practice allowance (BPA),
    2.3.1, Appendix 2

  payments on account, 2.3.8
  post graduate education allowance
    (PGEA), 2.3.3, Appendix 2
  seniority awards, 2.3.2, Appendix 2
  see also **Fees**
Anaesthetic fees, 2.6.3, Appendix 2
Ancillary staff refunds, 2.4.3
  abatement rule, 2.12
  payments on account, 2.4.9
Appeals
  notional rent assessment, 3.2
Architects' fees
  cost rent scheme, 3.4.1
Assessments
  partnership changes, 7.3–7.3.2,
    Figures 7.1, 7.2
  partnership taxation, 7.2
Assets
  acquired out of fund savings, 8.10.1
Audit of accounts, 1.5
  fundholding accounts, 8.6
  internal control questionnaire,
    Appendix 5

Bank interest and charges
  fundholding bank account, 8.11
  tax implications, 7.15–7.15.1
Bank overdrafts, 7.15.1
Bank reconciliations, 4.5
Bankruptcy of partner
  partnership implications, 5.12.2
Basic practice allowance (BPA), 2.3.1,
    Appendix 2
Building costs
  cost limit location factors, Appendix
    14
  cost rent limits, 3.4.1, Appendix 13
Business rates, 2.4.2
  accounting treatment, 6.4.6

Capital
  contribution by incoming partner,
    5.10

current accounts, 5.11, *Figure 5.8*, 6.4.2
fixed capital accounts, 5.8.1, *Figures 5.7, 5.8*
organisation in medical partnerships, 5.8–5.8.1, *Figures 5.4–5.9*
reorganisations of partnership, 7.5–7.5.2, *Figure 7.3*
Capital allowances, 3.10, 7.7.2
claim for residual cost not covered by capital grant, 7.16
GP fundholding, 8.11
new surgery developments, 7.4.3
Capital gains tax
private residence used for practice purposes, 7.6.6
Capital grants
accounting treatment, 6.3.6, Appendix 1
capital allowance on residual cost not covered by, 7.16
Capitation fees, 2.3.4, Appendix 2
Car allowance to GP trainees
National Insurance, 7.13
tax implications, 7.13
Car parking
refunds, 2.4.6
Cars
personal practice expenses claims, 7.7–7.7.2, *Figure 7.5*
private use factor when making claims, 7.7.1, *Figure 7.5*
Cash fees, 2.10, 7.12.2
Cash limiting
computer grants, 2.15
Cash reconciliations, 4.5
Central Services Agency (Northern Ireland), 1.2
Cervical cytology, 2.5, Appendix 2
Checklist for accounts preparation, Appendix 7
Child Health Surveillance list, 2.3.6, Appendix 2
Child immunisation, 2.5, Appendix 2
Childminders
personal practice expenses claims, 7.8.4
Claims
ancillary staff, 2.4.3
car parking, 2.4.6

computer grants, 2.4.8, 2.15, *Figure 2.9*, 8.9
dispensing practice, 2.8–2.8.6, *Figure 2.3*
drugs, 2.4.7
GP trainees, 2.4.5, 2.9–2.9.5
personal practice *see* **Personal practice expenses claims**
rates, 2.4.2, 6.4.6
refunds, 2.4–2.4.9
rents, 2.4.1
Cleaners
not regarded as ancillary staff, 2.4.3
Clinics
health promotion, 2.7.1
Co-operatives, 2.18
Community fundholding, 8.4, *Figure 8.2*
practice fund management allowance, 8.7
transitional allowance, 8.4, 8.7
Computer grants, 2.4.8, 2.15, *Figure 2.9*, 7.16
accounting treatment, 6.3.6, Appendix 1
GP fundholding practices, 8.9
Computer programs
GP accounts, 6.2
Computers
personal practice expenses claims, 7.6.11
Conferences
personal practice expenses claims, 7.6.13
Continuation election, 7.2
demerger of partnership, 7.2
Continuing education, 2.3.3
Contraceptive services, 2.6.4
Correspondent partner *see* **Nominated partner**
Cost rent scheme, 1.4, 3.1, 3.3–3.6.1, *Figures 3.2, 3.3*
area bands and factors, 3.4.2, Appendix 14
cost limit location factors, Appendix 14
cost of acquiring land, 3.4.1
cost of raising finance, 3.4.1
cost rent limits, 3.4.1, Appendix 13
fixed and variable rate of reimbursements, 3.5

professional and architects' fee,
3.4.1
total building cost, 3.4.1
Creditors
accounting treatment, 6.3.14
Cremation fees, 2.10, 7.12.2
Current accounts, 5.11, *Figure 5.8*
as source of disagreement, 6.4.2
overdrawn, 7.15.1
Current year basis of assesment,
2.2.3, 7.1
choice of year ends, 6.2

Date of retirement, 9.7, 9.17
Death gratuity, 9.10
Death of partner, 5.2
NHS pension benefits, 9.10
payment of share of capital, 5.9
Debtors
accounting treatment, 6.3.12
Defence Society subscriptions, 2.9.1,
2.9.5
Demerger of partnerships, 7.2
Depreciation
overdrawn current accounts, 7.15.1
Deprivation payments, 2.3.7,
Appendix 2
Development projects
surgery premises, 3.4.1, 3.6, 7.4.2
Dispensations
GP trainees' car allowance, 7.13
Dispensing practice, 2.8–2.8.6
accounting treatment, *Figure 2.3*,
6.3.8, 6.3.14
creditors, 6.3.14
payments on account, 2.8.2
private prescriptions, 2.8.5, *Figure
2.3*
profitability, 2.8.1
requirements to qualify, 2.8
valuation of stock, 2.8.4, 6.3.9
VAT, 7.11.4
Dissolution of partnerships, 7.2
District Valuer, 2.4.1
notional rent assessment, 3.2
Doctors and Dentists Review Body *see*
Review Body
Doctors' retainer scheme, 2.17
Domestic mortgage interest relief,
7.17
Donations

tax treatment, 7.14
Drawings, 5.12, *Figure 5.10*
current accounts, 5.11, 6.4.2
schedule, 6.4.3, Appendix 1
Drugs
dispensing practice, 2.8–2.8.6
refunds, 2.4.7, 2.8.2
valuation of stock, 2.8.4, 6.3.9

Early retirement, 9.9
due to ill health and NHS pension
benefit, 9.10
voluntary, 9.13, *Figure 9.5*,
Appendix 18
Earnings *see* **Income levels of GPs**
**Education and training of medical
students**
fees, 2.7.3, Appendix 2
Election
continuation, 7.2
Employee status, 5.4
Equitable Life, 9.9.3
Expenses
directly reimbursed, 2.2.2–2.2.3,
2.4–2.4.9, 6.3.1
GP trainees, 2.9.5
indirect reimbursement, 2.2.2–2.2.3
personal practice *see* **Personal
practice expenses claims**
statistics, 2.11.1

**Family Health Service Authorities
(FHSAs)**, 1.2
Fees, 2.3, 2.3.4–2.3.8, Appendix 2
accounting treatment, 6.3.12
anaesthetic/dental haemorrhage,
2.6.3, Appendix 2
capitation fees, 2.3.4, Appendix 2
child health surveillance, 2.3.6,
Appendix 2
contraceptive services, 2.6.4
deprivation payments, 2.3.7,
Appendix 2
dispensing practice, 2.8–2.8.6,
Figure 2.3
doctors' retainer scheme, 2.17
GP trainees, 2.4.5, 2.9–2.9.5
health promotion payments, 2.7.1,
Appendix 2
item of service, 2.6, 2.11.3, *Figure
2.5*, Appendix 2

maternal medical services
(MMS), 2.6.2, Appendix 2
minor surgery payments, 2.7.2,
Appendix 2
night visit, 2.6.1, 2.18, 5.5,
Appendix 2
payments on account, 2.3.8
registration fees (new patients),
2.3.5, Appendix 2
sessional payments, 2.7–2.7.3
sundry cash, 2.10, 7.12.2
target payments, 2.5, Appendix 2
temporary residents, 2.6.5
vaccinations and immunisations,
2.6.6
see also **Accountants' fees**
Female GPs
personal practice expenses claims,
7.8.4
Finance
surgery premises, 3.4.1, 3.6, 7.4.2
Fixed-share partners, 5.4
**Free-standing additional voluntary
contributions (FSAVCs),** 9.15.3
Fund savings, 8.3, 8.10–8.10.3
doctors leaving the practice, 8.10.3
ownership of assets acquired out of,
8.10.1
spent on surgery premises, 8.10.2
Fund savings account (FSA), 8.10
Fundholding accounts, 6.3.7, 8.6,
Figure 8.1, Appendix 1
audit, 8.6
connections with practice accounts,
8.8
year end, 8.6
see also **GP fundholding**
Fundholding bank account, 8.8
bank charges and interest, 8.11

**General Management Services
Committee**
accounting year ends, 6.2
General medical practitioners, 1.1
continuing education, 2.3.3
independent contractor status, 1.3
list size, 2.3.1, 2.11.6
seniority awards, 2.3.2, Appendix 2
Gifts
tax treatment, 7.14
Goodwill, 2.13, 3.9–3.9.1, 5.10

GP 96 form, 2.2.3, Appendix 3
GP co-operatives, 2.18
GP Contract, 1.2, 1.4
GP fundholding, 1.2, 8.1–8.11
admission to the scheme, 8.2
budget, 8.3
community, 8.4, 8.7, *Figure 8.2*
computer reimbursement scheme,
8.9
date of commencement, 8.2
eligibility rules, 8.2
origin, 8.1
practice fund management
allowance *see* **Practice fund
management allowance (PFMA)**
preparatory year, 8.2
role of the accountant, 8.5
savings *see* **Fund savings**
scope of fund, 8.3
taxation implications, 8.11
virement, 8.3
see also **Fundholding accounts**
GP trainees, 2.4.5, 2.9–2.9.5
accounting treatment of salaries,
6.4.7
car allowance, 7.13
payments on account, 2.4.9
pensions, 9.3
Grants *see* **Capital grants; Computer
grants; Improvement grants**
Gross income, 2.11.4
Group practices, 1.4, 5.1
see also **Partnership practices**

Health Authorities (HAs), 1.2
Health centres
accounting treatment of charges for
staff, rent and rates, 2.4.4
Health promotion payments, 2.7.1,
Appendix 2
Holiday camp residents, 2.6.5
Hospital service
NHS pension scheme, 9.12, 9.18,
Figure 9.8
salaried status of employees, 1.3
Husband and wife
job-sharing, 2.14.2
Husbands *see* **Spouses**

Ill-health retirement
NHS pension benefits, 9.10

Immunisations, 2.6.6
children, 2.5
Improvement grants, 3.10, 7.16
rates, 3.10
Income levels of GPs, 1.4
abatement rule, 2.12
case study, 2.11.7, *Figure 2.7*
non-NHS earnings, 2.10
proportions of NHS income, 2.11.2,
Figure 2.4
Review Body pay awards, 2.2–2.2.3,
Figures 2.1, 2.2
statistics, 2.11.4, *Figures 2.5, 2.6*
Income tax
declaration of non-NHS earnings,
2.10, 7.12.2
declaration of non-pooled income,
5.1.1
GP trainees, 2.9.1
see also **Capital allowances**; **PAYE**;
Schedule E
Income tax reserve
incoming partner, 5.10, 5.12.1.
5.12.2
overdrawn current accounts, 7.15.1
Incoming partner
capital contribution, 5.10
changes in NHS superannuation
contribution levels, 9.5
income tax reserve, 5.10, 5.12.1.
5.12.2
partnership deed, 5.6
partnership share of surgery
premises, 5.7
profit allocation, 5.3, 5.10, *Figure 5.1*
surgery premises, 3.9.1, 5.10
tax treatment expenses claims, 7.3.2
**Independent contractor status of
GPs,** 1.3
Inland Revenue
Extra-Statutory Concession A9, 9.6,
Appendix 17
Extra-Statutory Concession A37, 7.9
Extra-Statutory Concession A83,
7.6.12
Form P87, 7.13
Statement of Practice SP9/86, 7.2
Inland Revenue enquiry
GP 96 form, 2.2.3, Appendix 3
sampling process, 2.2.3, Appendix 3
Inland Revenue investigation

in-depth, 2.10, 5.1.1, 7.12–7.12.3
triggers leading to, 7.12.1
Inland Revenue press release
locum insurance, 7.6.12, Appendix
19
Inner-city practices
deprivation payments, 2.3.7,
Appendix 2
Interest charge
banks, 7.15–7.15.1
domestic mortgage interest relief,
7.17
project finance, 3.6, 7.4.2
tax relief for loans, 7.4.2, 7.15
Internal control, 1.4.1
questionnaire, Appendix 5
Internal management, 1.4.1
Investigations
in-depth Inland Revenue, 2.10,
5.1.1, 7.12–7.12.3
triggers leading to, 7.12.1
Item of service fees, 2.6, Appendix 2
statistics, 2.11.3, *Figure 2.5*

Jarman Index, 2.3.7
Job-sharing, 2.14.2

Land costs
cost rent scheme, 3.4.1
Leased cars
personal practice expenses claims,
7.7
Legacies
tax treatment, 7.14
Letter of acceptance, 4.9
Letter of engagement, 1.5, 4.8.1, 4.9
specimen, Appendix 9
Letter of representation, 4.10, 5.1.1
identification of prior shares of
profit, 5.5
specimen, Appendix 10
where no valid partnership deed
exists, 5.6
List sizes, 1.4, 2.11.6
basic practice allowance (BPA), 2.3.1
reconciliation, Appendix 8
Loan finance
surgery premises, 3.4.1, 3.6, 7.4.2
tax-efficient borrowing using
partnership capital, 7.5–7.5.2,
Figure 7.3

Local authority rates, 2.4.2, 6.4.6
Locums, 1.4
  accounting for payments to, 6.4.1
  payments to, 2.16, 6.4.1
  pensions, 9.3
  personal practice expenses claims,
    7.6.7
Locum insurance, 7.6.12
  Inland Revenue press release,
    Appendix 19
**Lump sum investments on
  retirement**, 9.16

Management Chart, 1.4.1
Management letter, 6.5
Management of a medical practice,
  1.4
  internal management and controls,
    1.4.1
Maternity medical services (MMS),
  2.6.2, Appendix 2
Maternity payments, 2.16
  accounting for, 6.4.1
Medical insurance premiums
  contributions paid on behalf of
    spouses, 7.8.6
Medical officers, fees for, 2.10
Medical Practices Committee, 2.13
Medical reports, fees for, 2.10,
  7.12.2
Minor surgery payments, 2.7.2,
  Appendix 2
Mortgage for surgery premises
  tax-efficient borrowing using
    partnership capital, 7.5.1
Motoring expenses
  personal practice claims, 7.7–7.7.2,
    Figure 7.5

National Audit Office, 8.6
National Health Service
  independent contractor status of
    GPs, 1.3
  organisation, 1.2
  pension scheme *see* **NHS pension
    scheme**
National Health Service Act 1977,
  2.13
**National Health Service and
  Community Care Act 1990**, 1.2,
  8.1

**National Insurance contributions
  (NIC)**
  Class 2, 1.3
  Class 4, 1.3
  GP trainees, 2.9.2
  GP trainees' car allowance, 7.13
  partners with earnings from outside
    appointments, 7.10
Negative equity
  accounting treatment, 6.4.4, *Figure
    6.3*
  surgery premises, 3.8–3.8.2, *Figure
    3.3*
Net income, 2.11.4
NHS pension scheme, 9.1–9.14
  abatement, 9.14–9.14.1
  additional voluntary contributions
    (AVCs), 9.9.3
  benefits of scheme, 9.8
  contribution levels, 9.5, *Figure 9.1*
  death and sickness benefits, 9.10
  dynamising (uprating) factor, 9.7,
    9.17, *Figure 9.3*
  Extra-Statutory Concession A9, 9.6,
    Appendix 17
  hospital service, 9.12, 9.18, *Figure
    9.8*
  leaving the scheme, 9.11
  membership, 9.3
  officer scheme, 9.2, 9.7, 9.12, 9.18
  opting out, 9.4
  partial retirement, 9.14–9.14.1
  partners with earnings from outside
    appointments, 9.12, 9.18, *Figure
    9.8*
  practitioner scheme, 9.2, 9.18
  purchases of added years, 9.9.1,
    Figure 9.4
  purchases of additional benefits, 9.9,
    Figure 9.4
  refund of contributions on leaving
    the scheme, 9.11
  transfer of contributions on leaving
    the scheme, 9.11
  unreduced lump sum, 9.9.2, *Figure
    9.4*
  voluntary early retirement, 9.13,
    Figure 9.8, Appendix 18
NIC *see* **National Insurance
  contributions**
Night visits

fees, 2.6.1, 2.18, 5.5, Appendix 2
GP co-operatives, 2.18
Nominated partner, 4.11, Appendix 12
Non-NHS earnings, 2.10, 7.12.2
abatement rule, 2.12
Notional rent allowances, 3.2

Opthalmic medical practitioners
NHS pension scheme, 9.3
Organisation
National Health Service, 1.2
partnership practices, 5.1–5.1.1
Out of hours visits *see* **Night visits**
Outgoing partners
allocation of fund savings, 8.10.3
payment of share of capital, 5.9
tax treatment of personal practice expenses claims, 7.3.2
Overdrawn current accounts, 7.15.1
Ownership of assets
acquired out of fund savings, 8.10.1
Ownership of surgery premises, 3.1–3.10
accounting treatment, 6.3.5, Appendix 1
partnership share, 5.7–5.7.2, *Figures 5.2, 5.3*
property capital accounts, 5.7.2, *Figure 5.3*
retiring partners, 5.7.1
taxation, 7.4–7.4.3

Part-time GPs, 2.14–2.14.2, *Figure 2.8*
basic practice allowance (BPA), 2.3.1, 2.14.1
Part-time practice, 2.14.1, *Figure 2.8*
Partial retirement
abatement, 9.14–9.14.1
NHS pension scheme, 9.14–9.14.1
'24-hour' retirement, 9.14
Partnership accounts *see* **Practice accounts**
Partnership Act 1890, 5.6
Partnership changes, 5.2
assessments on, 7.3–7.3.2, *Figures 7.1, 7.2*
death, 5.2
retirement, 5.2

treatment in partnership accounts, 6.3.2, *Figures 5.2, 6.1*
Partnership deed, 4.10, 5.6
identification of prior shares of profit, 5.5
requirements, 5.6
specimen, Appendix 4
Partnership practices, 1.1, 5.1–5.12.2
allocation of non-NHS earnings, 2.10, 7.12.2
changes *see* **Partnership changes**
nominated partner, 4.11, Appendix 12
organisation, 5.1–5.1.1
organising the capital structure, 5.8–5.8.1, *Figures 5.4–5.9*
ownership of surgery premises, 3.1–3.10, 5.7–5.7.2, *Figures 5.2, 5.3*, 6.3.5
pension contributions, 9.5.1
pooling of income, 5.1.1
prior shares of profit, 5.5, 6.3.3
profit allocation, 5.3, 5.10, *Figure 5.1*, 6.3.4, *Figure 6.2*, 7.3–7.3.2, *Figures 7.1, 7.2*, Appendix 1
succession, 5.1
see also **Practice accounts**
Partnership taxation
preceding year basis, 7.2
Partnerships
demergers, 7.2
dissolution, 7.2
see also **Partnership deeds**; **Partnership practices**
Patient lists
fees for child health surveillance, 2.3.6
fees for new registrations, 2.3.5
reconciliation of list sizes, Appendix 8
see also **List sizes**
PAYE
GP trainees, 2.9.1
partners with earnings from outside appointments, 7.9, *Figures 7.6, 7.7*
see also **Schedule E**
Payments on account, 2.3.8, 2.4.9, 2.8.2
Pension schemes
contributions paid on behalf of a spouse, 7.8.5

Extra-Statutory Concession A9,
9.6, Appendix 17
lump sum investments, 9.16
private, 9.15–9.15.4
see also **NHS pension scheme**
Permanent files, 4.7
Permanent health insurance, 7.6.12
Personal practice expenses claims,
2.2.2
accountancy fees, 7.6.8
accounting treatment, 6.3.11
computers and videos, 7.6.11
confirmation letter, Appendix 16
courses and conferences, 7.6.13
example, Appendix 15
locum fees, 7.6.7
motoring expenses, 7.7–7.7.2,
Figure 7.5
pension scheme contributions paid
on behalf of a spouse, 7.8.5
private telephone bills, 7.6.10
security expenses, 7.6.9
tax treatment, 7.3.2, 7.6–7.6.14,
Figures 7.1, 7.2
triggering an investigation, 7.12.1
use of the home for practice
purposes, 7.6.4–7.6.6, *Figure 7.4*
wives' salaries, 7.8.1
Petty cash, 4.5
Pooling of income, 5.1.1
**Post graduate education allowance
(PGEA)**, 2.3.3, Appendix 2
Practice accounts, 1.5, 6.1–6.6
accountants' certificate, 6.6
accounting for non-NHS earnings,
2.10, 7.12.2
accounting treatment of partnership
changes, *Figure 5.2*, 6.3.2, *Figure
6.1*
accounts preparation checklist,
Appendix 7
allocation of post graduate
education allowance (PGEA),
2.3.3, Appendix 1
allocation of seniority awards, 2.3.2,
Appendix 1
allowances, 6.3.12
basic practice allowance (BPA),
2.3.1, Appendix 2
business rates, 6.4.6
computer programs, 6.2

connections with fundholding
accounts, 8.8
creditors, 6.3.14
current accounts, 6.4.2
debtors, 6.3.12
dispensing practice trading account,
Figure 2.3, 6.3.8
draft, 4.5
drawings, 6.4.3, Appendix 1
fees, 6.3.12
fundholding management
allowances, 6.3.7, 8.7, *Figures 8.2,
8.3*, Appendix 1
grossing up of directly reimbursed
expenses, 6.3.1
isolation of prior shares of profit,
5.5, 6.3.3, Appendix 1
locums, payments to, 6.4.1
management information, 6.5
maternity payments, 6.4.1
negative equity, 6.4.4, *Figure 6.3*
nominated partner, 4.11, Appendix
12
payments to retained doctors, 2.17
personal expenses claim, 6.3.11
pre-payments, 6.3.13
profit allocation, 6.3.4, *Figure 6.2*,
Appendix 1
sickness, payments during, 6.4.1
specimen, Appendix 1
superannuation contributions,
6.3.10
surgery ownership, 6.3.5
tax provisions, 6.4.5
trainees' salaries, 6.4.7
treatment of notional and cost rent
allowances, 3.1
treatment of staff salaries, rent and
rates where GPs practice in health
centres, 2.4.4
valuation of drugs of a dispensing
practice, 2.8.4, *Figure 2.3*, 6.3.9
**Practice fund management allowance
(PFMA)**, 6.3.7, 8.7, *Figures 8.2,
8.3*, Appendix 1
computer reimbursement scheme,
8.9
eligible expenses, 8.7
excluded items, 8.7
taxation implications, 8.11
Practice managers, 1.4.1

internal control questionnaire,
Appendix 5
salary refunds, 2.4.3
Pre-payments
accounting treatment, 6.3.13
Pre-school boosters, 2.5, Appendix 2
Premises, surgery *see* **Surgery premises**
Prescribing doctors, 2.8.6
Prescriptions
private, 2.8.5, *Figure 2.3*, 6.3.8
see also **Drugs**
Preventative medicine
target payments, 2.5, Appendix 2
Prior share items, 5.5
accounting treatment, 6.3.3
tax treatment, 7.3.1
Private patients' fees, 2.10, 7.12.2
abatement rule, 2.12
see also **Medical insurance premiums**
Private pension schemes, 9.15–9.15.4
for spouses, 9.15.4
free-standing additional voluntary contributions, 9.15.3
'grossing-up', 9.15.1, *Figure 9.6*
lump sum investments, 9.16
renunciation of concessionary tax relief, 9.15.2, *Figure 9.7*
tax relief, 9.15, Appendix 17
Private prescriptions, 2.8.5, *Figure 2.3*, 6.3.8
Private residence
used for practice purposes, 7.6.4–7.6.6, *Figure 7.4*
Project finance
surgery premises, 3.4.1, 3.6, 7.4.2
Property *see* **Surgery premises**

Rates
abatement rule, 2.12
accounting treatment where GPs practice in health centres, 2.4.4
payments on account, 2.4.9
refund, 2.4.2, 6.4.6
Receipts, 4.5
Recommended reading, 1.1, Appendix 20
Records
expenses, 2.2.2

non-NHS earnings, 2.10
quality, 4.8.1
Red Book (SFA), 2.1
abatement rule, 2.12
anaesthetic/dental haemorrhage, 2.6.3, Appendix 2
basic practice allowance (BPA), 2.3.1, Appendix 2
child health surveillance, 2.3.6, Appendix 2
computer grants, 2.4.8, 2.15, *Figure 2.10*, 8.9
contraceptive services, 2.6.4
deprivation payments, 2.3.7, Appendix 2
doctors' retainer scheme, 2.17
drug refunds, 2.4.7
fees and allowances, 2.3–2.3.8, Appendix 2
GP trainees, 2.4.5, 2.9–2.9.5
GPs in health centres, 2.4.4
health promotion payments, 2.7.1, Appendix 2
improvement grants, 3.10
maternity medical services (MMS), 2.6.2, Appendix 2
minor surgery payments, 2.7.2, Appendix 2
night visit fees, 2.6.1, Appendix 2
payments during sickness and confinement, 2.16
payments on account, 2.3.8
post graduate education allowance (PGEA), 2.3.3, Appendix 2
rates, 2.4.2
registration fees (new patients), 2.3.5, Appendix 2
rents, 2.4.1
seniority awards, 2.3.2, Appendix 2
target payments, 2.5, Appendix 2
temporary residents, 2.6.5
training of medical students, 2.7.3, Appendix 2
vaccinations and immunisations, 2.6.6
Refunds
abatement rule, 2.12
ancillary staff, 2.4.3
car parking, 2.4.6
computer grants, 2.4.8, 2.15, *Figure 2.9*, 8.9

direct, 2.4–2.4.9
dispensing practice, 2.8–2.8.6,
   Figure 2.3
drugs, 2.4.7, 2.8.2
expenses, 2.2.2, 2.4–2.4.9
GP trainees, 2.4.5, 2.9–2.9.5
payments on account, 2.3.8, 2.4.9,
   2.8.2
rates, 2.4.2, 6.4.6
rents, 2.4.1
Refuse collection charges,
   2.4.2
Regional Health Authorities (RHA)
GP fundholding, 8.2–8.3
responsibilities, 1.2
Registration fees, 2.3.5, Appendix 2
Reimbursements *see* **Expenses**;
   Refunds
Removal expenses
GP trainees, 2.9.5
Rents
abatement rule, 2.12
accounting treatment where GPs
   practice in health centres, 2.4.4
payments on account, 2.4.9
refund, 2.4.1
Retention of income by partners,
   5.1.1
Retirement income of GPs, 1.3,
   9.1–9.18
see also **NHS pension scheme**
Retirement on grounds of ill health
NHS pension benefits, 9.10
Retiring partners, 5.2
age of retirement, 9.9, 9.17
changes in NHS superannuation
   contribution levels, 9.5
payment of share of capital, 5.9
shares in surgery premises, 5.7.1
tax treatment of personal practice
   expenses claims, 7.3.2
timing of retirement, 9.7, 9.17
Review Body, 1.3
evidence, 2.2, *Figure 2.1*
origins, 2.2
pay awards, 2.2–2.2.3, *Figures 2.1,*
   2.2
Reviewing of files, 4.6
Royal Institution of Chartered
   Surveyors
valuation guidelines, 3.9

Salaried partners *see* **Fixed-share**
   partners
Salaries
accounting treatment where GPs
   practice in health centres, 2.4.4
ancillary staff refunds, 2.4.3
fundholding budget, 8.3
Sale and leaseback scheme
surgery premises, 3.7
Schedule D, 1.3. 5.4
Schedule E, 5.4
partners with earnings from outside
   appointments, 7.9, *Figures 7.6,*
   7.7
see also **PAYE**
Scottish Office
Health Board, 1.2
Self-assessment, 2.2.3, 5.10, 5.12.2,
   7.1, 7.2
Self-employed, 1.3
Self-governing trusts, 1.2
Seniority awards, 2.3.2, Appendix 2
tax treatment, 7.3.1
Sessional payments, 2.7–2.7.3
health promotion payments, 2.7.1,
   Appendix 2
minor surgery payments, 2.7.2,
   Appendix 2
training of medical students, 2.7.3,
   Appendix 2
Sewerage rates, 2.4.2
Sickness
accounting for payments during,
   6.4.1
NHS pension benefit on early
   retirement due to ill health, 9.10
payments during, 2.16
Sole practitioners, 5.1
use of the home for practice
   purposes, 7.6.4–7.6.6, *Figure 7.4*
Specimen letters
appointment of nominated partner,
   Appendix 12
letter of engagement, Appendix 9
letter of representation, Appendix
   10
year end preparatory letter,
   Appendix 11
Spouses
medical insurance contributions
   paid on behalf of, 7.8.6

pension scheme contributions
   paid on behalf of, 7.8.5
pensions for, 9.15.4
salaries, 7.8.1, 7.8.4
Statement of Fees and Allowances *see*
   Red Book (SFA)
Statistics on medical practices, 2.11–
   2.11.8, *Figures 2.4–2.7*
   average list sizes, 2.11.6
   case study, 2.11.7, *Figure 2.7*
   expenditure levels, 2.11.1
   gross and net income, 2.11.4, *Figures
   2.5, 2.6*
   item of service fees, 2.11.3, *Figure
   2.5*
   proportions of NHS income, 2.11.2,
   Figure 2.4
Stock
   dispensing practice, 2.8.4, 6.3.9
Students
   fees for supervision and training of
   medical, 2.7.3, Appendix 2
   see also **GP trainees**
Succession
   partnerships, 5.1
Sundry cash fees, 2.10, 7.12.2
Superannuation, 9.1–9.18, Appendix
   17
   accounting treatment, 6.3.10
   dispensing GP, 2.8.3
   GP trainees, 2.9.3
   on outside appointments, 9.12, 9.18,
   Figure 9.8
   see also **NHS pension scheme**
Surgery premises
   capital allowances on plant and
   machinery for new developments,
   7.4.3
   cost rent scheme, 1.4, 3.1, 3.3–3.6.1,
   Figures 3.2, 3.3, Appendices 13
   and 14
   existing surgeries, 3.8.1, *Figure 3.4*
   fund savings spent on, 8.10.2
   incoming partner, 3.9.1, 5.7, 5.10
   negative equity, 3.8–3.8.2, 6.4.4
   notional rent allowances, 3.2
   ownership, 3.1–3.10, 5.7–5.7.2,
   Figures 5.2, 5.3, 6.3.5
   ownership by trust, 3.8.2
   sale and leaseback scheme, 3.7
   taxation, 7.4–7.4.3

use of the home for practice
   purposes, 7.6.4–7.6.6, *Figure 7.4*
valuation, 3.9–3.9.1
VAT on new developments, 7.11.2
see also **Rents**

Target payments, 2.5, Appendix 2
Tax provisions
   accounting for, 6.4.5
Tax relief
   interest charge on loans, 7.4.2, 7.15
   NHS pension contributions, 9.6,
   9.15, Appendix 17
   private pension contributions, 9.15,
   Appendix 17
   renunciation, 9.15.2, *Figure 9.7*
Tax reserve account, 5.10, 5.12.1,
   6.4.5
   implications of self-assessment,
   5.12.2
   overdrawn current accounts, 7.15.1
Taxation, 7.1–7.16
   declaration of non-NHS earnings,
   2.10, 7.12.2
   gifts and donations, 7.14
   GP fundholding, 8.11
   GP trainees' car allowance, 7.13
   seniority awards, 7.3.1
   surgery ownership, 7.4–7.4.3
Telephone bills
   personal practice expenses claims,
   7.6.10
Temporary residents, 2.6.5
Tender document, 4.9
Timing of retirement, 9.7, 9.17
Trainee GPs *see* **GP trainees**
Trainee supervision grant, 2.4.5, 2.9,
   2.9.5
Training of medical students
   fees, 2.7.3, Appendix 2
   see also **GP trainees**
Trusts
   property ownership, 3.8.2
'24-hour' retirement, 9.14

Uniform business rates, 2.4.2
   accounting treatment, 6.4.6

Vaccinations, 2.6.6
   children, 2.5
Valuation

notional rent, 3.2
rents, 2.4.1
Royal Institution of Chartered
   Surveyors guidelines, 3.9
stock of drugs in a dispensing
   practice, 2.8.4, 6.3.9
surgery premises, 3.9–3.9.1
VAT
accountants' fees, 4.8.1
dispensing practice, 7.11.4
exemptions, 7.11.1
new surgeries and self-supply,
   7.11.2
partial exemption and *de-minimis*
   rule, 7.11.3
private prescriptions, 2.8.5
stock of drugs in a dispensing
   practice, 2.8.4, 6.3.9, 7.11.4

Virement
GP fundholding, 8.3

Water rates, 2.4.2
Welsh Office
Health Board, 1.2
Wives *see* **Spouses**
Working hours, 1.4
Working papers, 4.3
accounts preparation checklist,
   Appendix 7
specimen master index, Appendix 6

Year end letter, 4.4
specimen, Appendix 11
Year ends, choice of, 6.2